HANDBOOKS
DOGS

SMITHSONIAN HANDBOOKS

DOGS

DAVID ALDERTON

Commissioned photography by
TRACY MORGAN

NEW EDITION

DK LONDON

Managing Editor Angeles Gavira Guerrero
Managing Art Editor Michael Duffy
Production Editor Andy Hilliard
US Editor Jennette ElNaggar
Senior Production Controller Meskerem Berhane
Jacket Design Development Manager Sophia MTT
Associate Publishing Director Liz Wheeler
Art Director Karen Self
Publishing Director Jonathan Metcalf

DK DELHI

Desk Editor Saumya Agarwal
Art Editor Shipra Jain
Managing Editor Saloni Singh
Senior Managing Art Editor Arunesh Talapatra
Jacket Designer Juhi Sheth
Senior DTP Designers Tarun Sharma, Harish Aggarwal
DTP Designers Umesh Singh Rawat, Anurag Trivedi,
Satish Chandra Gaur, Rajdeep Singh, Nand Kishor Acharya
Production Manager Pankaj Sharma
Pre-production Manager Balwant Singh
Editorial Head Glenda Fernandes
Design Head Malavika Talukder

Author David Alderton

FIRST EDITION

Project Editor Damien Moore
Art Editors Vicki James, Shaun Mc Nally
Series Editor Jonathan Metcalf

Series Art Editor Spencer Holbrook
Production Controller Caroline Webber

This American Edition, 2022
First American Edition, 1993
Published in the United States by DK Publishing
1450 Broadway, Suite 801, New York, NY 10018

A catalog record for this book
is available from the Library of Congress.
ISBN 978-0-7440-5810-9

DK books are available at special discounts when purchased
in bulk for sales promotions, premiums, fund-raising, or educational use.
For details, contact: DK Publishing Special Markets,
1450 Broadway, Suite 801, New York, NY 10018
SpecialSales@dk.com

Printed and bound in the UAE

For the curious
www.dk.com

MIX
Paper from
responsible sources
FSC™ C018179

This book was made with Forest
Stewardship Council™ certified
paper—one small step in DK's
commitment to a sustainable future.
For more information go to
www.dk.com/our-green-pledge

Contents

AUTHOR'S INTRODUCTION

DESPITE THE VARIETY of shapes and sizes in today's domestic dog breeds, all are directly related to the Gray Wolf. The process of domestication began more than 40,000 years ago, probably in disparate regions in the northern hemisphere, at a time when wolves had a far wider distribution than they do today. The early semi-wild dogs were probably kept for herding and guarding stock rather than as companions.

Archaeological evidence has now revealed that marked distinctions in the sizes of domestic dogs had already become apparent over 9,000 years ago, even in dogs living in the same region. This trend seems to have gathered momentum, with the characteristic build of many of today's breeds being established by Roman times. By this stage in their history, dogs were being kept largely for the same purposes as they are today: hunting; working with livestock; guarding property; and acting as companions. Highly selective breeding and natural adaptation to various climatic conditions led to the emergence of countless new forms of dogs through the Middle Ages. By the 1800s many of the gundog breeds known today had evolved. This process is ongoing, with new breeds still being created today, primarily as companions.

Ancient gods
Dating from about 200 BCE, this mummified dog was prepared by the Egyptians to resemble the jackal-god, Anubis.

BREED STANDARDS
In the past, many dogs may have been similar in general appearance to the way they are today, but they were not then classified in specific breeds. The most significant change in this respect occurred very recently in canine history.

As dog shows became fashionable in the late 19th century, the need arose for specific criteria against which individual dogs could be compared and judged. Enthusiasts in Great Britain grouped together in 1873 to form what became known as the Kennel Club. This led directly to the establishment of stud books and set standards for certain dog breeds. It also set basic rules for shows. Similar organizations followed in other countries: the American Kennel Club was formed in 1884 and its Canadian counterpart in 1888.

Off to the hunt
This medieval hunting scene depicts a distinctly greyhound-type breed in pursuit of its quarry. Leaner, sleeker dogs were better adapted for speed.

BREED RECOGNITION
Nowadays, certain breeds, such as the German Shepherd Dog, have become popular throughout the world. Others, however, such as the American coonhounds, remain far more localized, perhaps even restricted to one specific region of a single

Early foxhound
Many hounds have been developed to pursue a particular quarry; foxhounds are bred to have the pace, stamina, and tenacity needed for fox hunting.

country. The main purpose of this book is to serve as a guide to identifying these breeds, whether worldwide or local. Official recognition of breeds, however, depends largely on the individual countries and organizations. Breed standards often differ slightly between countries. Wherever possible, and with the cooperation of top breeders in countries throughout the world, this book includes illustrations of top class examples of the dogs as representatives of their breeds.

Charles Cruft
The founder of the famous Crufts dog show started his career as a dog food salesman.

Early show
Clumber Spaniels come under scrutiny at the 1933 Crufts dog show (below).

SHOWING

Not all opportunities to show a dog are dependent on the animal's adherence to breed standards. Nor are they as demanding, on dogs or owners, as championship shows such as Crufts. Open shows follow the same format as the championship shows, but they are considerably shorter: the best-of-breed winners compete for the best-in-show award. For dogs and owners new to showing, these can prove to be excellent venues at which to learn what is expected by judges.

Field trials (to put gundogs through their paces) and sheepdog trials are specialized events. At sheepdog trials, a dog herds a flock over a preset course into an enclosure. Points are given for speed and

Agility events

At an agility event, both pure-bred and mongrel dogs are judged on their competence in negotiating obstacles and obeying verbal commands.

concentration, and penalties incurred for barking and nipping when dogs grow impatient. The teamwork between handler and dog displayed at these events is perhaps the most striking example of the progress that has been made since humans and wolves embarked on their curious alliance over 40,000 years ago.

Top dog

The winner's cup or rosette is not only a reward for a good performance on the day; it is the culmination of months of dedicated hard work.

HOW THIS BOOK WORKS

FOLLOWING the Introduction and the Identification Key, the main breed section of the book is divided into seven dog groups: companion dogs, gundogs, herding dogs, hounds, terriers, working dogs, and designer dogs. The breeds are ordered according to their place of origin, ranging worldwide from the US to Australia. The annotated example below shows how a typical entry is organized.

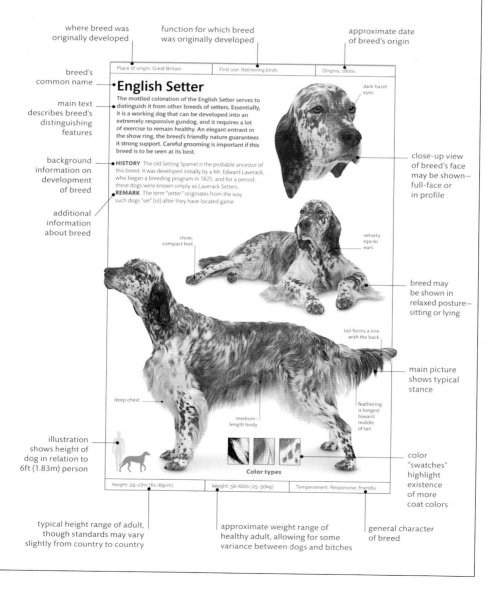

where breed was originally developed

function for which breed was originally developed

approximate date of breed's origin

breed's common name

Place of origin: Great Britain

First use: Retrieving birds

Origins: 1800s

•English Setter

dark hazel eyes

main text describes breed's distinguishing features

The mottled coloration of the English Setter serves to distinguish it from other breeds of setters. Essentially, it is a working dog that can be developed into an extremely responsive gundog, and it requires a lot of exercise to remain healthy. An elegant entrant in the show ring, the breed's friendly nature guarantees it strong support. Careful grooming is important if this breed is to be seen at its best.

background information on development of breed

•HISTORY The old Setting Spaniel is the probable ancestor of this breed. It was developed initially by a Mr. Edward Laverack, who began a breeding program in 1825, and for a period, these dogs were known simply as Laverack Setters.
•REMARK The term "setter" originates from the way such dogs "set" (sit) after they have located game.

additional information about breed

close-up view of breed's face may be shown— full-face or in profile

close, compact feet

velvety tips to ears

breed may be shown in relaxed posture— sitting or lying

tail forms a line with the back

main picture shows typical stance

deep chest

feathering is longest toward middle of tail

medium-length body

illustration shows height of dog in relation to 6ft (1.83m) person

Color types

color "swatches" highlight existence of more coat colors

Height: 24–27in (61–69cm)

Weight: 56–66lb (25–30kg)

Temperament: Responsive, friendly

typical height range of adult, though standards may vary slightly from country to country

approximate weight range of healthy adult, allowing for some variance between dogs and bitches

general character of breed

DOMESTIC DOG GROUPS

DOMESTIC DOGS may be classified in many different ways, but the fundamental means of separating breeds is on the basis of their function. Although many breeds are now kept as pets, irrespective of their origins, most were first used to carry out specific tasks, such as herding, hunting, and guarding. Their temperament, physique, and behavior have developed accordingly. For the purposes of this book, seven major categorizations have been employed.

COMPANION DOGS

The idea of keeping dogs as pets was popularized by the royal courts, where dogs have been fashionable for centuries. Companion dogs are generally characterized by small size and gentle nature.

GUNDOGS

Bred to work closely with people on a one-to-one basis, gundogs are characterized by their responsive, biddable natures, and high intelligence. The gundog category includes spaniels, setters, retrievers, poodles, and pointers. Many gundogs have multiple uses: they can track the game, indicate the target for the hunter, and retrieve the game if it is shot.

HERDING DOGS

This is an ancient category, with dogs having been employed to control the movements of livestock for many centuries. They are most commonly used to herd sheep and cattle but have also been used to control deer and even chickens. A good sheepdog is said to possess an "eye" with which it fixes the sheep, persuading them to move with the minimum of disturbance. The development of herding dogs has tended to be localized, which is reflected in the diversity of such breeds today. They are active, intelligent dogs with some of the more distinctive coats.

HOUNDS

This is probably the most ancient category of dog, bred to pursue game. It includes the fastest members of the dog family: the elegant sight hounds, such as the Saluki and the Greyhound. But other hounds, such as the Bloodhound, have been bred for stamina, and these, mostly short-coated, breeds will relentlessly pursue their quarry by scent rather than sight.

TERRIERS

These working breeds, whose development has been centred in Great Britain during the last 100 years, are small but tenacious. Bold and fearless by nature, they are also highly inquisitive. Terriers have fulfilled a wide range of roles down through the years, being highly valued in Victorian cities as rodent killers, while also working alongside foxhounds in the country. They make personable companions and enjoy exploring their surroundings.

WORKING DOGS

Around the world, dogs have been trained for a wide variety of specific tasks, including pulling sleighs across snow and ice. In many countries, they are employed to guard property and livestock; in others, they are little more than livestock themselves and have been traditionally used to provide food and fur.

DESIGNER DOGS

The development of dogs has been directly influenced by our lifestyles, and this trend is continuing, as reflected by the increasing popularity of so-called designer dogs. These are not standardized breeds however, but are the result of crossbreeding between breeds and so will not be seen at formal dog shows.

WHAT IS A DOG?

ALL DOGS are primarily carnivorous, with teeth especially adapted for eating meat and gnawing bones. As they were originally hunters, dogs are equipped with acute senses for detecting prey and have very powerful muscles, allowing them to run at a great pace, with bursts of speed when necessary.

All canids walk on their toes (rather than on the soles of their feet like bears), which allows them greater agility—often an important factor when they are tackling prey much larger than themselves. Dogs also evolved the ability to work together in a pack, thus overcoming the problem of hunting larger animals.

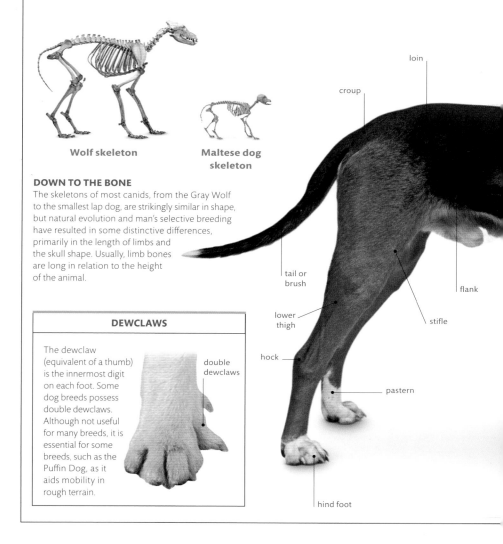

Wolf skeleton

Maltese dog skeleton

DOWN TO THE BONE
The skeletons of most canids, from the Gray Wolf to the smallest lap dog, are strikingly similar in shape, but natural evolution and man's selective breeding have resulted in some distinctive differences, primarily in the length of limbs and the skull shape. Usually, limb bones are long in relation to the height of the animal.

loin

croup

tail or brush

flank

lower thigh

stifle

hock

pastern

hind foot

DEWCLAWS

The dewclaw (equivalent of a thumb) is the innermost digit on each foot. Some dog breeds possess double dewclaws. Although not useful for many breeds, it is essential for some breeds, such as the Puffin Dog, as it aids mobility in rough terrain.

double dewclaws

SKULL SHAPE

The difference between the tiny, rounded (brachycephalic) skull of the selectively bred Japanese Chin and the elongate (dolichocephalic) skull of its ancestor, the Gray Wolf, illustrates the extent of man's influence on the development of the domestic dog.

Japanese Chin skull

Gray Wolf skull

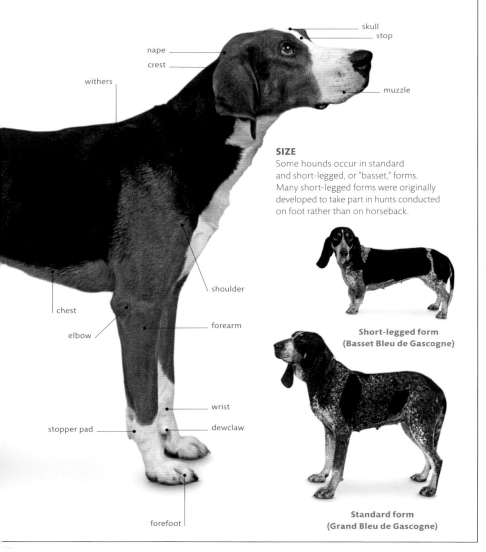

skull

stop

nape

crest

withers

muzzle

SIZE

Some hounds occur in standard and short-legged, or "basset," forms. Many short-legged forms were originally developed to take part in hunts conducted on foot rather than on horseback.

shoulder

chest

forearm

elbow

Short-legged form (Basset Bleu de Gascogne)

wrist

stopper pad

dewclaw

forefoot

Standard form (Grand Bleu de Gascogne)

COAT TYPES

A DOG'S COAT is comprised of two basic types of hair: the longer, outer, guard hairs, which are fairly coarse in texture; and the softer secondary hairs that make up the undercoat, and through which the guard hairs protrude. Variations on this basic pattern do occur, however, and not all breeds have both types of hair. A dog's coat is an important feature in its development: dogs bred in cold climates are likely to have dense coats; hunting dogs tend to have short, sleek coats; and terriers are often bred with wiry coats for protection against the elements.

CARE CONSIDERATIONS

The type of coat is an important consideration when choosing a dog. As a guide, those with short, smooth coats, such as Dalmatians, are easiest to care for, needing little more than a polish with a hound glove and an occasional bath. In contrast, dogs with wiry coats, such as Schnauzers, must be regularly combed. For show purposes, their coat must be stripped and plucked about once every three months; pets can be clipped about every two months and excess hair trimmed from around the eyes and ears. Breeds with longer coats, such as the Rough Collie, need daily grooming to prevent the coat from becoming matted. Many breeds will benefit from a bath every three months or so, both to keep their coat clean and to reduce their doggy odor. Excessive bathing is not recommended, however.

Desert dweller
Its short coat allows this Dingo to tolerate the Australian desert sun.

Long-haired coat

Wire-haired coat

Smooth coat

COLOR TYPES

Whereas some breeds occur in just a single color form, in other cases a much wider range of combinations exists. The color panels accompanying the breed entries in this book serve to give a general indication of some alternative color types for each particular breed. The panels themselves are not exact color replicas, but reflect major color groupings, as set out below.

In the case of patterned varieties, precise distribution of the colors may be laid down in the breed standard. Not all colors in a particular breed may be recognized for exhibition purposes. These can vary from country to country as well, or even between different registration bodies in the same country, as reflected by the breed standard.

Cream
Includes white, and light shades such as ivory, blond, and lemon.

Blue mottled with tan
Includes blue and brindle and bluish black and tan.

Black brindle
Includes "pepper and salt," a gray/black combination.

Red/Tan
Includes red, red-fawn, tawny, rich chestnut, orange roan, chestnut roan.

Black and white
Includes black or brindle markings with white.

Tan and white
A color combination seen in many breeds of hound.

Blue
Includes merle (blue-gray), and speckled blue (with black).

Black, tan, and white
Otherwise known as tricolor. The depth of tan coloration may vary.

Black
Some breeds are pure black but may become gray around the muzzle with age.

Dark brown
Includes mahogany and blackish brown.

Gray
Includes all shades from silvery to blue-black gray and gray or black brindle.

Gold and white
Includes white with lemon, gold, or orange spots.

Black and tan
Clearly defined colors that result in good contrast.

Liver and tan
A combination of two reddish shades.

Red brindle
Includes orange or mahogany brindle.

Gold
Includes russet gold, fawn, apricot, wheaten, and tawny.

Liver and white
A coloration often associated with gundog breeds.

Fur colors
A black and a yellow Labrador. There is also a liver-colored variety.

Chestnut red and white
Includes combinations of white with orange, fawn, red, chestnut.

Liver
Includes reddish brown, sable, and cinnamon shades.

SENSES AND INSTINCTS

SINCE THE PROCESS of domestication first began, selective breeding over 4,000 generations or more has changed the physical appearance of some dogs almost beyond recognition. But even the tiny Chihuahua (see p.37) still displays many of the behavioral characteristics of its ancestor, the wolf. Like the wolf, the domestic dog communicates by means of calls and body language, its ears and tail being especially expressive, and it retains the same strong social instincts.

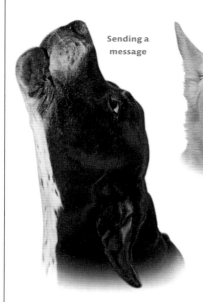

Sending a message

Sensitive ears

HEARING

Dogs generally have a very acute sense of hearing and are able to hear sounds that are too high-pitched for human beings. This greater hearing range assists dogs in tracking down their quarry and in communicating with each other. Dogs are sometimes used to help people suffering from loss of hearing, being trained to indicate such sounds as a ringing telephone.

SMELL

The keen sense of smell common to all dogs is most fully developed in breeds such as the Bloodhound, which uses it to track quarry. Dogs rely on the nose, as well as Jacobson's Organ in the mouth, to detect scent particles.

COMMUNICATION

Wolves keep in touch with each other by howling, a means of communication well developed in northern spitz breeds, which work in groups. Pack hounds tracking a scent may also bay, which is useful to the hunter when the dog is not visible.

On the scent

SIGHT

The position of the eyes, toward the sides of the head, gives dogs a wider field of vision than human beings, making them more aware of their environment. Dogs also have better vision at dusk because the cells in the retina, where the image is focused, respond well to low light. However, color vision is limited.

Keen eyesight

Identifying a stranger

SCENT MARKING

Dog urine contains highly individual chemical scent markers, or pheromones. A male will convey the boundaries of his territory to other dogs by using urine as a marker. After puberty, male dogs spray urine by lifting their leg, rather than squatting like a bitch, in order to hit a target such as a tree or a post. They may also scratch the ground, leaving a scent from the sweat glands between their toes. There is a distinct difference in scent marking between the sexes, and male dogs urinate perhaps three times more frequently than bitches.

AGGRESSION

Male dogs meeting in antagonistic situations carry out a well-defined series of gestures, indicating submission (right), or threatening aggression without actually attacking their opponent. The dog stands upright, tail erect, raising its hackles (the hairs along its back). The neck extends forward and the mouth opens into a snarl.

Offering no defense

Ready to fight

SUBMISSION

If a dog wants to submit, it will probably crouch down, with its tail between its legs and its ears down. In some cases, it may run off, with the dominant dog in pursuit. Alternatively, it may roll over on to its back, like a puppy, and may urinate a little if it has no easy means of retreat. A submissive dog is not likely to be attacked.

COMPANIONSHIP

Despite their need to establish a "pecking order," dogs are social by nature and generally get on well together. Dogs bred as companions tend to be less noisy than hounds, since barking is not considered a desirable trait where dogs are living in close proximity to people. Some toy breeds, however, such as Chihuahuas, can be vocal. A companion dog will wag its tail and open its mouth slightly in greeting when a member of the family returns home.

Faithful friend

PUPPIES

MOST PEOPLE prefer to own a dog from a puppy so that they can train it themselves. A puppy will settle more rapidly into unfamiliar surroundings than older individuals and is unlikely to display the behavioral problems that can be encountered in adult dogs. Even so, it is important to realize that some disruption and damage in the home is likely to follow its acquisition. Carpets, for example, may be soiled or chewed, and puppies may bark or yelp a great deal when first left on their own. This calls for tolerance on the part of owners. Sensible training and adequate attention to the puppy's needs should reduce such problems to a minimum. Dogs are creatures of routine and will soon learn to respond as required.

Golden Retriever and pups

THE BREEDING PERIOD

Domestic bitches (female dogs) usually have two periods of "heat" each year, whereas wild bitches come into season only once during this time. Both wolves and domestic dogs have a gestation period of about two months before the litter is born. The offspring, known as cubs or pups, respectively, are helpless at birth and are suckled and cleaned by their mother until they start to be weaned on to solid food at about four to six weeks old.

Playful Patterdales

HEALTHY PUPS

Young dogs tend to play vigorously and then sleep for long periods. This is not a sign of ill-health. Similarly, in a new home, a pup will be less active than an adult dog. Key health indicators to look for are a good appetite and firm motions with no trace of blood. The skin is normally loose but watch for a pot-bellied appearance, which could indicate worms. Deworming is a vital process for the pup's continued good health. Your vet will be able to advise you on essential vaccinations.

THE DEVELOPING PUP

The coat of a pup may be less profuse than its mother's (as in the example of the Old English Sheepdog, shown right), but the distribution of markings is unlikely to change as the pup matures.

By the time it is six months old, the pup should be house-trained. It should also be walking readily on a leash and can soon be allowed to exercise freely. Choose a quiet spot away from roads and away from distractions such as other dogs or farm animals. If the dog runs off, do not chase it, because it is likely to see this as a game. Instead, stand still and call it back. It should return after its enthusiasm for its newfound freedom wears off.

Old English Sheepdog and pup

Shar Pei pup   **Cocker Spaniel pup**

RELATIVE SIZES

All young puppies, no matter what their breed, are of a relatively similar size at birth. Only later do the larger breeds, like the Shar Pei (far left) start to grow at a faster rate than the smaller breeds, like the Cocker Spaniel (near left). Avoid exercising young dogs too strenuously, especially the larger breeds, because this puts stresses on their frame. It is better just to give them daily walks, with the opportunity to run free if they wish.

Australian Cattle Dog and pup

TOWARD ADULTHOOD

Changes become apparent as pups grow older. In certain breeds, such as the German Shepherd Dog, the ears will start to become erect. In a few cases, this does not happen, but generally the ears should have started to lift by the time the puppy is approaching six months old. In breeds in which pups are noticeably paler at birth than the adult dogs (as in the case of the Australian Cattle Dog, shown right), coat coloration is also likely to have darkened by six months. Other characteristics, such as eye color, may also be more adultlike by this age.

CHOOSING A DOG

WHEN CHOOSING A DOG, the potential owner is influenced by a number of factors, such as health, appearance, and character, but the size of the adult dog is generally the chief concern. However, size can often be deceptive, as some large dogs, such as the Greyhound, can be much less active in the home than smaller breeds. Unfortunately, the more dogs are kept as companions, the more their origins become obscured, though the instincts that first shaped their development often remain largely intact. Too many people choose a dog on the basis of its appearance alone without giving adequate consideration to the breed's ancestry, which is a factor that affects both its character and behavior.

HOUNDS

Some smaller hounds, such as the Beagle, have much to recommend them as pets, often having short, easy-care coats and lively, active natures. All scent hounds can be difficult to train, however, and will be reluctant to return to their owners if they pick up a scent. Pack dogs by nature, they can be greedy eaters.

Papillon

Beagle

SMALL IS BEAUTIFUL

Toy dogs such as the Papillon have a built-in advantage over larger breeds—their appetite is smaller and so they are less expensive to feed. They are quite easy to train and tend to be eager to please their owners. They thrive on affection and are usually good with children. However, it does not always follow that small dogs need less space; many small dogs, especially terriers, are very active and like nothing better than to run loose in open country.

SPANIELS

Gundogs were developed to have a close rapport with their owners, and breeds such as the English Springer Spaniel make admirable house companions, provided they have plenty of opportunity to exercise and plenty of time devoted to their needs. Grooming is a must, and particular attention should be paid to the heavy, pendulous ears, or they may become a source of problems in later life. Infections in the ears are common in spaniel breeds. One simple precaution is to invest in a very deep food bowl. The ears should then hang down outside the bowl, where they are less likely to become soiled by food.

English Springer Spaniel

POINTS TO CHECK

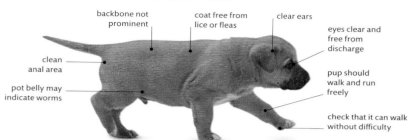

backbone not prominent

coat free from lice or fleas

clear ears

eyes clear and free from discharge

clean anal area

pot belly may indicate worms

pup should walk and run freely

check that it can walk without difficulty

CHOOSING A PUP

Having decided on the breed, you may be able to obtain a puppy locally. Breeders can be traced online or via the national kennel club. The cost of pups varies depending on their pedigree and the relative rarity of the breed. Pups are generally fully weaned and ready for their new home at about nine weeks old. Arrange for a veterinary check-up as soon as possible to ensure that the pup is in good health. However, not everybody wants, or can afford to buy, a pedigree dog and, in terms of companionship, rescue dogs or mongrel puppies (of no fixed breed) can be delightful pets. But remember that it may be hard to determine the ultimate size of a mongrel. As always, you want to see the parents.

GUARD DOGS

Breeds suitable for guard work, such as the Dobermann, are now popular as pets. However, many guard dogs retain strong working instincts and are dominant by nature. Consequently, they require firm training from a very early age if they are not to become a liability as they grow older. Never chose a breed just on its appearance. Investigate its background and what it was originally bred to do.

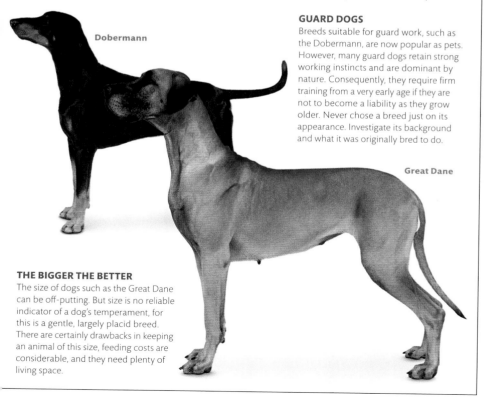

Dobermann

Great Dane

THE BIGGER THE BETTER

The size of dogs such as the Great Dane can be off-putting. But size is no reliable indicator of a dog's temperament, for this is a gentle, largely placid breed. There are certainly drawbacks in keeping an animal of this size, feeding costs are considerable, and they need plenty of living space.

PET CARE

A VARIETY OF EQUIPMENT is needed for grooming, feeding, and exercising a dog. However, it is important to choose the right equipment for your particular choice of breed, as requirements differ somewhat. Choosing the right equipment for the right stage in your dog's life will save you unnecessary trouble and expense. It may be better to defer the purchase of a bed, for instance, until the teething phase has passed, at around nine months of age. A cardboard box will do until then. Otherwise, your expensive purchase may be damaged beyond repair.

GROOMING AND COAT CARE

Regular grooming is vital from an early age, not only to keep the dog's coat in good condition but also to accustom it to the procedure, which the dog will then readily accept throughout its life. Some breeds require more coat care than others, depending on the quality of the hair, the length of the coat, and the lifestyle of the dog. Regular grooming sessions are a perfect opportunity for you to check for any health problems your dog may be experiencing, such as rashes, hair loss, sores or wounds, or any lumps or swellings that may need attention from a veterinarian. If you intend to show your dog, these sessions will also accustom the animal to being handled.

Combs and brushes

double-headed brush for finishing off

wire comb for untangling

flea comb

Brushing

Regular brushing to remove tangles and snags is the first step to keeping your dog's coat in good condition. You will have better access to all of the coat if you can persuade the dog to remain standing throughout this process. Start grooming your puppy at an early stage so it gets used to the process, picking up its feet and opening its mouth, too.

Sleeping quarters

Encouraging a dog to use its own sleeping quarters from an early age will deter it from sleeping on your bed. Getting a dog crate and placing the bed inside at the outset can be recommended.

DOG BEDS

When you decide that the purchase of a bed is in order, make sure that it is fully washable, for this is the site where fleas typically deposit their eggs. By cleaning the bed on a regular basis, you may be able to spare yourself an explosive epidemic of these troublesome parasites. If you are buying a bed for a young dog, make sure that it is sufficiently large to accommodate the dog comfortably once it is fully grown.

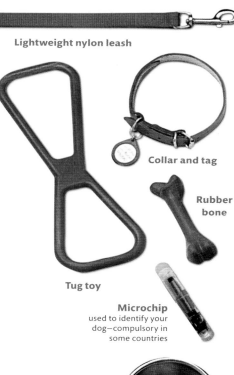

Lightweight nylon leash

Collar and tag

Rubber bone

Tug toy

Microchip
used to identify your dog—compulsory in some countries

Ceramic bowl

Stainless steel bowl

COLLARS, LEASHES, AND TOYS

Pups from six to seven weeks old should be introduced to wearing a collar. Proper training of all dogs must include learning to walk calmly on a collar and leash with their owner. A leather collar can be unbuckled and made longer as your dog grows. Adjust it so that it fits loosely but is not so slack that the dog can pull its head free of it. In case your dog wanders, you must attach a tag to the collar stating your address and telephone number.

Dogs, even when fully grown, enjoy play, and your pet store should have a wide range of suitable toys. Play sessions are not only fun for the dog; they also represent good exercise. Tug toys and rubber bones help keep the dog's teeth in good condition, but avoid small items that pups may swallow.

HEALTH CARE

TEETH CARE
You can now buy specially made toothpaste and brushes for your dog. These will help keep its teeth and gums in good condition.

GIVING MEDICINE
If your dog is cooperative, you should be able to administer medicine orally using a spoon. If not, use a syringe. Give it slowly or the dog is likely to spit it out.

EAR CLEANING
Remove dead hair with your fingers, use a dropper to put oily cleanser into the ear canal, massage the base of the ear to spread it, then clear oil or wax at the surface with cotton balls. Never poke into the ear canal.

NUTRITIONAL CARE

Food and water bowls should be made from a material that can be properly cleaned. Replace ceramic bowls once they are chipped or cracked, for such defects are sites where bacteria may breed.

Try not to vary the puppy's diet at first, even if you intend to change from canned to dry food, for example, at a later stage. This should help minimize the likelihood of any digestive upsets. If you decide to use a feeding supplement, be sure to follow the manufacturer's instructions carefully, because overdosing may well prove harmful.

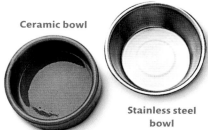

DOG IDENTIFICATION KEY

THE SYSTEM OF IDENTIFICATION used here assumes no prior knowledge of dog character or function but offers instead a method of recognition based on noting key physical characteristics, as defined below and opposite. On the following pages (pp.26–33), all the breeds in the book are separated into groups, first by size (small, medium, or large), then by head shape (round, long, or square), ear type (long, erect, or short), and finally by coat type (short, long, or wiry). At the end of this trail appears a typical dog of that type (e.g., small, round-headed, long-eared, and short-coated), together with the page numbers on which all breeds with similar features appear. In a few cases, a breed may appear in more than one group.

SIZE

This is the most evident feature that separates breeds. Three categories are used—small, medium, and large—and they refer to the highest point of the shoulder (the withers). This is also the measure for show purposes and is the figure given in the actual breed entries.

Size variants
The sizes shown are large, over 24in (61cm); medium, 18–24in (46–61cm); and small, under 18in (46cm).

HEAD SHAPE

This is obviously a less precise feature than height, but, again, the breeds have been divided into three broad categories: round-headed, long-headed, and square-headed. Round-headed breeds tend to be short-nosed; long-headed breeds have long noses, which may taper; square-headed breeds often have relatively short, muscular jaws.

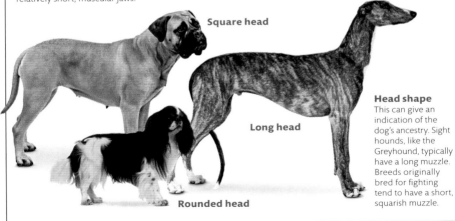

Large

Medium

Small

Square head

Long head

Rounded head

Head shape
This can give an indication of the dog's ancestry. Sight hounds, like the Greyhound, typically have a long muzzle. Breeds originally bred for fighting tend to have a short, squarish muzzle.

EAR SHAPE AND LENGTH

The shape and length of a dog's ears vary considerably. Erect ears trap sound waves most effectively, but in hounds that rely on their sense of smell to locate quarry, the ears tend to hang down. By obscuring the ear canal with the flap, the sensitive inner part of the ear is protected when the hounds are pursuing quarry through vegetation, and this also reduces the risk of seeds or thorns falling into the ear. Short ears allow dogs to go to ground more easily and are particularly encouraged in terrier breeds. A dog's appearance can be altered by cropping its ears, which is a surgical alteration that causes them to stand up. It is typically carried out on breeds such as the Dobermann and Great Dane, with a view to making them appear more aggressive. This surgery is, however, outlawed in many countries worldwide.

Long ears

Short ears

Naturally erect ears

COATS

Another significant feature that can help identify a dog is its coat type. Coats can be divided into short- or long-haired, on the basis of their length, while the third category, wire-haired, is distinguished by texture. Some breeds, such as the Dachshunds, have been developed in all three coat types, while others may occur in both short- and long-haired forms, although one type often tends to predominate today.

Short hair
Creates a smooth, sleek appearance, with the hair tight against the skin.

Long hair
Usually combines with a dense undercoat to give weatherproofing.

Wire hair
A harsh and dense type often found on breeds working in undergrowth.

TAILS

Tails show considerable variation in length and shape. Tails can be artificially shortened by docking, which entails cutting off part of the tail in young puppies, but this mutilation has now been banned in many countries.

Curly tail
Usually associated with spitz breeds.

Long tail
Used as a means of communication; enables a dog to be seen in undergrowth.

Feathered tail
Formed by longer hair on lower tail surface. Associated with setters and other gundogs.

SMALL DOGS

THIS GROUP INCLUDES all breeds under 18in (46cm) in height. Once you have established that the dog belongs to this category, you should identify the head shape (see p.24), followed by the ear and coat type. You will then be able to locate a breed of that physical type in one of the bands below or on pages 28–29, where there will also be page references for all similar breeds

BREEDS GROUPED BY KEY CHARACTERISTICS

ROUND-HEADED

Long-eared

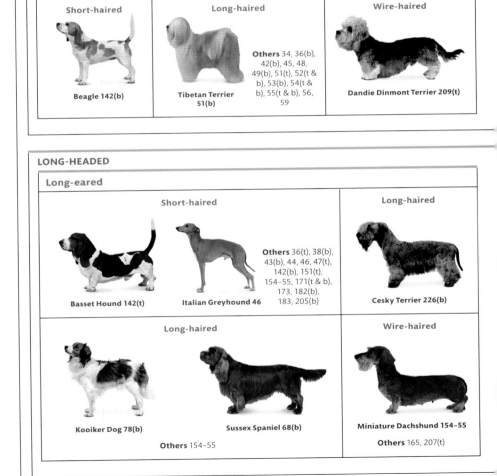

Short-haired

Beagle 142(b)

Long-haired

Tibetan Terrier 51(b)

Others 34, 36(b), 42(b), 45, 48, 49(b), 51(t), 52(t & b), 53(b), 54(t & b), 55(t & b), 56, 59

Wire-haired

Dandie Dinmont Terrier 209(t)

LONG-HEADED

Long-eared

Short-haired

Basset Hound 142(t)

Italian Greyhound 46

Others 36(t), 38(b), 43(b), 44, 46, 47(t), 142(b), 151(t), 154–55, 171(t & b), 173, 182(b), 183, 205(b)

Long-haired

Cesky Terrier 226(b)

Long-haired

Kooiker Dog 78(b)

Sussex Spaniel 68(b)

Others 154–55

Wire-haired

Miniature Dachshund 154–55

Others 165, 207(t)

featured in the book.
"Small" dogs include the so-called toy breeds, and many terriers. Their size makes them popular as companions today, although some were quite

localized earlier. Some terriers share a common ancestry and may resemble each other, whereas true companion dogs show a much wider variation in appearance.

Erect-eared

Long-haired	Wire-haired
	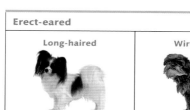
Continental Toy Spaniel: Papillon 43(t)	Affenpinscher 219(t)

Short-eared

Long-haired

Chihuahua 37(b)

Erect-eared

Short-haired			Long-haired
		Others 38(t), 50, 103(b), 107(t & b), 128(t), 193, 202, 206(b), 242(t), 245(b), 287(t), 291(b)	
Miniature Bull Terrier 208(t)	English Toy Terrier 206(t)		German Spitz: Mittel 40(b)

Wire-haired

Australian Terrier 216(b)

Podengo Portugueses Pequeño 193

Others 207(b), 213(t), 221

Others 35, 40(t), 41(t & b), 47(b), 53(t), 128(b), 217(t), 221

Shetland Sheepdog 105(b)

SMALL, LONG-HEADED DOGS *continued*

Short-eared

Short-haired

Parson Jack Russell Terrier 211(t)

Japanese Terrier 288(t)

Smooth Fox Terrier 212(t)

Others 214(t), 217(b), 218, 219(b), 224(b)

SQUARE-HEADED

Erect-eared

Short-haired	Long-haired	Wire-haired
Other 259(t)	**Other** 215(t)	**Other** 214(b)
Boston Terrier 204(b)	Skye Terrier 213(b)	Cairn Terrier 209(b)

MEDIUM-SIZE DOGS

THIS GROUP INCLUDES all breeds between 18–24in (41–61cm) in height. Once you have established that the dog belongs to this category, you should identify the head shape (see p.24), followed by the ear and coat type. You will then be able to locate a breed of that physical type below or on pages

ROUND-HEADED

Long-eared

Short-haired

Labrador 65

Other 132

Long-haired

Polish Lowland Sheepdog 119(t)

Others 62(b), 63(t), 91, 102, 119(b), 132, 262

Wire-haired

Wire Fox Terrier
211(b)

Lakeland Terrier
210(t)

Welsh Terrier
212(b)

Others 210(b),
211(t), 217(b),
220, 224(t)

Short-eared

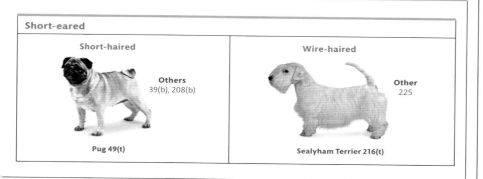

Short-haired

Others
39(b), 208(b)

Pug 49(t)

Wire-haired

Other
225

Sealyham Terrier 216(t)

30–33, where there will also be page references for all similar breeds featured in the book.

Many common breeds are medium-size, including various gundogs, sheepdogs, and hounds, though others remain localized, even within their place of origin. Nevertheless, rare breed shows are gradually introducing many of them to a wider audience.

Erect-eared

Long-haired

Chow Chow 284

Short-eared

Long-haired

Briard 113(t)

MEDIUM-SIZE, LONG-HEADED DOGS *continued*

Long-eared

Short-Haired	Long-Haired

Weimaraner 72-73

Afghan Hound 198

Others 57, 58, 63(b), 66, 68(t), 70, 75, 78(t), 83, 84–85, 86, 87, 88(t), 89, 94, 97, 98, 99, 100, 116–17, 134, 135(t & b), 136, 137, 138–39, 140, 141, 143, 147(b), 148, 149, 150(t & b), 151(b), 152, 153, 156(t & b), 157, 160, 161, 162–63, 164, 166–67, 168, 172, 176, 178, 179, 180–81, 184, 185(t), 186, 187, 191, 195, 197, 201, 226(t & b), 268, 270, 275, 276(t), 280(t)

Others 60, 61, 62(t), 64, 69, 71, 72–73, 76–77, 79(t & b), 80, 82, 90

Erect-eared

Short-Haired	Long-Haired

Pharaoh Hound 189   **Saarloos Wolfdog 121**

Keeshond 42(t)

Others 105(t), 108, 109, 112(b), 115, 125, 188(b), 190, 194, 200, 229(b), 230–31, 235(t), 241(t & b), 242(b), 243(t & b), 244, 245(t), 277, 280(b), 281(t & b), 282, 283(t), 286, 288(b)

Others 104, 110(t&b), 120, 122, 124

Short-eared

Short-Haired

Sloughi 199

Chinook 229(t)

Others 103(t), 146, 147(t), 182(t), 192

Wire-Haired

Irish Red and White Setter 81

Others 92, 99, 101, 106, 130(t & b), 131, 133, 145, 263, 266–67, 271, 276(t), 291(t)

Spinone 96

Others 74, 93(t & b), 95, 118, 161, 174, 175(b), 169, 176, 177, 185(b), 188(t)

Briquet Griffon Vendéen 175(t)

Wire-Haired

Berger de Picard 114

Others 235(b), 239, 258, 264(t)

Laekenois 123

Others 190, 222

Podengo Portugueses Medio 194

Long-Haired

Wire-Haired

Soft-coated Wheaten Terrier 223

Border Collie 103(t)

Airedale Terrier 205(t)

MEDIUM-SIZE, SQUARE-HEADED DOGS *continued*

Long-eared

Short-Haired	Long-Haired

Dogue de Bordeaux 259(b) Others 234, 238, 256, 269, 276(b), 289	**Bouvier des Flandres 126–27** **Others** 129(b), 269

LARGE DOGS

THIS GROUP INCLUDES all breeds over 24in (61cm) in height. Once you have established that the dog belongs to this category, you should identify the head shape (see p.24), followed by the ear and coat type. You will then be able to locate a breed of that physical type

LONG-HEADED

Long-eared

Short-Haired	Long-Haired

Great Dane 248–49 **Others** 239, 279, 287(b)	**Pyrenean Mastiff 274** **Others** 196, 254–55, 257, 260–61, 278

SQUARE-HEADED

Long-eared

Short-Haired

Neapolitan Mastiff 272

Mastiff 232–33

Erect-eared

Long-Haired

Pumi 129(b)

Short-eared

Short-Haired

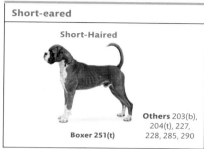

Boxer 251(t)

Others 203(b), 204(t), 227, 228, 285, 290

in one of the bands below, where there will also be page references for all similar breeds featured in the book.

As might be expected, these breeds are relatively few in number, though some can trace their ancestry back to the oldest forms of the domestic dog.

Wire-Haired

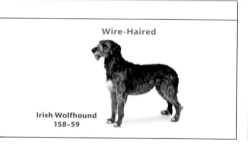

Irish Wolfhound
158–59

Short-eared

Wire-Haired

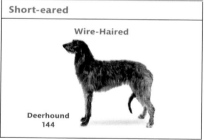

Deerhound
144

Short-eared

Long-Haired

Landseer
252–53

Newfoundland
236–37

COMPANION DOGS

BRED ESSENTIALLY AS PETS and not as working dogs, companion dogs appear in a wide variety of shapes and sizes. They are often simply scaled-down versions of much larger dogs, but some, such as the Chihuahua (see p.37), were created specifically as companions, with no hint of a working ancestry. Others, like the Bulldog (see p.35) and the Basenji (see p.47), were developed from former working stock.

Companion dogs are typically loyal and affectionate by nature, but concerns have been expressed regarding the constitution of some members of this group. A hindlimb weakness centered on the knees (called luxating patellas) is one type of problem found in some companion breeds. However, by careful selection of adult breeding stock, breeders are continually seeking to eliminate such weaknesses.

Place of origin: US	First use: Companion	Origins: 1972

Kyi Leo

The Kyi Leo is a small, solidly built animal with a profuse covering of long hair and an alert, friendly face. Usual coat coloration is black and white, but other colors are also commonly seen.

HISTORY The ancestry of this breed is in no doubt at all: it is the result of crossings between the Lhasa Apso (see p.52) and the Maltese (see p.53). Originating in California, the Kyi Leo is specifically designed for life as a companion dog and does not regard the lack of a garden or yard as a particular hardship.
REMARK The Kyi Leo is an "easy-care" dog. Its long coat does require frequent brushing to remain in good condition but no clipping is necessary.

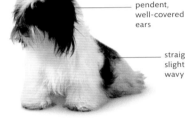

pendent, well-covered ears

straight or slightly wavy hair

hair forms parting on back

well-muscled physique

pronounced stop

Color types

Height: 9–11in (23–28cm)	Weight: 13–15lb (6–7kg)	Temperament: Gentle, loyal

Place of origin: US	First use: Companion	Origins: 1900s

American Eskimo Dog

Popularly known as Eskies, three distinct sizes of this attractive breed are recognized. Aside from the toy and miniature forms seen here, there is also a standard variation. They are descended from European spitz stock. The face, coat, and lush tail of this dog identify it as a spitz-type breed. The pointed muzzle and erect ears are foxlike, its coat is long and thick, and its tail is well plumed and carried in a curl over the back. Although a small dog, it is nevertheless sturdy, well muscled, and powerful with a broad back. These dogs are white or biscuit and white in color.

HISTORY Descended from the German Spitz, this breed was scaled down from farm dogs used by German immigrants in the American Midwest.

REMARK An American Eskimo Dog was a highly successful tight-rope walker in Barnum & Bailey's famous circus.

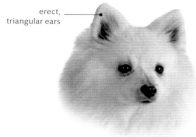

erect, triangular ears

the distinctive biscuit-cream shade is evident in the fur in this case

plumed tail, set high and carried over the back

short, sturdy legs

Toy

pure white fur

Black rim around the eyes

Miniature

Manelike ruff of fur

Height: 9–19in (23–48cm)	Weight: 6–35lb (3–16kg)	Temperament: Affectionate, obedient

Place of origin: Great Britain	First use: Companion	Origins: 1920s

Cavalier King Charles

An early 20th-century recreation of the old type of King Charles Spaniel (below), the Cavalier can be distinguished by its longer nose and heavier build. Both breeds have identical coloration. The chestnut and white of each breed is described as the Blenheim, after the estate of the Duke of Marlborough, where spaniels of this color were first developed.

HISTORY Toy spaniels were a common sight around the palaces of Europe during the 17th century and were often portrayed in paintings of the period. Cavaliers were first registered by the British Kennel Club as a separate breed in 1945.

REMARK The prefix "Cavalier" was chosen to distinguish it from the King Charles Spaniel.

Ruby

long, well-feathered ears

relatively flat, undomed skull

Blenheim

long, silky coat with no curls

Color types

Height: 12–13in (31–33cm)	Weight: 10–18lb (5–8kg)	Temperament: Friendly, obedient

Place of origin: Great Britain	First use: Companion	Origins: 1600s

King Charles Spaniel

Squarely built with a distinctive domed skull, this breed's affectionate nature has made it a popular pet for centuries. The large, dark eyes are particularly appealing.

HISTORY This breed was greatly favored by King Charles II of England (1630–1685). He regularly exercised his dogs in St. James's Park, London.

REMARK The breed today is larger than its ancestors.

OTHER NAMES English Toy Spaniel.

Blenheim

domed skull

short nose, with wide, turned-up muzzle

short back

deep, broad chest

Tricolor

Color types

Height: 10–11in (25–27cm)	Weight: 8–14lb (4–6kg)	Temperament: Obedient, affectionate

Place of origin: Mexico	First use: Companion	Origins: 1800s

Chihuahua

Differing coat lengths separate the two varieties of this tiny, plucky dog. The smooth-coated form has a glossy, short coat, while the long-haired form has a significantly longer, slightly wavy coat. Today's long-haired form is the result of crossings of Smooth-coated Chihuahuas with Yorkshire Terriers (see p.215) and Papillons (see p.43). Selective breeding has since taken place to ensure that in all other respects the two forms are indistinguishable. Common colors are fawn, chestnut, steel-blue, and silver, often seen in combinations.

HISTORY The name "Chihuahua" derives from the Mexican state of that name where this dog may have originated. It was first seen in the US toward the end of the 19th century, before being taken to Europe. Most of today's bloodlines are descended from the original 50 dogs taken to the US.
REMARK They can be quite noisy dogs by nature.

short, pointed muzzle

relatively muscular hindquarters

short, soft, and glossy coat

Short-haired Chihuahua

ruff on neck

muscular, well-feathered legs

Long-haired Chihuahua

coat may be slightly wavy but never curled

long tail resembles a plume

dainty feet

Color types

Height: 6–9in (15–23cm)	Weight: 2–6lb (1–3kg)	Temperament: Bold, playful

| Place of origin: Mexico | First use: Companion | Origins: 1500s |

Mexican Hairless

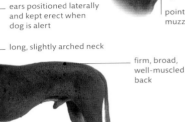
traces of hair apparent on top of head

Three forms of this breed are now recognized: the Standard (shown here), the Miniature, and the smaller Toy version. There is also a so-called "Powder-puff" version of each size, which does have a coat of hair but cannot be exhibited. The Mexican Hairless has a noble stance, not unlike that of a sight hound, and the build of a terrier.

HISTORY Utilized as bed-warmers, pets, and, less comfortably, as ritual sacrifices, this dog was widely kept in ancient Aztec settlements.

REMARK A breeding program initiated by the Mexican Kennel Club in the 1950s saved this dog from certain extinction. They are, however, still quite scarce, even today.

OTHER NAMES Tepeizeuintli, Xoloitzcuintli.

ears positioned laterally and kept erect when dog is alert

pointed muzzle

long, slightly arched neck

firm, broad, well-muscled back

exposed skin is susceptible to sunburn

straight, parallel forelegs

tip of tail shows traces of hair

Color types

| Height: 11–12in (28–31cm) | Weight: 9–18lb (4–8kg) | Temperament: Lively, alert |

| Place of origin: Peru | First use: Warming beds | Origins: 1200s |

Inca Hairless Dog

This group of dogs is found in three distinct categories, based on size. It is not clear whether all the New World hairless breeds are related, but these particular dogs are seen in both solid and spotted variants.

HISTORY Although rare in their homeland today, they were once the favored companions of the Incas.

REMARK As with the Mexican Hairless (above), "Powder-puff" versions of these dogs also occur.

OTHER NAMES Peruvian Hairless Dog.

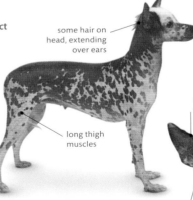

some hair on head, extending over ears

ears set low on head

long thigh muscles

small, dark eyes

Color types

| Height: 10–28in (25–71cm) | Weight: 9–55lb (4–25kg) | Temperament: Affectionate, loyal |

| Place of origin: Russia | First use: Watchdog and ratter | Origins: 1700s |

Russian Toy

This breed had close ties to the Russian aristocracy, up until the Russian Revolution of 1917, after which it became very scarce. It has since been recreated, with the long-coated form emerging in 1958.

HISTORY Renewed interest in the Russian Toy followed the creation of a breed club during 2006 in Russia. Just two years later, the breed reached the UK and was seen in North America at this stage, too.

REMARK The coat of a long-coated individual takes three years to develop fully.

OTHER NAMES Russkiy Toy, Moscow Toy Terrier, Moscovian Miniature Terrier.

prominent high-set, triangular ears

Smooth-haired form

strong, straight back

long-legged, fine-boned appearance

semi-long feathering

Long-haired form

Color types

| Height: 8–11in (20–28cm) | Weight: Up to 6½lb (3kg) | Temperament: Loyal, often vocal |

| Place of origin: Great Britain | First use: Baiting bulls | Origins: 1800s |

Bulldog

With a musculature almost out of proportion to its size, the Bulldog is a diminutive but powerful mastiff-type dog. Its head is proportionately large and its circumference may equal its height. Its eyes are set low. White often predominates in the coat, although there are plenty of red, brindle, and fawn Bulldogs.

HISTORY Until the banning of bull baiting in England in 1835, this breed was very popular. Since then it has been made considerably gentler by selective breeding and has become a popular companion today.

REMARK Birth by Cesarean section is not uncommon, as the large head size of the pups may block the birth canal.

OTHER NAMES English Bulldog.

very short, broad nose

undershot lower jaw

powerful, compact body

extremely wide chest

Color types

| Height: 12–14in (31–36cm) | Weight: 50–55lb (23–25kg) | Temperament: Affectionate, docile |

Place of origin: Germany	First use: Companion	Origins: 1800s

Giant German Spitz

The face of this breed is a little foxlike. The outercoat is long and harsh, while the undercoat is dense and soft. The Giant German Spitz is not actually as large as the Keeshond (see p.42)—the fifth member of this group. It is bred in solid colors only.

HISTORY The ancestors of these dogs were probably brought to Holland and Germany by the Vikings.
REMARK Certain colors became associated with particular regions, such as the black with Wurttemberg.
OTHER NAMES Deutscher Gross Spitz.

tail curls up and lies over back

erect, triangular-shaped ears

rounded, catlike feet

Color types

Height: 16in (41cm)	Weight: 40lb (18kg)	Temperament: Lively, playful

---

Place of origin: Germany	First use: Working on farms	Origins: 1800s

German Spitz: Mittel

The Mittel, or standard, form of the German Spitz is the third largest of the five varieties. Like the Giant (above), it is usually bred in solid colors, but in Britain, all varieties and markings are acceptable.

HISTORY The watchful demeanor of these dogs initially led to their being highly valued on farms, but they also make rewarding companions.
REMARK Like the other German Spitz, the Mittel has a harsh, long outercoat and a soft, woolly undercoat.
OTHER NAMES Deutscher Mittel Spitz.

luxuriant tail

oval-shaped eyes

compact, firm condition

Color types

Height: 11½–14in (29–36cm)	Weight: 25lb (11kg)	Temperament: Lively, playful

| Place of origin: Germany | First use: Lap dog | Origins: 1800s |

German Spitz: Klein

The German Spitz breeds are compact and squarely built and can be distinguished essentially on the basis of size. The Spitz is protected from harsh weather by its thick coat, which varies greatly in color and has a dense undercoat.

HISTORY The German Spitz is descended from much larger, sledge-pulling spitz breeds.
REMARK Since 1985, this breed has undergone a revival outside Germany.
OTHER NAMES Deutsche Spitz.

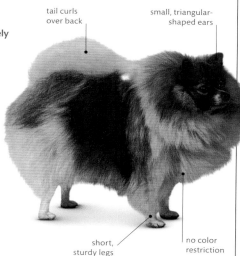

tail curls over back

small, triangular-shaped ears

no color restriction

short, sturdy legs

Color types

| Height: 9–11in (23–28cm) | Weight: 18–22lb (8–10kg) | Temperament: Lively, playful |

| Place of origin: Germany | First use: General companion | Origins: 1800s |

Pomeranian

The smallest member of the German Spitz group, the Pomeranian is characterized by an upright tail that tilts forward over its body. The coat takes three years to reach full maturity. This breed is an affectionate companion. A variant called the "Teacup Pomeranian" appeared during the 19th century, when the Pomeranian was selectively bred down to "toy" size.

HISTORY This breed is thought to have developed in northern Germany from larger spitz dogs.
REMARK Despite its diminutive size, it makes a good watchdog.

erect, foxlike ears

harsh, long hair on tail

Color types

| Height: 11in (28cm) | Weight: 4–5½lb (2–3kg) | Temperament: Friendly, active |

Place of origin: Netherlands	First use: Barge companion	Origins: 1500s

Keeshond

This lively breed is distinguished by its wolf-gray coat. Its coloration tends to be lighter on the head, creating the impression of dark "spectacles" around the eyes.

HISTORY It is named after the Dutchman de Gyselaer, whose nickname was Kees.
REMARK A fine watchdog, the Keeshond provides good security as well as company.
OTHER NAMES Wolf Spitz, Chien Loup.

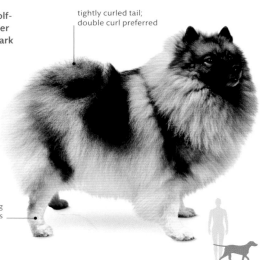

tightly curled tail; double curl preferred

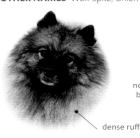

no feathering below hocks

dense ruff

Height: 17–19in (43–48cm)	Weight: 55–66lb (25–30kg)	Temperament: Independent, affectionate

Place of origin: Belgium	First use: Companion	Origins: 1600s

Continental Toy Spaniel: Phalene

Closely related to the Papillon (opposite), the Phalene can be readily distinguished from it by its ears, which hang down on the sides of its head.

HISTORY The breed was popular in Italy during the Renaissance and was well known in European royal circles.
REMARK In the US, the Phalene is not distinguished from the Papillon, which is accepted in both ear forms.
OTHER NAMES Épagneul Nain, Continental Phalene.

white blaze on face

high-set bushy tail

Color types

harelike feet

Height: 8–11in (20–28cm)	Weight: 9–10lb (4.1–4.5kg)	Temperament: Friendly, alert

Place of origin: France	First use: Companion	Origins: 1600s

Continental Toy Spaniel: Papillon

This dainty little dog is closely related to the Phalene (opposite), but it can easily be distinguished by its erect ears. Its name, *Papillon*, the French for "butterfly," refers to the shape of its ears.

HISTORY This breed often featured in paintings by the Flemish artist Van Dyke.
REMARK Daily grooming is essential.
OTHER NAMES Épagneul Nain.

symmetrical head markings and blaze

slightly round skull

very large, well-fringed ears

fine, harelike feet with long hair between toes

Height: 8–11in (20–28cm)	Weight: 9–10lb (4–4.5kg)	Temperament: Friendly, alert

Place of origin: France	First use: Companion	Origins: 1400s

Toy Poodle

Identical in all respects to its larger relatives except in height, this is the smallest of the three varieties of poodle. Pictured here is the lion trim, preferred for showing.

HISTORY Miniaturization of the Standard Poodle (see p.250) gave rise to this dog. They were portrayed by the German artist Dürer in 1500.
REMARK The coat of this and other poodles is not molted, so it needs clipping approximately every six to eight weeks.
OTHER NAMES Caniche.

tail carried at an angle to body

long, fine head

deep, relatively wide chest

dense, very profuse coat

well-sprung ribs

Color types

small, oval-shaped feet

Height: 10–11in (25–28cm)	Weight: 15lb (7kg)	Temperament: Loyal, sociable

| Place of origin: France | First use: Water dog | Origins: 1600s |

Miniature Poodle

Well-proportioned and squarely built, the Miniature Poodle lies between the larger Standard (see p.250) and the tiny Toy (see p.43) in size. This intelligent breed has a sporty disposition and is easy to train.

HISTORY Poodles probably derive from the Pudel, an old German water dog.
REMARK From the late 1940s to the 1960s, the Miniature Poodle was the most popular dog breed in the world.
OTHER NAMES Barbone, Caniche.

long, wide ears

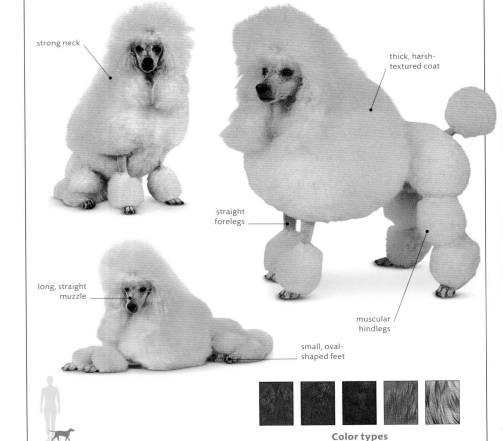

strong neck

thick, harsh-textured coat

straight forelegs

long, straight muzzle

muscular hindlegs

small, oval-shaped feet

Color types

| Height: 11–15in (28–38cm) | Weight: 26–30lb (12–14kg) | Temperament: Intelligent, lively |

Place of origin: France	First use: Companion	Origins: 1500s

Löwchen

With its long, silky coat trimmed in the traditional "lion clip," this dog is easily distinguished from other members of the bichon group. The tail is clipped along part of its length, leaving just a plume of hair, completing this attractive, lively breed's distinctive parody of the "king of the beasts".

HISTORY This breed found favor with the European aristocracy at an early stage in its development. It was featured in a painting by Goya of the Duchess of Alba in the late 1700s. However, its popularity declined to the extent that by 1960 it was considered to be the world's rarest dog breed.
REMARK This intelligent, good-natured breed has now undergone a welcome growth in popularity, particularly in the US.
OTHER NAMES Little Lion Dog.

short head with dark nose

long, silky "mane"

large, dark, round eyes

tail curls forward over back

well-muscled hindquarters

long, pendent, well-fringed ears

long, wavy but not curly coat

Color types

Height: 10–13in (25–33cm)	Weight: 8–18lb (4–8kg)	Temperament: Active, affectionate

Place of origin: Italy	First use: Lady's companion	Origins: 500 BCE

Italian Greyhound

A miniature form of the Greyhound (See p.146), this breed is far less fragile than it looks. It has a gait similar to the larger dog's, and the same rapid acceleration, facilitated by long, muscular hindquarters. The long, graceful neck heightens its refined air.

HISTORY This breed has survived since the time of the pharaohs. However, it suffered from the introduction of English Toy Terrier blood (see p.206) in the 1800s, in an attempt to miniaturize these dogs further.
REMARK Similar dogs have been found, mummified, in Egyptian tombs.
OTHER NAMES Piccolo Levrieri Italiani.

ears well back on head

flat and narrow skull

Italian Greyhound puppies and mother

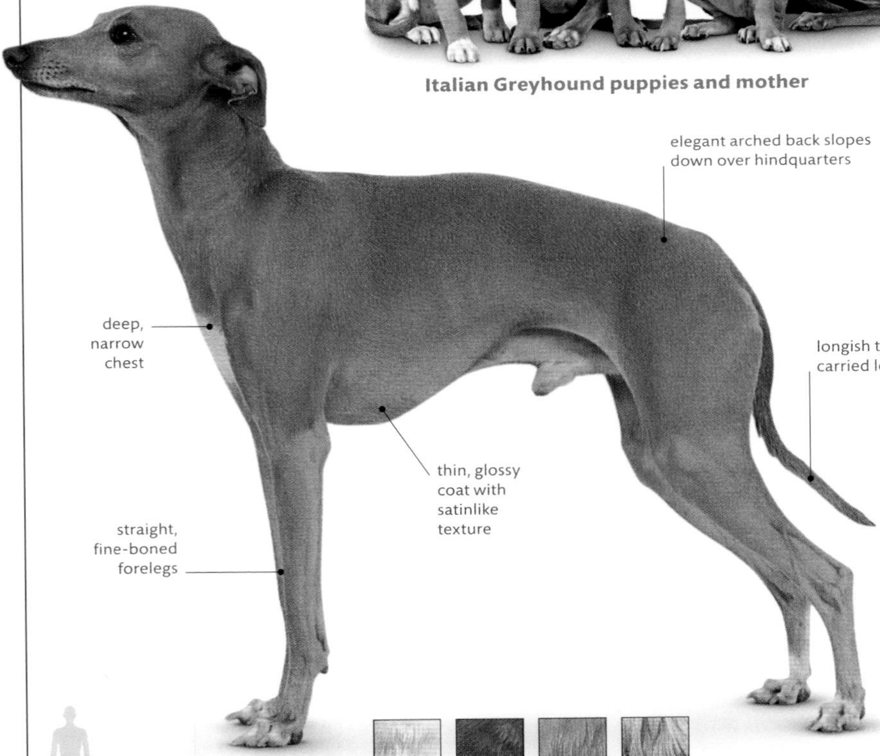

elegant arched back slopes down over hindquarters

deep, narrow chest

longish tail carried low

thin, glossy coat with satinlike texture

straight, fine-boned forelegs

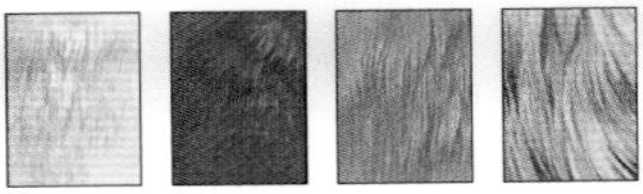

Color types

Height: 13–15in (33–38cm)	Weight: 8lb (3.6kg)	Temperament: Quiet, affectionate

Place of origin: Zaire	First use: Hunting dog	Origins: 1500s

Basenji

The most distinctive feature of the alert, finely built Basenji becomes apparent only when it is disturbed—instead of barking like other dogs, it has unique yodeling and chortling calls.

HISTORY The Basenji was developed as a hunting dog in the Congo and it may be related to similar dogs portrayed on ancient Egyptian artifact. The breed caused a sensation when it was first shown at Crufts, in England, in 1937. The owner called them "basenji," which is an African word for "bush thing."

REMARK Green vegetables are favored by these dogs and should form part of their regular diet. Bitches come on heat only once a year instead of twice.

OTHER NAMES Congo Dog.

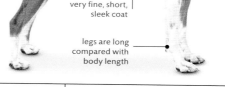

pointed, erect ears

wrinkled forehead

tightly curled tail

very fine, short, sleek coat

legs are long compared with body length

Color types

Height: 16–17in (41–43cm)	Weight: 21–24lb (9.5–11kg)	Temperament: Intelligent, affectionate

---

Place of origin: Italy	First use: General companion	Origins: 1600s

Volpino Italiano

This small Italian breed is unmistakably a spitz type, its face being not unlike that of a fox, with the muzzle short, straight, and rather pointed. The Volpino is usually pure white in coloration, the sable form now being rare. A fawn variety existed at one time, but this has now been lost.

HISTORY The early ancestors of the Volpino Italiano were originally brought from northern Europe in the 1600s, but the breed itself was developed entirely within Italy. Today, it is quite scarce in its homeland.

REMARK The name "Volpino" originates from the Italian word, *volpe*, which translates as "fox."

OTHER NAMES Cane de Quirinale.

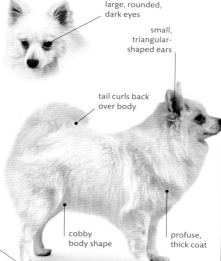

large, rounded, dark eyes

small, triangular-shaped ears

tail curls back over body

dainty hindfeet

cobby body shape

profuse, thick coat

Color types

Height: 11in (28cm)	Weight: 10lb (5kg)	Temperament: Affectionate

Place of origin: China	First use: Companion	Origins: 100s

Pekingese

The Pekingese is a short-legged breed of
dog with a characteristic rolling gait. It has
a relatively compact, flattened face fringed
with longer hair, which gives the impression
of the dog having a mane. This breed makes
a bold and alert watchdog for the home.

HISTORY It was first seen in the West after
the British overran Beijing (formerly known in
Europe as Peking) in 1860. Prior to this, the
Pekingese had been the jealously guarded,
exclusive possession of the Chinese emperor.
REMARK Pekingese used to be known
as "sleeve dogs" because they could be
carried in the long, flowing sleeves of
Chinese courtiers.
OTHER NAMES Peking Palasthund.

large, round,
dark eyes

very evident
stop to nose

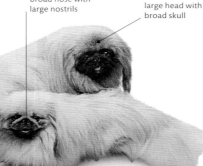

well-feathered tail is
set high and curled
over to one side

long, silky coat

broad nose with
large nostrils

large head with
broad skull

heart-shaped
ears set level
with skull

skull is flat
between ears

Color types

Height: 6–9in (15–23cm)	Weight: 7–12lb (3–6kg)	Temperament: Independent, lively

Place of origin: China	First use: Companion	Origins: 1500s

Pug

Squarely and solidly built, the Pug is a compact yet very well-proportioned little breed with an unmistakable, flat, wrinkled face. It has a very distinctive, endearing expression.

HISTORY Originally developed in China, the breed came to Europe in the 16th century, where it gained immense popularity. It was later perfected in Britain.
REMARK This intelligent, long-lived dog may have been larger in the earliest days of its development.
OTHER NAMES Carlin, Mops.

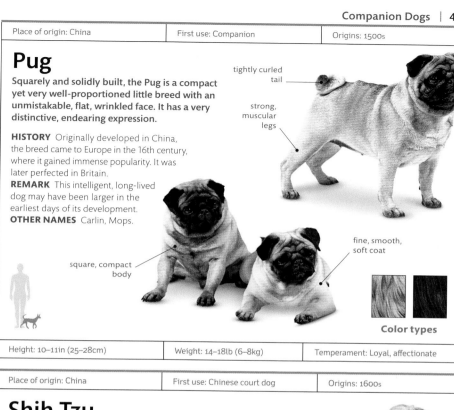

tightly curled tail

strong, muscular legs

square, compact body

fine, smooth, soft coat

Color types

Height: 10–11in (25–28cm)	Weight: 14–18lb (6–8kg)	Temperament: Loyal, affectionate

---

Place of origin: China	First use: Chinese court dog	Origins: 1600s

Shih Tzu

Often confused with the Tibetan Lhasa Apso (see p.52), the Chinese Shih Tzu has a denser, slightly wavy coat and a face that has been described as similar to a chrysanthemum. This impression is given by the tendency of the hair on the bridge of the dog's nose to grow upward. Generally, this facial hair is tied up on the top of its head.

HISTORY The Shih Tzu was developed in Beijing, China, by crossing miniature Chinese breeds with Tibetan breeds.
REMARK For many years, this breed was a great favorite of the Emperors of China.
OTHER NAMES Chrysanthemum Dog.

well-spaced eyes

long facial hair

tail held high and heavily plumed

long, dense outercoat with good undercoat

Color types

Height: 10½in (27cm)	Weight: 10–16lb (5–7kg)	Temperament: Gentle, loyal

| Place of origin: China | First use: Companion | Origins: 100 BCE |

Chinese Crested Dog

This nimble little dog comes in two varieties. One form, the Hairless, has hair only as a crest on its head and toes, and a plume on its tail. The Powder Puff variety is covered with long, soft hair. Both are found in a mixture of colors.

HISTORY Known for centuries in China, this dog first came to prominence in the Han dynasty but was not exhibited in the West until the Westminster Show in New York in 1885. It was only during 1975 that a specialist breed club was established in the US. **REMARK** The texture of the skin of the Hairless should be smooth and fine-grained. This dog is vulnerable to sunburn.

Powder Puff

ears are normally erect

long, slightly rounded skull

deep, broad chest

Powder Puff has undercoat and a soft veil of long hair

skin may be plain or spotted, and may lighten in summer

long, tapering, fairly straight tail

no hair above first joint of leg

ears sometimes droop under weight of hair

Hairless

hairless body

harelike feet

| Height: 9–13in (23–33cm) | Weight: 5–12lb (2–5½kg) | Temperament: Affectionate, lively |

Place of origin: Tibet	First use: Companion in monasteries	Origins: 1600s

Tibetan Spaniel

Although known as a spaniel, the dog's name is rather misleading. The breed appears more closely related to the Pekingese (see p.48) but is not so exaggerated in terms of its type. The face of the Tibetan Spaniel is less compressed and its coat not as profuse.

HISTORY This highly intelligent dog was associated with the monasteries of Tibet, and reputedly turned the prayer wheels.
REMARK The Tibetan Spaniel is a loyal, affectionate dog and has an energetic nature.

slightly domed skull

slightly bowed forelegs

strong, well-made hindquarters

Color types

Height: 10in (25cm)	Weight: 9–15lb (4–7kg)	Temperament: Intelligent, assertive

---

Place of origin: Tibet	First use: Herding and guarding stock	Origins: 1700s

Tibetan Terrier

Despite its diminutive size, this breed is still used to herd stock in its native Tibet. This dog is not a true terrier, however, and is more like a small Old English Sheepdog (see p.106).

HISTORY The breed was introduced to Europe by Dr. Greig, who brought a pair to England in the 1930s.
REMARK Many Tibetan Terriers can trace their ancestry back to the original pair.
OTHER NAMES Dhokhi Apso.

V-shaped, heavily feathered ears

double coat

straight or wavy coat

large, round feet

Color types

Height: 14–16in (36–41cm)	Weight: 18–30lb (8–14kg)	Temperament: Friendly, alert

| Place of origin: Tibet | First use: Companion in monasteries | Origins: 600s |

Lhasa Apso

Although small in stature, the Lhasa Apso is a hardy dog, has a fine sense of hearing, and makes an excellent watchdog. While the name "Lhasa" probably refers to the capital of Tibet, "apso" may mean "goat-like"—a reference to this breed's long, coarse coat. The luxuriant coat is its most distinctive feature. Hair falls well over its eyes, and it has a prominent beard and moustache.

HISTORY This is the most recent of the Tibetan breeds to have reached Europe. The giving of a Lhasa Apso was a traditional gift of the Dalai Lama.
REMARK The Lhasa Apso's long, cascading coat needs plenty of grooming.

long parting from back of head

feathered ears

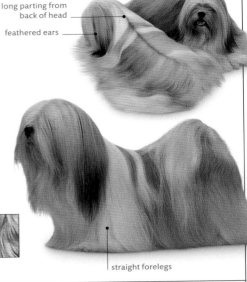

Color types

straight forelegs

| Height: 10–11in (25–28cm) | Weight: 13–15lb (6–7kg) | Temperament: Gentle, loyal |

| Place of origin: Japan | First use: Companion to aristocracy | Origins: 700s |

Japanese Chin

There is a distinct similarity between this breed and the Pekingese (see p.48), but the Japanese Chin is both taller and of a lighter build. The coat of a puppy is relatively short compared with that of an adult dog.

HISTORY Queen Victoria, a keen dog lover, had two Japanese Chins.
REMARK Early examples of the breed were apparently quite delicate and tended to be even smaller than those seen today.
OTHER NAMES Japanese Spaniel, Chin.

large, dark eyes

long hair on ears

slender feet

Color types

| Height: 9in (23cm) | Weight: 4–7lb (2–3kg) | Temperament: Intelligent, alert |

Place of origin: Japan	First use: Companion	Origins: 1800s

Japanese Spitz

This delightful spitz breed has a striking, long coat, which must always be pure white in color. This feature can serve to distinguish it from the miniature form of the American Eskimo (see p.35), which is otherwise extremely similar.

HISTORY The Japanese Spitz is thought to bear no direct relationship to the American Eskimo; rather, it is believed to have been developed from the native Siberian Samoyed (see p.283).
REMARK The Japanese Spitz has gained popularity worldwide. The breed was first seen outside its homeland in Sweden.

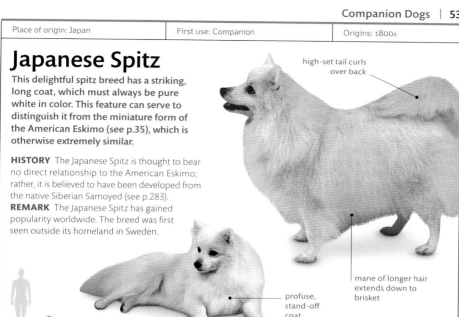

high-set tail curls over back

mane of longer hair extends down to brisket

profuse, stand-off coat

catlike feet

Height: 12–14in (30–36cm)	Weight: 11–13lb (5–6kg)	Temperament: Lively, intelligent

Place of origin: Malta	First use: Catching rats	Origins: 500 BCE

Maltese

Of bichon stock, this tiny, attractive dog has a long, silky, pure-white coat that contrasts starkly with its dark, oval-shaped eyes and black eye rims. The coat may have slight lemon-colored markings, notably in the vicinity of the head.

HISTORY Possibly the oldest of Europe's toy breeds, the ancestors of the Maltese were thought to have been introduced to Malta by the Phoenicians. This lively, intelligent breed has since attracted countless generations of enthusiastic owners.
REMARK Belying its "chocolate-box" appearance, this dog, once called a Maltese Terrier, was a renowned rat-catcher.
OTHER NAMES Bichon Maltese, Bichon Maltais.

pure black nose

stop is centred between tip of nose and occiput

dark brown eyes

long, straight coat should not impede the dog's action

Height: 10in (25cm)	Weight: 4–6lb (2–3kg)	Temperament: Friendly, alert

Place of origin: Tenerife	First use: Companion to royalty	Origins: 1400s

Bichon Frise

This bichon is distinguished by its double coat, which gives it a fluffy appearance. The coat is fine and silky, consisting of soft, corkscrew curls. These are trimmed back over the eyes to emphasize the rounded appearance of the face.

HISTORY Originally, the Bichon Frise was popular in the royal courts of Europe. By the 1800s, however, the breed had lost favor and was more likely to be seen in circuses or accompanying organ grinders.

REMARK Its long association with people makes the Bichon Frise a responsive pet.

OTHER NAMES Tenerife Dog.

narrow, delicate ears

tail curls over back

naturally agile

tight, round feet

silky, corkscrew curls

strong, straight forelegs

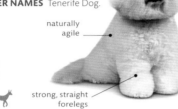

Height: 9–12in (23–31cm)	Weight: 7–12lb (3–6kg)	Temperament: Friendly, active

---

Place of origin: Madagascar	First use: Companion	Origins: 1600s

Coton de Tulear

The name of this breed points to its most obvious feature – an extravagant, cotton-fluff coat of long, white hair. The Coton de Tulear is a member of the bichon group of breeds.

HISTORY It is thought that early bichon stock was taken by French troops to Madagascar, where this breed developed. The similar, but now extinct, Chien Coton was popular on the island of Réunion located off the east coast of Madagascar.

REMARK The breed is virtually unknown outside its homeland.

round, black nose

small, flat skull

cottonlike coat texture

rounded feet with black nails

Color types

Height: 10–12in (25–30cm)	Weight: 12–15lb (5½–7kg)	Temperament: Lively, loyal

| Place of origin: Italy | First use: General companion | Origins: 1200s |

Bolognese

flat cheeks

Descended from bichon stock, and so having the characteristic white, cottony coat associated with this group, the Bolognese may in fact have blond markings, although these are not considered desirable. This is a square-built and solid dog for its size.

HISTORY The breed's ancestry dates back to the bichons that first appeared in southern Italy in the 13th century. It became a popular court dog but is now relatively scarce.

REMARK The Bolognese has always been a companion dog and bonds very closely with people.

OTHER NAMES Bichon Bolognese.

round, black, shiny nose

soft hair forms tufts, with no undercoat

small, rounded feet

| Height: 10–12in (25–31cm) | Weight: 5½–9lb (3–4kg) | Temperament: Friendly, loyal |

| Place of origin: Cuba | First use: Companion | Origins: 1700s |

Havanese

This dog has a bichon ancestry and is related to such breeds as the Bichon Frise (opposite). It has a profuse double coat and is usually cream, gold, silver, blue, or black.

dense crest of long hair on head

tail carried forward in a curl

HISTORY Its ancestors are believed to have been brought to Cuba by sailors from the Canaries.

REMARK This breed is becoming popular in the US.

OTHER NAMES Bichon Havanais.

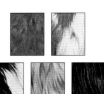

Color types

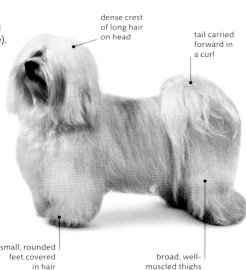

small, rounded feet covered in hair

broad, well-muscled thighs

| Height: 8–11in (20–28cm) | Weight: 7–12lb (3–6kg) | Temperament: Responsive, friendly |

GUNDOGS

ORIGINALLY a sporting companion, the lively, loyal nature of the gundog has won it a place in the home as a family pet. Setters, spaniels, pointers, and retrievers are all classified as gundogs and are characterized by their very responsive and friendly dispositions. However, they do require a great deal of exercise. Their longish, water-resistant coats protect them in all weather, a feature bred into them in their sporting days. A number of gundog breeds have a localized distribution, while others, such as the Spinone (see p.96), are now well known in show rings around the world. Field trials are held regularly to test and maintain their working abilities.

Place of origin: US	First use: Hunting small game	Origins: 1800s

American Cocker Spaniel

Smaller than its English counterpart (see p.59), and with a much longer coat, the American Cocker Spaniel was developed in the US in the last century. A black American Cocker must be jet black, with no trace of brown or liver shadings. To be classified as black and tan, tan markings must comprise no less than 10 percent of the coat. The color "tan" can vary from shades of cream to dark red.

HISTORY This dog was bred from English Cocker Spaniels taken to the US. It was first recognized as a separate breed in 1946.
REMARK This keen and industrious breed specialized in retrieving quails.
OTHER NAMES Cocker Spaniel.

clearly defined stop

lobular ears

rounded head shape

muscular, well-boned hindquarters

rounded, firm feet with thick pads

profuse covering of wavy or flat silky hair

Color types

Height: 14–15in (36–38cm)	Weight: 24–28lb (11–13kg)	Temperament: Active, friendly

Place of origin: US	First use: Retrieving waterfowl	Origins: 1800s

Chesapeake Bay Retriever

The broad skull, wedge-shaped forehead, and powerful jaws of this breed make it ideal as a retriever, and its very dense coat serves to protect it from the cold waters of the Chesapeake Bay region of the US, where it was first developed. The oily texture of the hair gives this retriever a rather distinctive smell.

broad, rounded head

distinctive yellow or amber eyes

HISTORY The breed evolved from two pups rescued from a ship that ran aground off the coast of Maryland in 1807. The two dogs were trained to retrieve duck, a skill that was refined through crossings with Flat (see p.63) and Curly-coated (see p.60) Retrievers and Otterhounds (see p.145). **REMARK** The webbed toes of this breed assist in swimming.

thin, not pendulous, lips

Color types

tail thick at base, with some feathering

powerful hindquarters provide thrust when swimming

harelike feet with well-rounded toes

Height: 21–26in (53–66cm)	Weight: 55–75lb (25–34kg)	Temperament: Responsive, industrious

| Place of origin: Great Britain | First use: Tracking and retrieving game | Origins: 1800s |

Clumber Spaniel

This large, bulky spaniel is not as speedy in the field as some of its more streamlined relatives, but it is vigorous and works well, especially in areas of heavy cover. The Clumber has a large, wide head, a pronounced stop, and deep-set eyes. Its attractive, pure-white, silky coat is heavily feathered on the neck and chest. Lemon- or orange-colored markings are permissible.

HISTORY The Duke of Newcastle was instrumental in developing this breed in Britain at the family home in Clumber Park. He may have obtained the ancestral stock from France. Later, Queen Victoria's husband, Prince Albert, as well as his son, who became King Edward VII, both favored this spaniel, as did King George V.
REMARK Despite royal patronage, this spaniel has never been generally popular.

massive, square skull with heavy brow and deep stop

lemon markings on ears preferred

long ears, shaped like vine leaves

plain white body preferred

well-feathered tail

thick, powerful neck

short, well-boned legs

exceedingly powerful hindquarters

| Height: 19–20in (48–51cm) | Weight: 65–80lb (29–36kg) | Temperament: Dedicated, responsive |

| Place of origin: Great Britain | First use: Retrieving game | Origins: 1800s |

Cocker Spaniel

This breed of gundog has a broad nose for scenting, a generous, square muzzle, a pronounced stop, and a precise yet delicate bite, ideal for retrieving game. Its long coat is silky in texture but not curly. In solid-colored dogs, white markings are permissible only on the chest.

HISTORY The Cocker Spaniel was originally developed in Wales and southwestern parts of England to flush woodcock, a popular game bird.
REMARK Its long ears hang close to the ground and often harbor ticks and burrs, which can lead to disease and injury.
OTHER NAMES English Cocker Spaniel.

long, silky hair on ears

Puppy

strong, compact body

ears set low, level with eyes

flat, silky coat with feathering

tail set low

medium-length, muscular neck merging into sloping shoulders

stifles well-bent

straight, well-boned legs

thickly padded feet

Color types

| Height: 15–16in (38–41cm) | Weight: 28–32lb (13–15kg) | Temperament: Responsive, affectionate |

| Place of origin: Great Britain | First use: Retrieving waterfowl | Origins: 1800s |

Curly-coated Retriever

This robust, agile breed of retriever has a generally neat appearance. Its body is covered with a tightly curled, black- or liver-colored coat, which does not need trimming. By contrast, its facial hair is distinctively smooth.

HISTORY The precise ancestry of the Curly-coated Retriever is unclear, but Water Spaniels are probably responsible for its distinctive coat. Early Labradors (see p.65) may also have contributed to its development, as may poodles.

REMARK The Curly-coated Retriever is one of the oldest breeds of retriever and is still a popular choice in Australia and New Zealand for quail and waterfowl hunting. They enter water without hesitation, and their water-resistant coat dries quickly.

long head

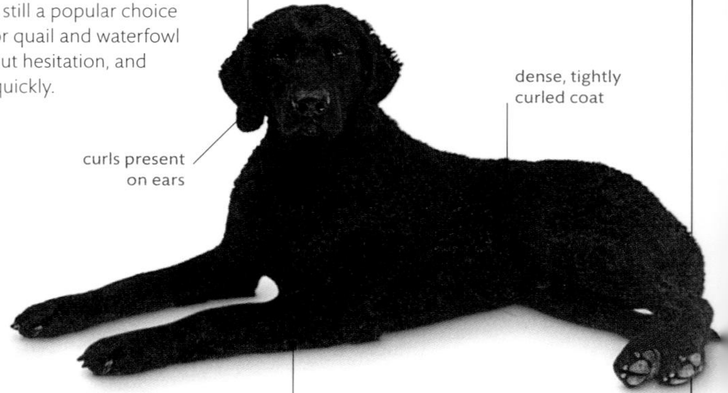

small ears
lying close
to head

dense, tightly
curled coat

curls present
on ears

moderately long legs

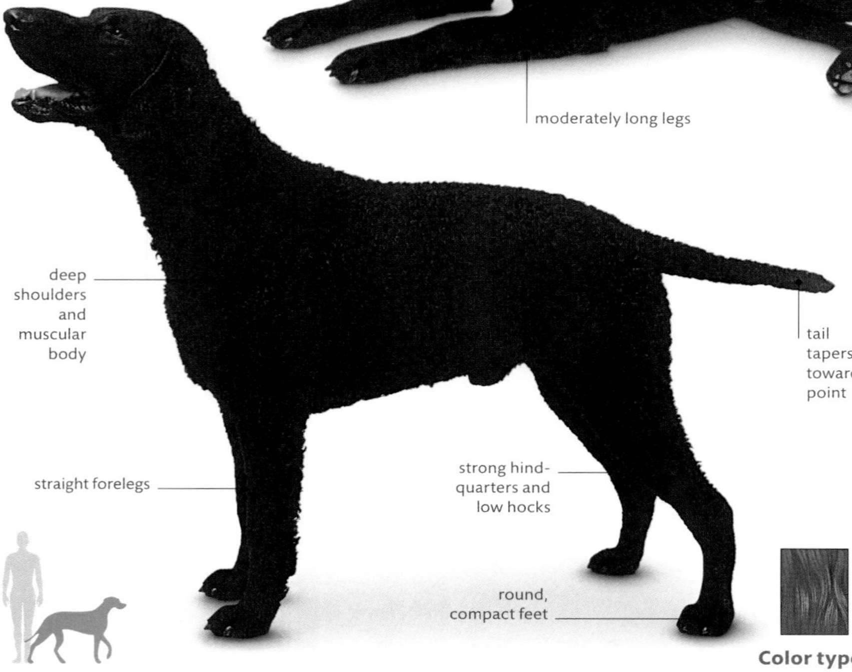

deep
shoulders
and
muscular
body

tail
tapers
toward
point

straight forelegs

strong hind-
quarters and
low hocks

round,
compact feet

Color types

| Height: 25–27in (64–69cm) | Weight: 70–80lb (32–36kg) | Temperament: Responsive, friendly |

Place of origin: Great Britain	First use: Retrieving birds	Origins: 1800s

English Setter

dark hazel eyes

The mottled coloration of the English Setter serves to distinguish it from other breeds of setters. Essentially, it is a working dog that can be developed into an extremely responsive gundog, and it requires a lot of exercise to remain healthy. An elegant entrant in the show ring, the breed's friendly nature guarantees it strong support. Careful grooming is important if this breed is to be seen at its best.

HISTORY The old Setting Spaniel is the probable ancestor of this breed. It was developed initially by a Mr. Edward Laverack, who began a breeding program in 1825, and for a period, these dogs were known simply as Laverack Setters.

REMARK The term "setter" originates from the way such dogs "set" (sit) after they have located game.

velvety tips to ears

close, compact feet

tail forms a line with the back

deep chest

feathering is longest toward middle of tail

medium-length body

Color types

Height: 24–27in (61–69cm)	Weight: 56–66lb (25–30kg)	Temperament: Responsive, friendly

Place of origin: Great Britain	First use: Retrieving birds	Origins: 1600s

Gordon Setter

The black-and-tan coloration of the Gordon is distinctive among setters. It is an adept sporting dog, being skilled at locating game, and is also an impressive sight in the show ring. Puppies are slow to mature, however, and appear rather uncoordinated.

HISTORY The Gordon Setter was developed by the 4th Duke of Richmond and Gordon, at his ancestral seat in Banffshire, Scotland, from various breeds, including bloodhounds and collies.
REMARK It is the only setter developed in Scotland.

clearly defined stop

forelegs are well feathered

long muzzle

silky, glossy coat

Height: 24½–26in (62–66cm)	Weight: 56–65lb (25–30kg)	Temperament: Obedient, loyal

Place of origin: Great Britain	First use: Flushing out game	Origins: 1800s

English Springer Spaniel

As well as being the ancestor of most other contemporary spaniels, the English Springer is also one of the tallest. A division between working and show strains has arisen, the former being shorter and stockier.

HISTORY This gundog was originally used to "spring" (flush) game from the ground.
REMARK The Springer makes a good family pet if it receives sufficient exercise.

strong jaws

lobe-shaped ears

weather-resistant coat

Color types

Height: 19–20in (48–51cm)	Weight: 49–53lb (22–24kg)	Temperament: Willing, active

Place of origin: Great Britain	First use: Retrieving birds	Origins: 1800s

Field Spaniel

The Field Spaniel has a long body in relation to its height and a silky, flat coat. The breed was originally divided into two categories, the lighter of which became the Cocker Spaniel (see p.59).

HISTORY After the Field Spaniel was separated from the Cocker in 1892, crossings with Sussex Spaniels (see p.68) led to a temporary deterioration in type and soundness, which threatened the breed's existence.

REMARK Although popular as a gundog, the breed has not done well in the show ring.

long, well-feathered ears

wide, almond-shaped eyes

very long rib cage

Color types

Height: 18in (46cm)	Weight: 35–50lb (16–23kg)	Temperament: Responsive, friendly

Place of origin: Great Britain	First use: Retrieving fowl	Origins: 1800s

Flat-coated Retriever

As its name suggests, the coat of this retriever lies close to the body. It is dense and fine-textured, with feathering on the legs and tail.

HISTORY Although a British dog, it derives from two American breeds—the Labrador (see p.65) and the Newfoundland (see pp.236–237).
REMARK The breed declined after the First World War, having been kept largely as a working dog.

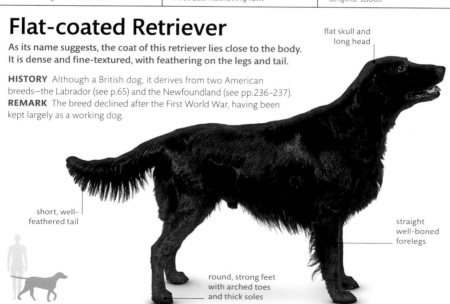

flat skull and long head

short, well-feathered tail

straight well-boned forelegs

round, strong feet with arched toes and thick soles

Height: 22–23in (56–58cm)	Weight: 60–70lb (27–32kg)	Temperament: Attentive, friendly

Place of origin: Great Britain	First use: Retrieving birds	Origins: 1800s

Golden Retriever

The coloration of this retriever has helped make it one of the most popular of all breeds. The coat can vary from shades of cream to gold, but must not be red. The Golden Retriever is a responsive dog to train, and provided it receives plenty of exercise it makes an excellent family companion.

HISTORY Although it has been suggested that this retriever evolved from Russian circus dogs, it is more likely it was bred from crossings that started with a yellow Flat-coated Retriever (see p.63) and a Tweed Water Spaniel, with Irish Setter (see p.82), Labrador (see p.65), and Bloodhound (see pp.162–163) introduced later.

REMARK Until 1920 it was known as the Golden Flat-coat.

OTHER NAMES Yellow Retriever, Russian Retriever.

broad skull and powerful muzzle

well-spaced, brown eyes

ears level with eyes

black nose preferred

well-defined stop

wavy or flat coat

tail level with back, and carried horizontally

straight, well-boned forelegs

round, rather catlike feet

good feathering on tail

Height: 20–24in (51–61cm)	Weight: 60–80lb (27–36kg)	Temperament: Responsive, alert

Place of origin: Canada	First use: Helping fishermen	Origins: 1800s

Labrador Retriever

The tail is the most distinctive feature of this intelligent, short-coated retriever. It has a thick base, tapering along its length, with no signs of feathering. A short-coupled, solid dog, it has a broad skull, wide nose, and powerful neck.

HISTORY The Labrador Retriever came from Newfoundland, where it used to help haul the fishermen's nets ashore. Today, apart from being a gundog, Labradors often act as guide dogs, have been trained to detect drugs and explosives, and are popular as companions.
REMARK Unless regularly exercised, Labradors tend toward obesity.

wide skull and slightly pronounced brow

smooth, black, chocolate, or yellow double coat

long shoulders

otterlike, medium-length tail

well-developed hindquarters

well-arched toes and thick pads

wide, powerful, chest with barrel-shaped rib cage

Color types

Height: 21½–22½in (54–57cm)	Weight: 55–75lb (25–34kg)	Temperament: Responsive, friendly

Place of origin: Great Britain	First use: Tracking hares	Origins: 1600s

Pointer

This breed has an agile and athletic build. The muzzle has a distinctively concave profile and is often raised high as the dog tests the air. The Pointer is prized for its exceptional sense of smell and displays considerable pace on the field, covering enormous distances. This elegant dog retains strong working instincts and requires a great deal of exercise if it is to be kept as a pet.

HISTORY The Pointer has been a hunting dog since the 17th century. Originally, it was trained to detect hares, which were then run down, or "coursed," by greyhounds.
REMARK In the presence of game, this dog freezes in a characteristic "pointing" stance to indicate the quarry's direction.
OTHER NAMES English Pointer.

well-defined stop
on the muzzle

medium-length ears,
lying close to head

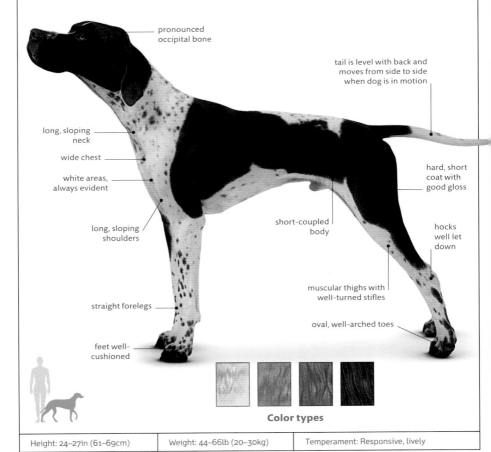

pronounced
occipital bone

tail is level with back and
moves from side to side
when dog is in motion

long, sloping
neck

wide chest

white areas,
always evident

hard, short
coat with
good gloss

long, sloping
shoulders

short-coupled
body

hocks
well let
down

muscular thighs with
well-turned stifles

straight forelegs

oval, well-arched toes

feet well-
cushioned

Color types

Height: 24–27in (61–69cm)	Weight: 44–66lb (20–30kg)	Temperament: Responsive, lively

Place of origin: Slovakia	First use: Multipurpose gundog	Origins: 1950s

Slovakian Rough-haired Pointer

Initial crossings between the Czesky Fousek (see p.93) and the German Wire-haired Pointer (see p.74) were made, with the Weimaraner (see pp.72–73) then contributing its distinctive silver-gray coloration to this wire-coated breed.

HISTORY It was created to track and point and retrieve on land or in water.
REMARK Only proven working gundogs can be officially registered for breeding in Slovakia.
OTHER NAMES Slovenský Hrubosrstý Stavač.

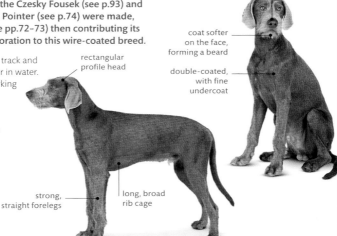

large, dark nose

coat softer on the face, forming a beard

double-coated, with fine undercoat

rectangular profile head

strong, straight forelegs

long, broad rib cage

Height: 23–27in (58–69cm)	Weight: 55–57lb (25–35kg)	Temperament: Responsive, intelligent

Place of origin: Spain	First use: Hunting	Origins: 1100s

Spanish Water Dog

This breed has undertaken a wide variety of roles during its long history, and has a very active herding instinct combined with plenty of stamina.

HISTORY These dogs also used to help with mooring boats returning to port, and catching fish.
REMARK Few breeds are more versatile, being able to work with sheep, goats, pigs and cattle.
OTHER NAMES Perro de Agua Español.

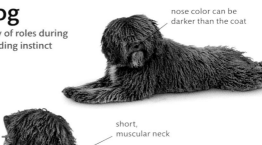

nose color can be darker than the coat

short, muscular neck

woolly-textured coat, being corded when long

Color types

Height: 18–19½in (40–50cm)	Weight: 31–48lb (14–22kg)	Temperament: Good-natured, adaptable

Place of origin: Great Britain	First use: Springing hidden game	Origins: 1500s

Welsh Springer Spaniel

Although possibly sharing common origins with the English Springer (see p.62), the Welsh Springer Spaniel is generally smaller, has a finer head, and always has rich, dark-red markings on a white coat.

slightly domed skull

HISTORY A clue to the possible age of this breed comes from a 16th-century manuscript, which refers to what could be an early ancestor of the Welsh Springer Spaniel.

REMARK The description "springer" refers to the breed's ability to "spring" hidden game, forcing it into the open.

long, muscular neck

square, medium-length muzzle

silky, dense coat, never wavy or wiry

Height: 18–19in (46–48cm)	Weight: 35–45lb (16–20kg)	Temperament: Attentive, friendly

Place of origin: Great Britain	First use: Scenting game	Origins: 1700s

Sussex Spaniel

The Sussex is a lower, longer, slower dog than other spaniels. Its abundant, flat coat is rich golden liver in color, with the hairs becoming golden at their tips.

broad skull and wrinkled brows

HISTORY This is one of the oldest spaniel breeds, first recognized in 1855.

REMARK Unusually for spaniels, the Sussex will "give tongue" (bay) when on the scent of game, in the fashion of hounds.

short, strong legs

long body

Height: 15–16in (38–41cm)	Weight: 40–50lb (18–23kg)	Temperament: Friendly, determined

| Place of origin: Canada | First use: Retrieving waterfowl | Origins: 1800s |

Nova Scotia Duck Tolling Retriever

This muscular, medium- to heavy-boned retriever has a dense, water-repellent coat. The feathering is paler than the ground color, which can be various shades of red, often with white markings.

HISTORY This Retriever was developed in Canada in the late 19th century to perform a unique role in hunting. It is used to toll (lure) curious ducks within range of the concealed hunters' guns by creating a disturbance at the water's edge. **REMARK** Foxes occasionally lure their prey toward them in this cunning fashion.

wedge-shaped head

brown nose

deep chest

pale feathering

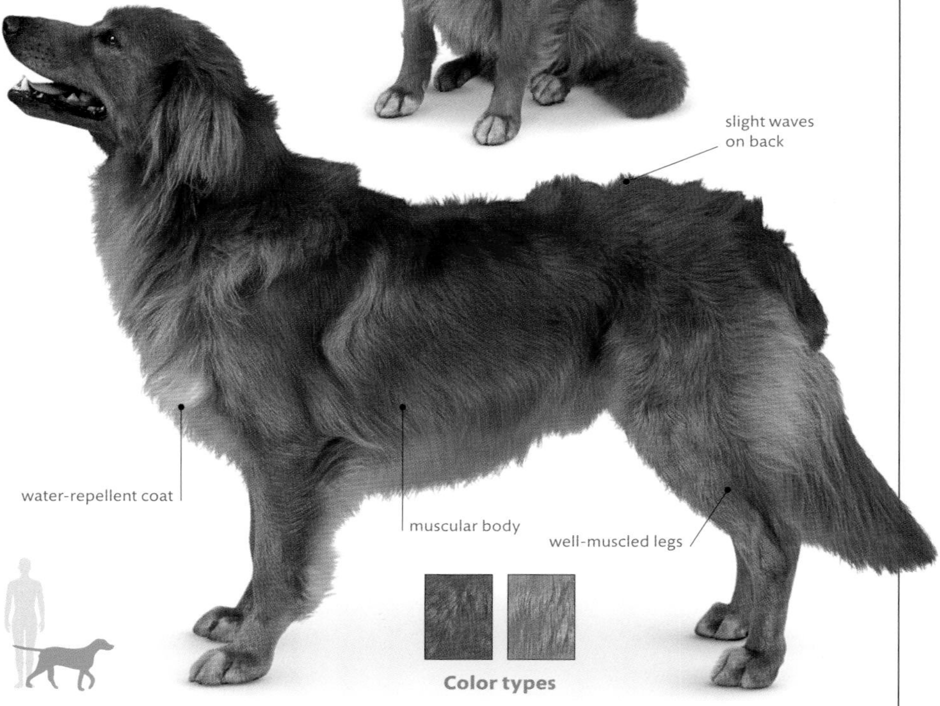

slight waves on back

water-repellent coat

muscular body

well-muscled legs

Color types

| Height: 17–21in (43–53cm) | Weight: 37–51lb (17–23kg) | Temperament: Responsive, active |

| Place of origin: Denmark | First use: Scenting and pointing game | Origins: 1700s |

Old Danish Pointer

By the standards of most pointers, this dog is not tall, but it is nevertheless a robust animal, well-balanced, with muscular thighs, a heavy head, and a long and powerful neck with dewlap. Its short coat is brown and white in color, some ticking being permitted.

HISTORY The origins of the Old Danish Pointer are uncertain, but it may have resulted from crossings between Spanish Pointers, brought to Denmark and then mated with local bloodhound breeds. The breed is little known outside its Danish homeland.

REMARK Its excellent scenting abilities makes it ideal for tracking wounded animals.

OTHER NAMES Gammel Dansk Honsehund.

long, pendent ears, rounded at tips

broad forehead

liver-colored nose

some ticking evident in coat

hazel-colored eyes

long neck with dewlap

broad, muscular chest

broad, straight back

short, dense coat

tapering tail, thick at base

well-developed, powerful thighs

| Height: 20–23in (51–58cm) | Weight: 40–53lb (18–24kg) | Temperament: Active, responsive |

Place of origin: Germany	First use: Hunting quail	Origins: 1900s

German Spaniel

Although somewhat similar in appearance to the English Springer Spaniel (see p.62), the German Spaniel is slightly shorter in the leg. This versatile dog operates as a talented retriever, often working in marshland. It resembles hounds in that it is also highly respected as a tracker.

HISTORY Various breeds contributed to its development, including the old German Stöber.
REMARK Essentially a working dog, this breed is not widely kept as a pet in Germany.
OTHER NAMES Deutscher Wachtelhund.

predominantly smooth coat on head

broad, brown nose with large nostrils

pendent ears covered with longer hair

slight feathering on tail

body is long compared with its height

feathering present on backs of forelegs

thick, medium-length, wavy coat

long ears hang back, behind eyes

elongated, but not pointed, muzzle

Color types

Height: 16–20in (40–51cm)	Weight: 44–66lb (20–30kg)	Temperament: Gentle, obedient

| Place of origin: Germany | First use: Tracking large game | Origins: 1600s |

Weimaraner

A sleek, uniformly gray coat color and fine, aristocratic features are the main hallmarks of this medium-size hunting dog. It has a strong muzzle and only a moderate stop. The Weimaraner, originally known as the Weimar Pointer, comes from a long tradition of German hunting dogs, many of which have found favor in other countries all over the world. This indefatigable breed has long, muscular limbs, a good sense of smell, and an obedient and friendly nature—all the attributes of a good, all-around hunting dog. It is one of only seven breeds of hunt, point, and retrieve dogs. Long- and short-haired forms of the Weimaraner are found, although the long-haired form is not officially recognized in the US. The coat color is slightly lighter on the head and on the ears.

HISTORY There is no confirmed history of the development of this dog. One theory suggests that the Weimaraner is the result of an albino mutation that appeared in some of the ancient German pointers. It may have descended from the German Braken, or from crossings between a regular pointer and an unnamed yellow pointer, overseen by Grand Duke Karl August of Weimar.

REMARK The exact origins of this dog are unknown. However, it can be positively dated to the 1600s when it appeared in an early painting by the Flemish artist Van Dyck.

OTHER NAMES Weimaraner Vorstehhund.

back slopes slightly down from the withers

well-developed, muscular hindquarters

coat length 1–2in (3–6cm)

color of head and ears slightly lighter than rest of coat

coat has almost metallic sheen

fringing evident

Long-haired Weimaraner

| Height: 22–27in (56–69cm) | Weight: 70–86lb (32–39kg) | Temperament: Responsive, alert |

long, lobular
ears with
rounded tips

short, smooth,
and sleek coat

long muzzle

moderately long,
clean-lined neck

amber-
colored
or blue-gray
eyes

well-developed
neck and deep
shoulders

**Short-haired
Weimaraner**

firm, compact
feet and well-
arched toes

Place of origin: Germany	First use: Retrieving birds	Origins: 1800s

German Wire-haired Pointer

The harsh, wiry coat and the longer hair above the eyes and on the jaws distinguish this sturdy breed from the other forms of German pointer. The distinctive texture of the coat helps prevent twigs and other debris from becoming entangled when the dog is working.

HISTORY First recognized in Germany in 1870, the appearance of the breed has been influenced by the infusion of German Shepherd and griffon blood.
REMARK Highly valued as a gundog, it is able to fulfill a variety of tasks.
OTHER NAMES Deutscher Drahthaariger Vorstehhund.

medium-length head

pronounced beard

harsh, flat outercoat

tail often kept nearly horizontal

powerful muzzle

straight forelegs

deep chest

well-arched toes with sturdy nails

Color types

Height: 22–26in (56–66cm)	Weight: 45–75lb (20–34kg)	Temperament: Active, responsive

| Place of origin: Germany | First use: Pointing | Origins: 1800s |

Small Münsterländer

This sturdy breed can be distinguished from its larger relative (see pp.76–77) not only by its size but also by its coloration, which is invariably liver and white. It is otherwise of similar type, being a powerful, muscular dog very well suited to working in the field for long periods.

HISTORY The breed's origins can be traced back to Westphalia in Germany. It was developed from crossings involving French spaniels and dogs similar to the Dutch Partridge Dog (see p.78). It was used as a bird dog, and valued especially for its pointing skills. It reached its greatest prominence in the early 1900s.
REMARK This good-natured dog is now becoming more popular outside Germany.
OTHER NAMES Kleiner Münsterländer Vorstehhund, Heidewachtel, Spion.

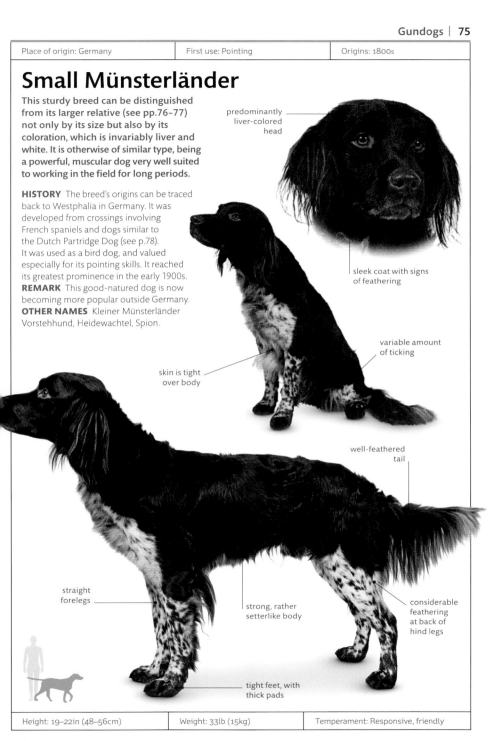

predominantly liver-colored head

sleek coat with signs of feathering

variable amount of ticking

skin is tight over body

well-feathered tail

straight forelegs

strong, rather setterlike body

considerable feathering at back of hind legs

tight feet, with thick pads

| Height: 19–22in (48–56cm) | Weight: 33lb (15kg) | Temperament: Responsive, friendly |

| Place of origin: Germany | First use: Tracking and retrieving game | Origins: 1800s |

Large Münsterländer

The Large Münsterländer can be instantly distinguished from its smaller relative (see p.75) by its distinctive coloration, which is a striking combination of black and white, rather than liver and white. The larger breed should also have ticking or roaning in the white.

HISTORY Originally, the German Long-haired Pointer Club accepted only liver-and-white dogs for registration, and so black-and-white pups were often simply given away. It was from these that the Large Münsterländer evolved.

REMARK The first breed club for this dog was formed in 1919.

OTHER NAMES Grosser Münsterländer Vorstehhund.

strong, muscular neck

broad, slightly rounded head

wide chest with good depth

straight forelegs

strong, black nails

| Height: 23–24in (59–61cm) | Weight: 55–65lb (25–29kg) | Temperament: Responsive, friendly |

dark brown, medium-size eyes

broad, round-tipped ears, lying flat on the sides

solid back, sloping slightly downward

well-formed black nose

tail is in line with back, tapering to the tip

taut abdomen

dense hair between toes

Place of origin: Netherlands	First use: Hunting game	Origins: 1600s

Dutch Partridge Dog

The coat of this medium-size, strongly built breed appears long, mainly because of fringes present on the ears. These extend down the neck, and on the legs and tail. When walking, the tail is extended horizontally and is slightly curled at the tip but is held down when the dog is at rest.

HISTORY This breed originated in the Drentse district of the Netherlands; it probably stems from the same ancestral stock as today's spaniels and setters. It frequently hunts pheasants and rabbits, as well as partridges.

REMARK The Dutch Partridge Dog tends to rotate its tail in a circle when it has located game.

OTHER NAMES Drentse Partijshond.

fringes on ears

coarse, straight coat

strong, sturdy legs with thick pads on feet

Color types

Height: 22–25in (56–64cm)	Weight: 50lb (23kg)	Temperament: Responsive, loyal

Place of origin: Netherlands	First use: Hunting small game	Origins: 1700s

Kooiker Dog

This lightly-built, well-proportioned dog has well-feathered ears, a slightly wavy, moderate-length coat, and pronounced fringing to the ears, legs, chest, and tail. In general appearance it is not unlike a small setter with a long, bushy tail.

HISTORY This breed is well known in the Netherlands and is reputed to have foiled an assassination attempt on Prince William II of Orange (1626–1650) by barking and waking him just in time.

REMARK The bushy tail of the Kooiker is used to lure wild ducks so that they can be banded and then released.

OTHER NAMES Kooikerhondje.

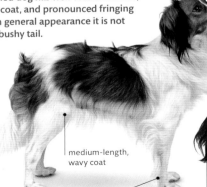

ears set high on head

conspicuous black nose

white blaze on face

medium-length, wavy coat

well-feathered forelegs

well-feathered ears with black tips

Height: 14–16in (35–41cm)	Weight: 20–24lb (9–11kg)	Temperament: Industrious, intelligent

Place of origin: Netherlands	First use: Catching moles	Origins: 1600s

Stabyhoun

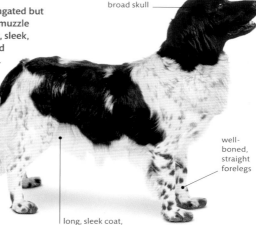

broad skull

This spaniel-like breed has a slightly elongated but well-balanced body, a wide head, and a muzzle tapering toward the nose. Its coat is long, sleek, and well feathered and is seen in dappled colors of black, brown, orange, and blue.

HISTORY The breed originated in Friesland, in the Netherlands. Crossings between the Drentse Patrijshond (opposite), a larger Dutch gundog, and spaniels probably underlie its development.

REMARK This popular gundog is able to locate, point, and retrieve game. It adapts well to family life.

well-boned, straight forelegs

long, sleek coat, with feathering evident

Color types

Height: 19½–21in (50–53cm)	Weight: 33–44lb (15–20kg)	Temperament: Responsive, gentle

---

Place of origin: Netherlands	First use: Hunting otters	Origins: 1600s

Wetterhoun

spatula-shaped ears on a broad head

The Wetterhoun is a dog for all seasons. Its coat provides a covering of tight, water-resistant curls, except on the head and legs, and its solid and rugged build made it an ideal hunter of otters.

HISTORY The Wetterhoun, Dutch for "water dog," probably descended from the now-extinct Old Water Dog.

REMARK This strong-willed dog benefits from good training when young.

OTHER NAMES Otterhoun, Dutch Spaniel.

curly coat except for head and legs

powerful, thick-set neck

Color types

Height: 21–23in (53–58cm)	Weight: 33–44lb (15–20kg)	Temperament: Independent, active

| Place of origin: Ireland | First use: Retrieving water-fowl | Origins: 1800s |

Irish Water Spaniel

Standing taller than any other breed of spaniel, and with a unique coloration showing a purplish hue described as puce liver, this breed has a powerful presence. The coat is comprised of tight ringlets and is naturally oily and water-repellent. The first 4in (10cm) of tail has curly hair, whereas the rest to the tip is either bare skin or is covered with straight hair.

HISTORY The Irish Water Spaniel may have been developed from the Portuguese Water Dog (see p.99) or a poodle, crossed with native Irish spaniels. The breed's founder, Justin McCarthy, kept the breed's origins a closely guarded secret and refused to reveal details of its precise ancestry.

REMARK This spaniel is a powerful swimmer and is large enough to retrieve game the size of geese from deep water.

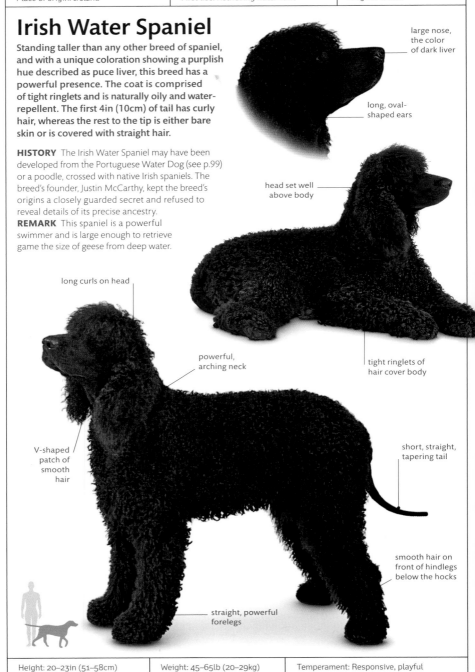

large nose, the color of dark liver

long, oval-shaped ears

head set well above body

long curls on head

powerful, arching neck

tight ringlets of hair cover body

V-shaped patch of smooth hair

short, straight, tapering tail

smooth hair on front of hindlegs below the hocks

straight, powerful forelegs

| Height: 20–23in (51–58cm) | Weight: 45–65lb (20–29kg) | Temperament: Responsive, playful |

Place of origin: Ireland	First use: Retrieving game	Origins: 1700s

Irish Red and White Setter

Well-proportioned and athletic, the Irish Red and White Setter is a powerful, good-natured dog. Similar to the Irish Setter (see p.82), it is more heavily built with a broader head and a more prominent occipital peak. The finely textured, feathered coat has a pure white ground color with solid red patches. Some mottling or flecking is common; roaning, however, is frowned upon in show circles. Setters are renowned for their highly developed sense of smell and ability to excel at any kind of hunting in any type of terrain or weather conditions.

domed skull

solid red patches

HISTORY Originally called the Parti-colored Setter, this hardy breed derives from the same rootstock as the graceful Irish Setter. Although the Irish Red and White Setter is an excellent working dog in the field, it came very close to extinction before undergoing a revival in the late 20th century.

REMARK The Irish Red and White Setter makes an affectionate family pet, but requires a great deal of exercise and rigorous training.

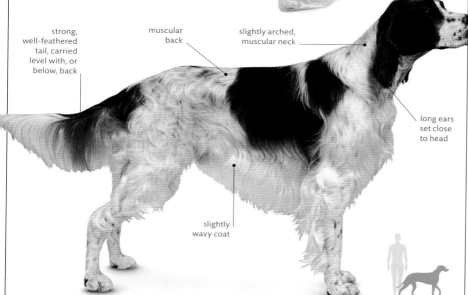

strong, well-feathered tail, carried level with, or below, back

muscular back

slightly arched, muscular neck

long ears set close to head

slightly wavy coat

Height: 23–27in (58–69cm)	Weight: 60–70lb (27–32kg)	Temperament: Active, affectionate

Place of origin: Ireland	First use: Retrieving game	Origins: 1700s

Irish Setter

In spite of its formal name, the Irish Setter is often better known simply as the Red Setter, due to its distinctive coloration. Built on racier lines than its red and white cousin (see p.82), it is a lively, active dog, perpetually ready for fun. It is popular as a pet but must have plenty of exercise. To ensure obedience, it requires more training than other similar breeds, but in the end, the Irish Setter should become a superb working companion.

HISTORY The breed evolved in Ireland, where Irish Water Spaniels, Gordon Setters, and Springer Spaniels are all believed to have played a part in its development.
REMARK A small amount of white on the chest is quite common and will not lead to disqualification from a show ring.
OTHER NAMES Red Setter.

ears hang close to head

square muzzle

rich, chestnut coat

long, muscular neck

feathered, low-set tail

deep, narrow chest

straight, sinewy forelegs

long, fine feathering on back of legs

Height: 25–27in (64–69cm)	Weight: 60–70lb (27–32kg)	Temperament: Active, affectionate

| Place of origin: France | First use: Hunting small game | Origins: 1700s |

Braque St. Germain

This pointer has a predominantly white coat broken by orange areas of variable size. Although slightly leggier than the English Pointer (see p.66), the elegant Braque St. Germain is a dog of fine proportions.

HISTORY The breed's ancestry traces back to two English Pointers given to King Charles X of France. When one died, the other was mated with a Braque Francais. The offspring laid the foundations of this breed.

REMARK This dog is not favored for retrieving from water as its coat does not provide sufficient insulation when it is wet.

OTHER NAMES St. Germain Pointer.

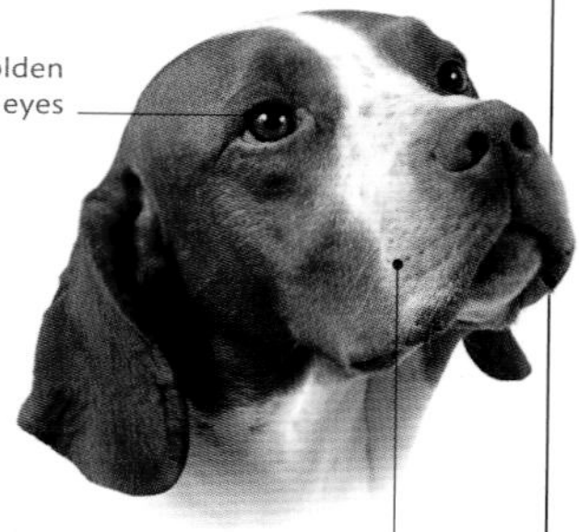

distinctive golden yellow eyes

long muzzle

well-defined orange patches

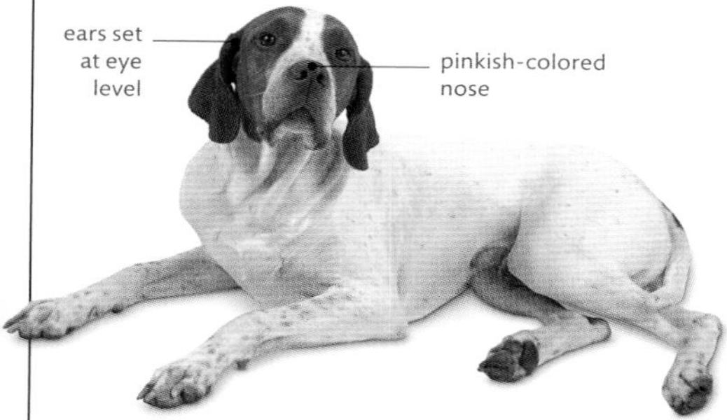

ears set at eye level

pinkish-colored nose

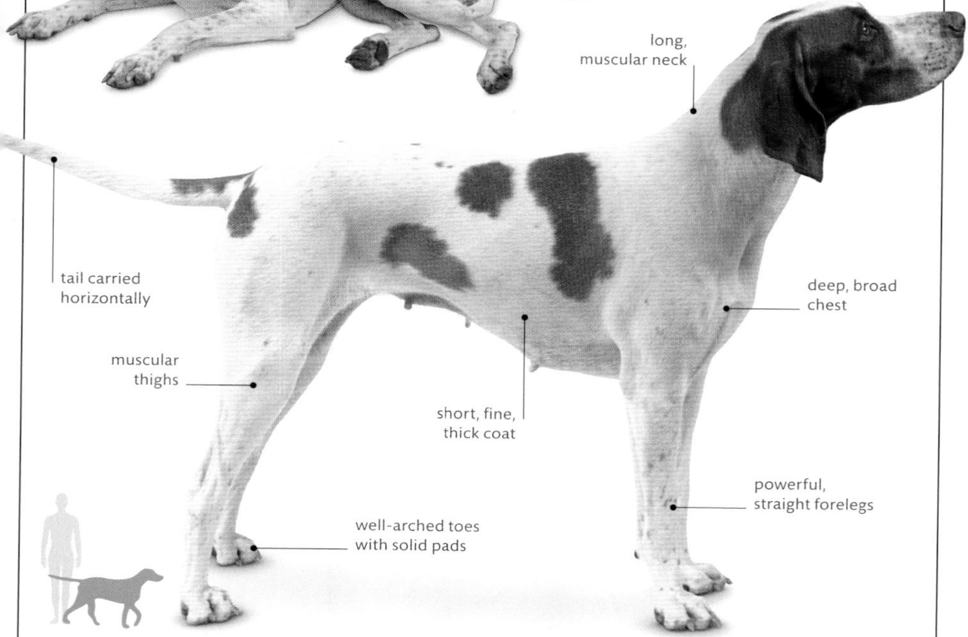

long, muscular neck

deep, broad chest

tail carried horizontally

muscular thighs

short, fine, thick coat

powerful, straight forelegs

well-arched toes with solid pads

| Height: 20–24in (51–61cm) | Weight: 40–57lb (18–26kg) | Temperament: Obedient, loyal |

| Place of origin: France | First use: Scenting and pointing game | Origins: 1600s |

Large French Pointer

One of France's oldest breeds, the Large French Pointer is
an imposing dog, with a strong, well-muscled physique.
The breed, which originated in the Pyrenean region
of France, is a slightly taller dog than the better-known
English Pointer (see p.66), but in general physique
they are very similar. A smaller version of the breed,
from Gascony, has a more refined appearance.

HISTORY It is popularly believed that the Large French
Pointer is descended from the old, extinct Southern
Hound and that it is also closely related to the Italian
and Spanish Pointers (see pp.97 and 98). There is
certainly a houndlike aura attaching to this breed,
which lends credence to this belief.

REMARK During the latter part of the 19th century,
the breed declined in popularity and was in danger
of dying out. However, recent efforts among
enthusiasts have resulted in a considerable boost in the
numbers of these pointers. Although not common, its
future does now seem assured, as a new generation
of hunters learns to appreciate its working skills.

OTHER NAMES Braque Francais de Grande Taille.

head often held upwards to
detect scent when working
in open surroundings

ticking present
on this specimen

broad, deep
chest

convex head
has broad,
rectangular
muzzle

fine hair
covering on
ears and head

straight,
well-boned
forelegs

ears show signs
of pleats

| Height: 22–27in (56–68cm) | Weight: 45–71lb (20–32kg) | Temperament: Well-balanced, steady |

short, dense, thick coat

chestnut or dark yellow eyes

broad, chestnut-colored nose

well-muscled hindquarters

sound rump and strong hindlegs

oval-shaped, well-cushioned feet

Place of origin: France	First use: Pointing and retrieving game	Origins: 1800s

Auvergne Pointer

The Auvergne Pointer is a large and relatively heavy gundog, with distinctive coloration and markings. It is an important breed characteristic that the ears and the area around the eyes are black. Elsewhere on the body, blue roaning, resulting from overlapping black and white hairs, is desirable. This patterning is known as "charbonnée," or "charcoaled," although some Auvergnes show clearly defined black markings on a white background.

HISTORY It is thought that Gascony Hounds (see pp.166–167) contributed to the breed's ancestry, although any residual traces of tan markings now merit disqualification in the show ring.
REMARK This pointer is still kept essentially for sporting purposes.
OTHER NAMES Braque d'Auvergne.

black markings on ears and around eyes are essential

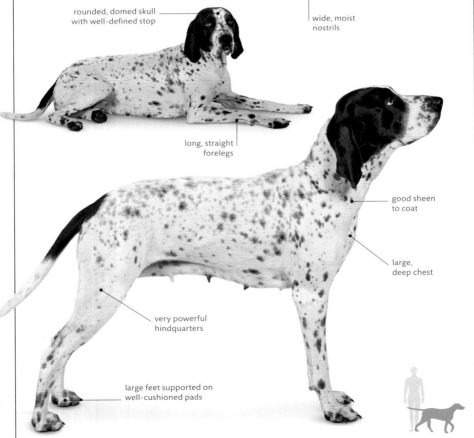

rounded, domed skull with well-defined stop

wide, moist nostrils

long, straight forelegs

good sheen to coat

large, deep chest

very powerful hindquarters

large feet supported on well-cushioned pads

Height: 22–24in (56–61cm)	Weight: 49–62lb (22–28kg)	Temperament: Responsive, lively

Place of origin: France	First use: Hunting game	Origins: 1500s

Braque du Bourbonnais

The coat of the Braque du Bourbonnais is basically white with very evident roaning and as few clear patches of coloration as possible. This moderately large pointer is born with either no tail or a very rudimentary stump.

HISTORY As its name implies, the Braque du Bourbonnais originated in the French province of Bourbon, and a dog very similar to today's breed can be found in paintings dating back to the 16th century. The breed flourished in France during the 1800s but then declined from about the First World War. Enthusiasts have, however, now pooled their breeding stock to ensure its continued success as a fine French pointing dog.

REMARK This versatile breed is equally at home in scrubland or marshes and is happy hunting all manner of game.

OTHER NAMES Bourbonnais Pointer.

slightly curled, pendent ears

dark amber eyes

strong, broad muzzle

short, muscular neck and slight dewlap

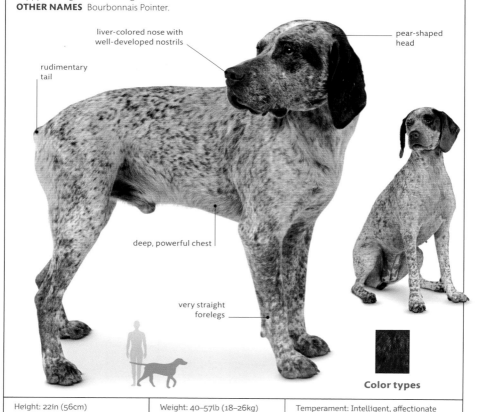

liver-colored nose with well-developed nostrils

pear-shaped head

rudimentary tail

deep, powerful chest

very straight forelegs

Color types

Height: 22in (56cm)	Weight: 40–57lb (18–26kg)	Temperament: Intelligent, affectionate

| Place of origin: France | First use: Flushing and retrieving game | Origins: 1600s |

Épagneul Français

Being relatively tall and powerfully built, the Épagneul Français, one of the oldest breeds of French spaniel, shows a distinct relationship to the setters. Its head is square, with a short neck that joins a muscular body of fine proportions. The coat is short and flat with some feathering.

HISTORY Competition from other gundogs brought it close to extinction at the start of the 20th century, but it is now firmly reestablished.
REMARK The breed is not well-known outside its native France.
OTHER NAMES French Spaniel.

long, flat, feathered ears

strong-boned legs

feathered underparts

long, feathered tail

flat, straight coat with liver markings

| Height: 21–24in (53–61cm) | Weight: 44–55lb (20–25kg) | Temperament: Intelligent, responsive |

| Place of origin: France | First use: Retrieving waterfowl | Origins: 1700s |

Épagneul Picard

This is another of the older French breeds of spaniel that displays an obvious relationship to the setters. The Picard can be distinguished by its characteristic tricolored appearance, with tan, liver, and white areas apparent in its coat.

HISTORY Closely related to the Épagneul Français (above), the Picard's ancestry is equally uncertain.
REMARK This spaniel is highly prized as a waterfowl retriever, working in the marshlands of Picardy, France.
OTHER NAMES Picardy Spaniel.

broad, round skull

finer, longer hair on ears

flat, straight coat

ticking clearly evident in coat

feathering apparent at back of legs

large feet for body size

| Height: 22–24in (56–61cm) | Weight: 44lb (20kg) | Temperament: Intelligent, friendly |

Place of origin: France	First use: Retrieving game	Origins: 1700s

Brittany

Frequently described as a spaniel, in behavior the rather square-built Brittany appears to have more in common with the setters, certainly in terms of height. It is not a particularly gainly dog, the legs appearing rather out of proportion to the body. The tail is naturally short in length.

HISTORY An old breed, it underwent a revival in its native France in the early 1900s. It has since become popular in the US.

REMARK A good all-arounder in the field, the Brittany can hunt, point, and retrieve.

OTHER NAMES Épagneul Breton.

wide-open nostrils enable scent to be detected more easily

medium-length, tapering muzzle

rather short ears, with rounded tips

height at withers corresponds to length of body

broad hind-quarters

stifles well bent, feathering extends to midthigh

strong, yet relatively small, feet with thick pads

Color types

Height: 18–20½in (46–52cm)	Weight: 28–33lb (13–15kg)	Temperament: Loyal, obedient

Place of origin: France	First use: Flushing and retrieving game	Origins: 1600s

Épagneul Pont-Audemer

The presence of a curly top-knot gives this spaniel a distinctive appearance. The rest of the liver, or liver-and-white, coat is long and curly, covering a medium-size, well-built dog.

HISTORY Crosses involving the Irish Water Spaniel (see p.80), or similar ancestral stock, gave rise to this breed. Old French spaniels also probably contributed to the bloodline. The breed was developed in the area of Pont-Audemer in Normandy. After the Second World War, the breed declined drastically, and Irish Water Spaniels were used to increase numbers.

REMARK The Épagnuel Pont-Audemer remains scarce. They were valued for working with waterfowl and, even today, are most often kept as working gundogs.

OTHER NAMES Pont-Audemer Spaniel.

short hair on face

long, pendent, well-feathered ears

weather-resistant, wavy coat

ticking may be apparent in white areas of coat

well-proportioned body

Color types

Height: 20–23in (51–58cm)	Weight: 40–53lb (18–24kg)	Temperament: Responsive, docile

Place of origin: France | First use: Retrieving waterfowl | Origins: 1600s

Barbet

The coat of the Barbet is thick and woolly, protecting the dog even from freezing water conditions. It is shiny and may be curly or wavy, with a rather becoming tasseled appearance. The Barbet has played a central role in the development of many of today's water dogs.

HISTORY Although the precise ancestry of the Barbet is unknown, it is an ancient breed and is thought to be the forerunner of such breeds as poodles, Irish Water Spaniels (see p.80), and Otterhounds (see p.145). It is also thought to resemble the now-extinct English Water Dog.
REMARK As well as retrieving waterfowl, the Barbet would also return the fallen arrows of hunters who had missed their target.
OTHER NAMES Griffon d'Arret à Poil Laineux.

good covering of long, water-resistant hair

long, pendent ears lying close to the head

large, prominent nostrils

solid, muscular body

tail with slight upward curve

powerful, well-boned legs

large, rounded feet with webbing between toes

Color types

Height: 18–22in (46–56cm) | Weight: 33–55lb (15–25kg) | Temperament: Intelligent, obedient

Place of origin: France	First use: Hunting snipe	Origins: 1800s

Épagneul Bleu de Picardie

The distinctive blue roan coloration of this breed helps to distinguish it from the Épagneul Picard (see p.88), another form of the same dog but with flecks and patches of liver and tan in its coat. In terms of its size, general proportions, and head shape, the breed conforms more to today's definition of a setter than a spaniel, and it looks a little like the engravings of early Gordon Setters (see p.62).

HISTORY This form of the Picard was developed in the French province of Picardy and is descended from crossings of the blue belton (blue mixed with white) English Setter with the Picard itself. The result is a taller, lighter-boned dog with a better nose than the old type of French spaniel.

REMARK The Épagneul Bleu de Picardie is an exceedingly hardworking gundog and develops a very close bond with its master.

OTHER NAMES Blue Picardy Spaniel.

hair longer and finer on ears

flat, relatively long, straight coat

dark brown, expressive eyes

good covering of hair on feet

ram-shaped muzzle with prominent nose

hair longer on tail than on body

deep chest

strong, well-boned legs

large feet

Height: 22–24in (56–61cm)	Weight: 44lb (20kg)	Temperament: Intelligent, friendly

| Place of origin: France | First use: Hunting and retrieving game | Origins: 1800s |

Wire-haired Pointing Griffon

The hard, coarse coat of this dog gives it rather an unkempt appearance. In reality, it requires little grooming, aside from periodic brushing. Facially, this breed is characterized by bushy eyebrows and a heavy beard of long, thick hair.

HISTORY The breed was developed by Dutchman Eduard Karel Korthals, possibly by crossing griffons with French Pointers.

REMARK As well as pointing and retrieving, the versatile Wire-haired Pointing Griffon will also hunt rodents and pursue foxes.

OTHER NAMES Korthals Griffon.

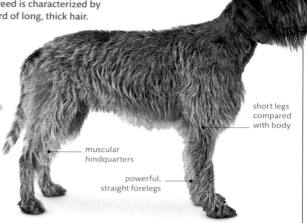

long, large head

short legs compared with body

muscular hindquarters

powerful, straight forelegs

Color types

| Height: 22–24in (56–61cm) | Weight: 50–60lb (23–27kg) | Temperament: Independent, intelligent |

| Place of origin: Czech Republic | First use: Pointing game | Origins: 1800s |

Czesky Fousek

The rough-textured coat of this breed varies in length from 1–3in (2.5–7.5cm) and is longest over the back and sides of the body. This is offset against a soft, thick undercoat.

HISTORY Originated in Czech Republic, this dog was popular up until about 1914, but it was only the infusion of German Short-haired Pointer blood in the 1930s that saved it from extinction.

REMARK The Fousek needs to be worked hard and does not take readily to domesticity.

beard present on face

legs are long in relation to body

bristly texture to coat

Color types

pendent ears set well back on head

ticking may be evident on coat

| Height: 24–26in (61–66cm) | Weight: 60–75lb (27–34kg) | Temperament: Intelligent, responsive |

Place of origin: Hungary	First use: Hunting and retrieving game	Origins: 1000s

Hungarian Vizsla

This medium-size, athletic gundog gives an immediate impression of being lean, lively, and muscular. Its coat is particularly striking, being smooth, shiny, sleek, and golden russet in color. White patches are undesirable.

HISTORY It is thought that the ancestors of the Vizsla accompanied the Magyars in their invasion of Hungary. Its bloodline probably includes the ancient Transylvanian Hound and the Turkish Yellow Dog, with more recent additions of pointer blood.
REMARK The Vizsla is adept at hunting, pointing, and retrieving in any terrain, including marshes.
OTHER NAMES Magyar Vizsla.

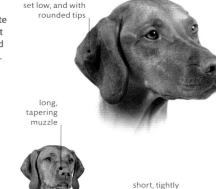

long, thin ears, set low, and with rounded tips

long, tapering muzzle

short, tightly fitting coat

lean, elegant head

robust, medium-boned frame

moderately long, muscular neck

deep chest with prominent breastbone

well-developed, powerful thighs

tail set low

straight, strong forelegs

catlike feet with thick pads

Height: 22½–25in (57–64cm)	Weight: 48½–66lb (22–30kg)	Temperament: Gentle, responsive

| Place of origin: Hungary | First use: Gundog | Origins: 1930s |

Wire-haired Vizsla

The wire-haired form of the vizsla is less common than its smooth-coated counterpart (opposite). It has grown in popularity, thanks to its good looks, and has obtained separate show recognition in various countries. In its Hungarian homeland, it is favored for working in water because it is less vulnerable to the cold.

HISTORY Cross-breedings between the German Wire-haired Pointer (see p.74) and vizslas, which took place during the 1930s, gave rise to this breed.
REMARK The Hungarian word *vizsla* translates as "responsive," "alert."
OTHER NAMES Drótszörü Magyar Vizsla.

noble head with tapering muzzle

beard and eyebrows evident

nails slightly darker than coat

tail set low on back

muscular shoulders

well-developed thighs

long forelegs

rounded feet

| Height: 22–24in (56–61cm) | Weight: 48–66lb (22–30kg) | Temperament: Responsive, intelligent |

Place of origin: Italy	First use: Retrieving game	Origins: 1200s

Spinone

Solid and squarely built, the Spinone is one of the most talented of all the hunting dogs. Long appreciated in its homeland, it has now become popular elsewhere in Europe and in the US. Its tracking abilities are particularly keen, and few dogs have a "softer" mouth for retrieving game unspoiled.

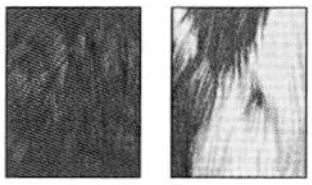

Color types

friendly expression

HISTORY The ancestry of this dog dates back many centuries, and probably originated from griffon stock.
REMARK A 15th-century fresco at the Ducal Palace in Mantua, Italy, depicts an early representation of the breed.
OTHER NAMES Spinone Italiano, Italian Spinone.

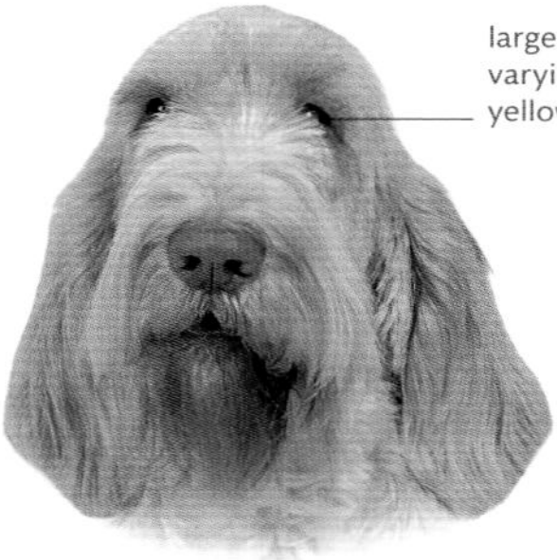

large eyes, varying from yellow to ocher

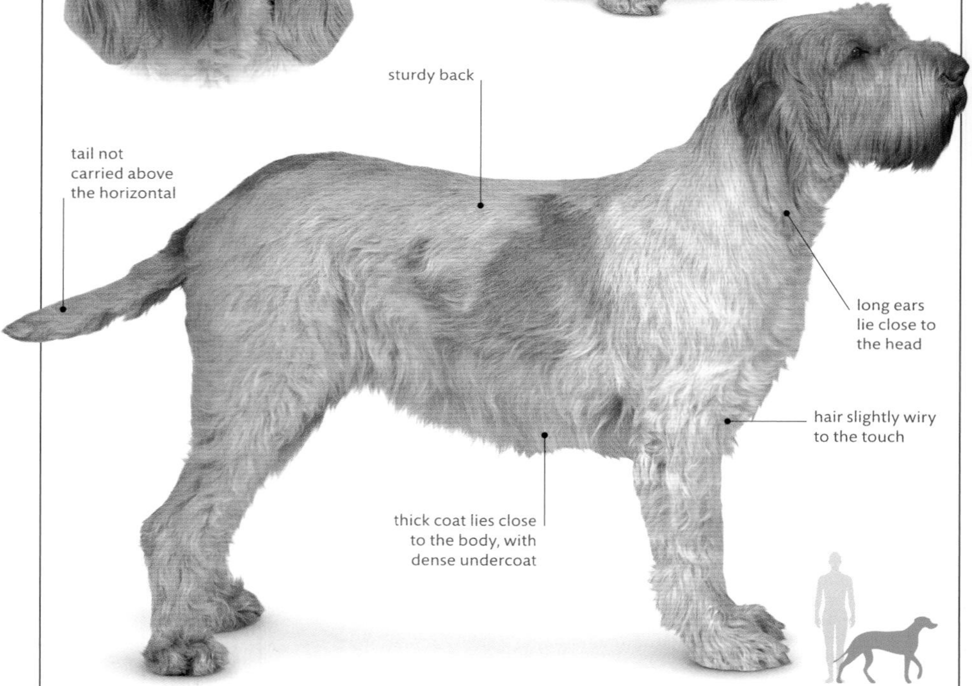

sturdy back

tail not carried above the horizontal

long ears lie close to the head

hair slightly wiry to the touch

thick coat lies close to the body, with dense undercoat

Height: 24–26in (61–66cm)	Weight: 71–82lb (32–37kg)	Temperament: Responsive, loyal

Place of origin: Italy	First use: Gundog	Origins: 1700s

Bracco Italiano

This agile, square-framed dog is one of the oldest surviving gundog breeds and shows very clear signs of its origins from ancient hound stock. The muzzle is unusual, being square almost to the point of convex when viewed in profile. Its coat, which is short and dense, has a finer quality on the head, neck, and lower body. The body of the Bracco Italiano resembles other pointer breeds in overall appearance.

Color types

HISTORY This was a popular dog during the Renaissance period and was often given as a gift from Italy to countries such as France and Spain. Numbers had declined by the early 20th century, but enthusiasts saved the breed, and the Italian Kennel Club drew up a standard for it in 1949.

REMARK It has changed little over the centuries and tends to be a little stubborn.

OTHER NAMES Italian Pointer.

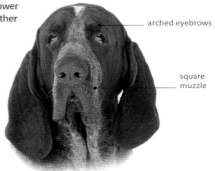

arched eyebrows

square muzzle

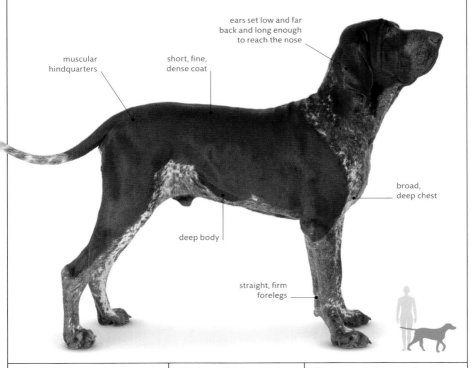

ears set low and far back and long enough to reach the nose

muscular hindquarters

short, fine, dense coat

broad, deep chest

deep body

straight, firm forelegs

Height: 22–26½in (56–67cm)	Weight: 55–88lb (25–40kg)	Temperament: Responsive, loyal

Place of origin: Spain	First use: Hunting deer	Origins: 1600s

Perdiguero de Burgos

This breed of pointer has a massive head in relation to a rather slender, well-muscled body. Its coat is short and of a fine texture, being exclusively liver and white in coloration, often with prominent ticking.

HISTORY The ancestry of this dog is not certain, but it undoubtedly is linked to an old breed, possibly one related to the ancient Sabueso Hound.

REMARK The earlier form of this dog hunted deer; the quarry of today's breed is more likely to be partridge.

OTHER NAMES Burgos Pointer, Burgalese Pointer.

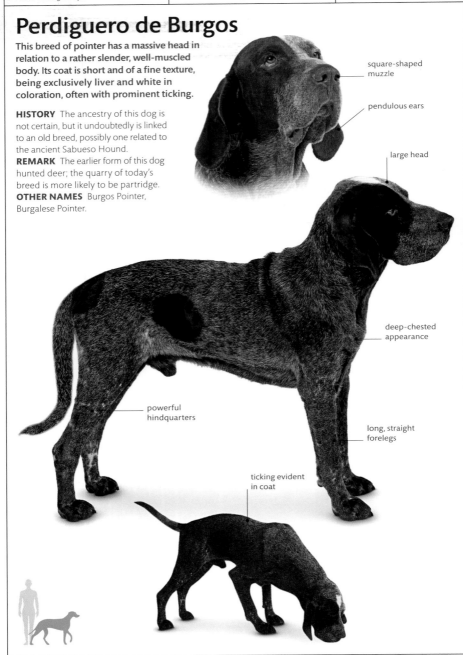

square-shaped muzzle

pendulous ears

large head

deep-chested appearance

powerful hindquarters

long, straight forelegs

ticking evident in coat

Height: 26–30in (66–76cm)	Weight: 55–66lb (25–30kg)	Temperament: Alert, responsive

Place of origin: Portugal | First use: Retrieving from the sea | Origins: 1500s

Portuguese Water Dog

There are two coat types associated with this breed, neither of which has an undercoat. In the first form, the hair is longish and wavy, with loose curls. In the second, the coat is shorter and thicker and with more compact curls.

HISTORY This breed is centuries old and was a valued fisherman's dog in the Algarve region of Portugal, capable of retrieving objects lost overboard and carrying messages between boats.

REMARK Numbers of this breed fell to just 50 in 1960, and it is still quite scarce today.

OTHER NAMES Cão de Água, Cão Pescador Português.

long, wavy hair

characteristic plume on tail

short, straight, muscular neck

profuse coat

deep chest

angulated hindquarters

powerful forelegs

Color types

Height: 16–22in (41–56cm) | Weight: 35–55lb (16–25kg) | Temperament: Obedient, friendly

| Place of origin: Portugal | First use: Hunting and retrieving game | Origins: 1200s |

Perdiguerio Portugueses

This is a medium-size breed of pointer, which is still kept for working purposes in its homeland. The long-haired form is now relatively scarce, with the smooth-coated type predominating. It has a broad head and a distinctive stop to the nose.

HISTORY So effective are the hunting abilities of this ancient breed that game suffered a dramatic decline. An ownership ban, from which only royalty was exempt, was imposed in the late 16th century.

REMARK The name "Perdiguerio" comes from the Portuguese word for partridge, the breed's chief quarry.

OTHER NAMES Portuguese Pointer.

ears have rounded tips

smooth, short coat

large, preferably dark eyes

triangular-shaped ears

broad, black nostrils

round, straight, powerful neck

short, broad body

well-arched toes

Color types

| Height: 20½–22in (52–56cm) | Weight: 35–60lb (16–27kg) | Temperament: Active, obedient |

HERDING DOGS

ORIGINALLY, HERDING DOGS tended to be large and powerful, capable of protecting livestock from predators such as wolves and bears. As such threats declined, smaller, more agile breeds were adopted to take a more active role in controlling the movements of the herds. With various exceptions such as the German Shepherd Dog (see p.115), European herding breeds are less likely to be seen in the show ring, or in the home as family pets, but are still used for herding purposes. However, this is changing. Some breeds, such as the Tervuren (see p.124), are losing their popularity as herders but finding new roles often as companions and show dogs.

Place of origin: US	First use: Herding sheep	Origins: 1800s

Australian Shepherd

This attractive, long-haired breed often has a bobtail and a striking and remarkably varied, coat coloration—every dog has a unique pattern of markings. Eye coloration, too, is highly variable.

HISTORY Despite its name, this breed was developed mainly in the US. It is descended from collie stock, possibly crossed with other herding breeds. Its original ancestry can be traced back to the Basque region of France and Spain.

REMARK This breed is highly prized wherever obedience is of vital importance, such as in search and rescue work.

Color types

triangular ears set high on head

thick ruff of fur on neck and chest

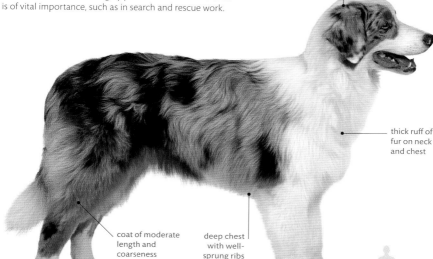

coat of moderate length and coarseness

deep chest with well-sprung ribs

Height: 18–23in (46–58½cm)	Weight: 35–70lb (16–32kg)	Temperament: Active, intelligent

Place of origin: Great Britain	First use: Herding sheep	Origins: 1500s

Bearded Collie

Not dissimilar to the Old English Sheepdog in appearance (see p.106), the Bearded Collie is much lighter and more slender in shape. It has a medium-length, tousled coat covering an agile and athletic, strong-limbed body.

HISTORY The Bearded Collie is thought to have descended from Polish Lowland Sheepdogs brought to Scotland centuries ago by visiting sailors. Although an attentive and industrious worker, it has also become popular in agility competitions and as a pet.
REMARK Hardy and well protected, it is quite content to sleep outdoors.
OTHER NAMES Beardie.

flat, broad skull

ears largely covered with hair

straight, level back

tail set low on back

strong, well-boned forelegs

legs covered with shaggy hair

medium-size ears

oval-shaped feet with hair between toes

medium-length, harsh coat

Color types

Height: 20–22in (51–56cm)	Weight: 40–60lb (18–27kg)	Temperament: Friendly, active

| Place of origin: Great Britain | First use: Herding sheep | Origins: 1700s |

Border Collie

This graceful breed can be recognized by its distinctive black and white coloration, although a variety of colors are permissible. Its coat may be moderately long or smooth.

HISTORY A standard was approved by the Kennel Club of Britain in 1976, but this dog had long been valued by farmers in the border region between Scotland and England as an excellent sheep herder.
REMARK The Border Collie has an effortless gait, lifting its feet just a short distance off the ground.

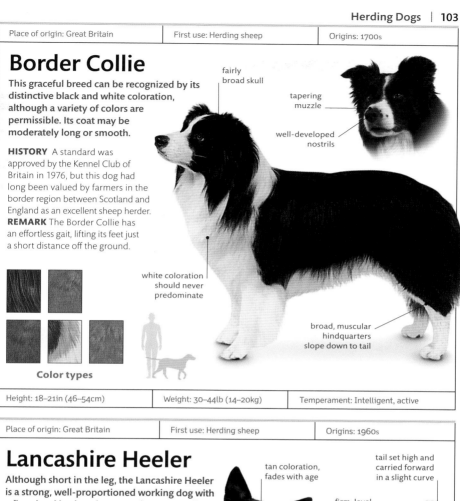

fairly broad skull

tapering muzzle

well-developed nostrils

white coloration should never predominate

broad, muscular hindquarters slope down to tail

Color types

| Height: 18–21in (46–54cm) | Weight: 30–44lb (14–20kg) | Temperament: Intelligent, active |

| Place of origin: Great Britain | First use: Herding sheep | Origins: 1960s |

Lancashire Heeler

Although short in the leg, the Lancashire Heeler is a strong, well-proportioned working dog with a firm, level back and an engaging personality.

HISTORY This breed derives from Welsh Corgis crossed with Manchester Terriers (see p.206), which imparted their coloration and vermin-catching skills.
REMARK The Lancashire Heeler has strong, natural herding instincts.
OTHER NAMES Ormskirk Terrier.

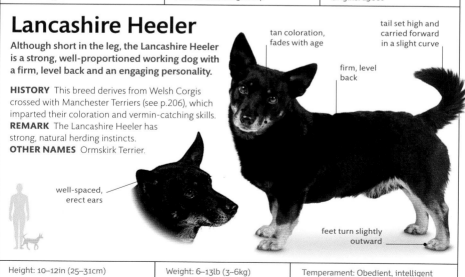

tan coloration, fades with age

tail set high and carried forward in a slight curve

firm, level back

well-spaced, erect ears

feet turn slightly outward

| Height: 10–12in (25–31cm) | Weight: 6–13lb (3–6kg) | Temperament: Obedient, intelligent |

| Place of origin: Great Britain | First use: Herding sheep | Origins: 1500s |

Rough Collie

Truly spectacular in full coat, the Rough Collie is one of the most glamorous breeds in the world. It is unmistakable with its profuse mane and frill and has a highly intelligent expression.

HISTORY Essentially the same breed as the Smooth Collie (opposite), it derived from the same Scottish working collie stock. It enjoyed royal patronage when Queen Victoria kept the breed at Balmoral Castle, Scotland.

REMARK The greatest of all movie star dogs, Lassie, was a Rough Collie.

OTHER NAMES Rough-haired Collie.

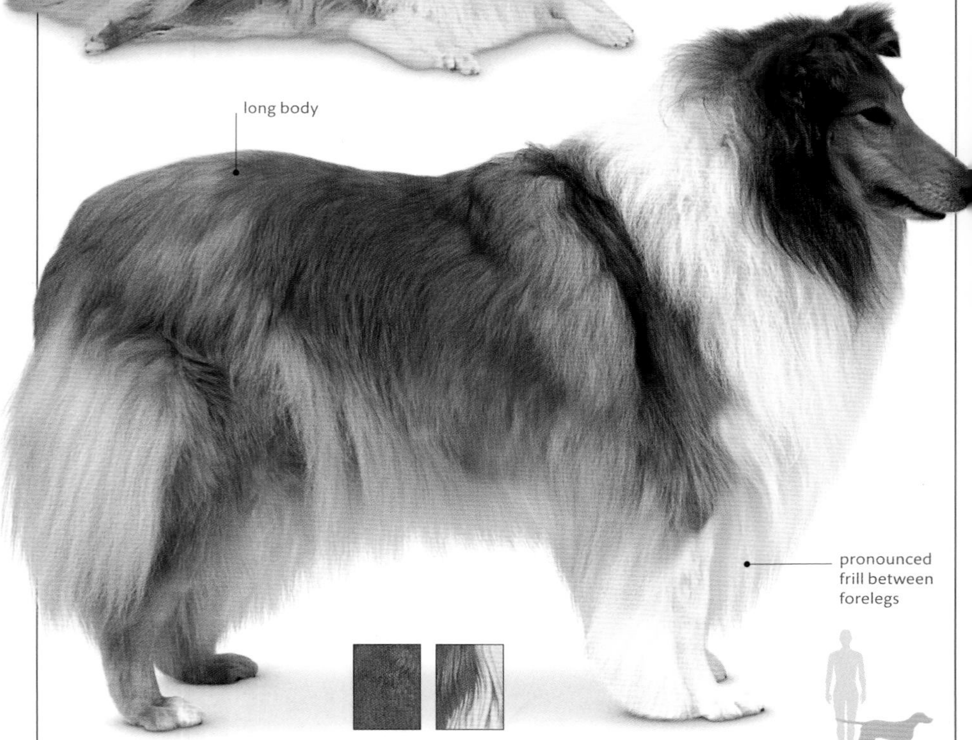

small, tipped ears

bushy tail

top of the skull is flat

long, tapering muzzle

long body

pronounced frill between forelegs

Color types

| Height: 20–24in (51–61cm) | Weight: 40–65lb (18–30kg) | Temperament: Loyal, responsive |

| Place of origin: Great Britain | First use: Herding sheep | Origins: 1500s |

Smooth Collie

Easily distinguishable from its rough-coated relative (opposite), the Smooth Collie has a short, somewhat harsh, flat coat, as well as a dense, weather-resistant undercoat. The blue merle (blue and black mixed with tan) form often shows blue coloration in the eyes.

ears erect when alert, with tips hanging forward

HISTORY This breed's history can be traced back to a dog called Trefoil, a tricolored collie born in 1873.
REMARK The Smooth Collie has not enjoyed the popularity of the rough form.
OTHER NAMES Smooth-haired Collie.

sweet expression in almond-shaped eyes

powerful, arched neck

muscular thighs

straight, muscular forelegs

Color types

| Height: 20–24in (51–61cm) | Weight: 40–65lb (18–29½kg) | Temperament: Loyal, responsive |

| Place of origin: Great Britain | First use: Herding sheep | Origins: 1700s |

Shetland Sheepdog

Noticeably smaller in size than a Rough Collie (opposite), this small but glamorous sheepdog has a double coat with a distinctive frill and mane around its head.

small ears set close together

HISTORY Bred originally on the Shetland Islands off Scotland, this sheepdog is now common around the world.
REMARK Affectionate with its owner, this dog does not take so readily to strangers.

level back

distinctive mane

feathering on back of forelegs

Color types

| Height: 14–14½in (35–37cm) | Weight: 14–16lb (6–7kg) | Temperament: Active, intelligent |

| Place of origin: Great Britain | First use: Herding sheep | Origins: 1800s |

Old English Sheepdog

The immense, shaggy coat is the distinctive feature of this breed and requires a great deal of grooming. Thick-set and muscular, this strong, square-built dog has great symmetry and a distinctive rolling gait.

HISTORY Developed from drover's dogs in the 1800s, it is probably related to shepherd's dogs found in mainland Europe, such as the Bergamasco (see p.131).
REMARK This breed requires plenty of exercise if it is to remain healthy and happy.
OTHER NAMES Bobtail.

hair extends over eyes

Adult and puppy

small ear on side of head, hidden by hair

coat is shaggy, not curly

thick-set, compact body

strong, straight forelegs

Color types

small, rounded feet

| Height: 22–24in (56–61cm) | Weight: 66lb (30kg) | Temperament: Active, protective |

| Place of origin: Great Britain | First use: Droving cattle | Origins: 1200 BCE |

Cardigan Welsh Corgi

The Cardigan is distinguishable from the Pembroke Welsh Corgi (below) by its long, fox's brush tail. The Cardigan's ears are also larger and more widely spaced, and the feet tend to have a more rounded appearance.

HISTORY The Corgi is traditionally a droving dog; its small size enabled it to dodge in and bite the lower legs of cattle, forcing them to move where required.

REMARK Until the 1850s, the Cardigan Welsh Corgi was the only dog known to be kept in some Welsh communities.

erect, rounded ears

wide skull and foxlike head

powerful, muscular neck

long body in relation to height

Color types

| Height: 10½–12½in (27–32cm) | Weight: 25–38lb (11–17kg) | Temperament: Active, obedient |

| Place of origin: Great Britain | First use: Droving cattle | Origins: 1000s |

Pembroke Welsh Corgi

In spite of its size, this bold, inquisitive dog is still powerful, and has a surprisingly loud bark. Unlike the Cardigan (above), the Pembroke has only a short tail, and it is bred in a more restricted color range.

HISTORY The Welsh Corgi may be related to the Swedish Vallhund (see p.128), but its precise origins are not known. Its presence has been recorded in Wales since the Domesday Book of 1086.

REMARK This breed is now internationally known as the favorite pet of Queen Elizabeth II.

pricked, medium-size ears

powerful neck

flat skull

round, brown eyes

slightly tapering muzzle

short tail and strong hindquarters

Color types

| Height: 10–12in (25–31cm) | Weight: 20–26lb (10–12kg) | Temperament: Active, obedient |

| Place of origin: Australia | First use: Herding cattle | Origins: 1800s |

Australian Cattle Dog

This strong, compact dog was first developed in Australia to drive herds of cattle on long, arduous treks to market. Its key qualities are its amazing stamina, versatility, and endurance. It is essentially silent when working, controlling cattle with precision and the minimum of effort.

HISTORY A number of different breeds contributed to its ancestry. The most significant of these was the dingo, the feral dog of the First Australians, which was too unruly to perform the task of cattle-driving competently.

REMARK This breed holds the record for canine longevity—29 years.

OTHER NAMES Australian Queensland Heeler, Blue Heeler.

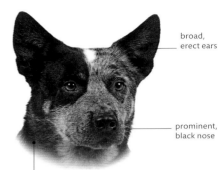

broad, erect ears

prominent, black nose

thick-set neck

puppies are born white, due to Dalmatian blood in ancestry

Puppies

strong back and couplings

tail hangs in slight curve

harsh, dense outercoat

deep, muscular chest

strong, rounded feet

Color types

| Height: 17–20in (43–51cm) | Weight: 35–45lb (16–20kg) | Temperament: Bold, determined |

Place of origin: Australia	First use: Herding livestock	Origins: 1800s

Australian Kelpie

The work rate of this tough little sheepdog has become a legend in its native Australia. An economical, compact body, well-muscled but lean, is supported on strong, firm-boned legs. The Kelpie has a tough, weather-resistant outercoat and a short, dense undercoat. A wide range of coat colors is seen; black dogs are sometimes known as barbs.

HISTORY A New South Wales grazier named Allen imported a pair of English collies into Australia in 1870. These dogs mated on board ship and one of the offspring was bred with a local black-and-tan bitch named *Kelpie*. Her progeny formed the basis of this breed, which was first exhibited in 1908.
REMARK Australian Kelpies seem to have the ability to mesmerize and control sheep simply by staring at them.
OTHER NAMES Kelpie, Barb.

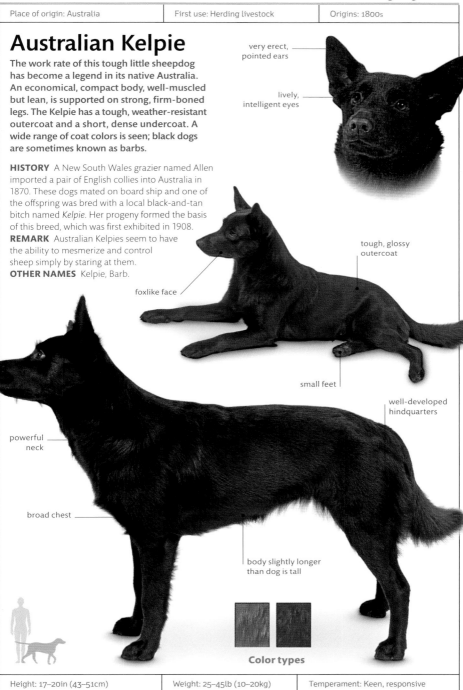

very erect, pointed ears

lively, intelligent eyes

tough, glossy outercoat

foxlike face

small feet

well-developed hindquarters

powerful neck

broad chest

body slightly longer than dog is tall

Color types

Height: 17–20in (43–51cm)	Weight: 25–45lb (10–20kg)	Temperament: Keen, responsive

| Place of origin: Finland | First use: Herding reindeer | Origins: 1600s |

Finnish Lapphund

This medium-size breed is typically spitz-like in appearance, with a beautiful, fluffy coat occurring in a large range of colors.

HISTORY Originally kept by the Sámi people who have long inhabited northernmost Europe, it is probably related to the Samoyed (see p.283) evolved by the Samoyede tribes of the Urals.

REMARK In the parti-colored dog, the colored area must predominate, with white markings small and symmetrical.

OTHER NAMES Lapinkoira.

square-shaped skull

foxlike head

mane of longer hair evident on neck

muscular hindquarters

Color types

| Height: 18–20½in (46–52cm) | Weight: 44–47lb (20–21kg) | Temperament: Responsive, intelligent |

| Place of origin: Finland | First use: Herding reindeer | Origins: 1600s |

Lapinporokoira

This herding dog has a loosely curled tail, which may be held against the thigh rather than over the back. Its body is longer than that of the Finnish Lapphund (above).

HISTORY Having been kept primarily as a working breed for many years, in the 1960s, a show standard was at last created for the Lapinporokoira by the Finnish Kennel Club.

REMARK Working dogs from the north are brought south to mate with bitches; male offspring are then sent north to herd. This helps maintain the breed's working instinct.

OTHER NAMES Lapland Reindeer Dog.

widely spaced, erect ears

coarse outercoat in wide range of colors

relatively short muzzle

long tail, well covered with hair

Color types

soft, woolly undercoat

| Height: 19–22in (48–56cm) | Weight: 60–66lb (27–30kg) | Temperament: Alert, responsive |

| Place of origin: Central Asia | First use: Livestock guardian | Origins: 1600s |

Caucasian Shepherd Dog

These large formidable dogs originate from the Caucasus Mountains. Regional variants were recognized, which could differ in size and coat length.

HISTORY The biggest examples of this breed were those from the mountains, rather than the steppes, where they could be challenged by bears. This called for bravery and loyalty. In more recent times, these dogs have been used by the military.

REMARK Caucasian Shepherd Dogs are now standardized for show purposes and have grown in popularity during the 21st century. Their size means they are costly dogs to keep.

OTHER NAMES Caucasian Ovcharka, Azerbaijani Shepherd Dog, Circassian Sheepdog, Kars.

triangular ears set high

smooth, short hair on the muzzle and forehead

powerful tail

Puppy

very large paws

large, broad head

well-muscled, powerful front legs

oval-shaped feet

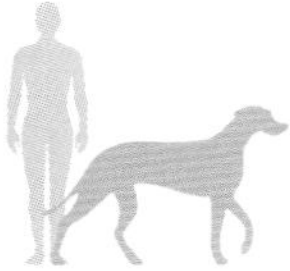

Color types

| Height: 26–35in (65–90cm) | Weight: 121–220lb (55–100kg) | Temperament: Independent, watchful |

Place of origin: New Zealand	First use: Herding sheep	Origins: 1800s

Huntaway

These herding dogs are still kept primarily for controlling the movements of sheep in upland areas of New Zealand. They vary considerably in appearance and size. What sets the Huntaway apart from other herding dogs is the fact that it will bark, meaning it can be located from afar.

HISTORY The Huntaway is the first breed created in New Zealand, originating in the late 1800s. The emphasis has always been on its working ability rather than appearance, although they are usually black and tan.
REMARK These dogs are now being kept in other countries, including Australia and Japan. They are quite noisy by nature.
OTHER NAMES New Zealand Huntaway.

usually floppy-eared

coat type variable

deep-chested

powerful legs and feet

strong hindquarters, with muscular thighs

Color types

Height: 22–26in (56–66cm)	Weight: 55–88lb (25–40kg)	Temperament: Independent, energetic

Place of origin: France	First use: Hunting boar	Origins: 1500s

Beauceron

One of the best-known sheepdogs in France, the Beauceron is somewhat reminiscent of the Dobermann (see pp.246–247) in overall appearance but can be distinguished by its long tail and double dewclaws.

HISTORY Originally used for hunting wild boar, its intelligent and adaptable nature was later employed for herding sheep, and even for carrying messages during wartime.
REMARK The alternative name of Bas Rouge refers to the tan markings on the legs of this breed.
OTHER NAMES Bas Rouge, Berger de Beauce.

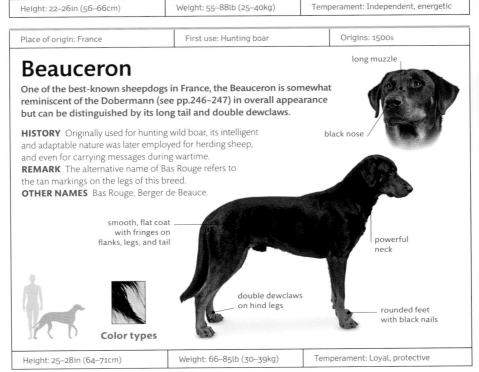

long muzzle

black nose

smooth, flat coat with fringes on flanks, legs, and tail

powerful neck

double dewclaws on hind legs

rounded feet with black nails

Color types

Height: 25–28in (64–71cm)	Weight: 66–85lb (30–39kg)	Temperament: Loyal, protective

| Place of origin: France | First use: Guarding and herding stock | Origins: 1200s |

Briard

This large, muscular breed of French sheepdog is one of the oldest of northern Europe. Although a fierce and protective guardian of its flock, it is an amiable giant and is easy to train. Its slightly wavy and very dry coat gives protection against the elements and needs little grooming.

HISTORY The Briard is named after the French province of Brie, although the breed appears to have been kept all over France.
REMARK One of the most unusual features of the Briard is its double dewclaws.
OTHER NAMES Berger de Brie.

prominent, black nose

rectangular-shaped skull

angulated hindquarters

firm, level back

strong, powerful forelegs

flexible and powerful hindquarters

strong, slightly rounded feet

Color types

| Height: 23–27in (57–69cm) | Weight: 75lb (34kg) | Temperament: Lively, protective |

| Place of origin: France | First use: Herding sheep | Origins: 1600s |

Pyrenean Sheepdog

These relatively small sheepdogs originated in the mountainous Pyrenean region, separating France and Spain, where they have been kept for centuries. They are well protected by their coats against the harsh weather.

HISTORY Although smaller than many sheepdogs, the Pyrenean is noted for its stamina, having worked for centuries watching over flocks in this difficult terrain. As companions, they need plenty of exercise if they are to thrive.
REMARK Hair on the muzzle is short and unusually grows away from the eyes and nose.
OTHER NAMES Le Berger des Pyrénées.

triangular-shaped head when viewed from above

low-set, sometimes naturally stumpy tail

longer-coated dogs may have a naturally corded coat

straight, rather sinewy front legs

Color types

| Height: 15–20in (38–50cm) | Weight: 31–55lb (14–25kg) | Temperament: Independent, alert |

Place of origin: France	First use: Herding sheep	Origins: 800s

Berger de Picard

This is the oldest of the French sheepdogs and is thought to have been brought to northern France around the 9th century. In size, the Berger de Picard is about as tall as a German Shepherd (opposite), with a rough, durable outercoat and a thick, waterproof undercoat. The breed is usually fawn or gray in coloration, the white markings confined to the chest and legs.

HISTORY The Celts are thought to have introduced the Berger de Picard into France. Its origins, however, are obscure, and the few that remain in France are largely working dogs. The breed is seen infrequently outside its native France.

REMARK Members of this breed make excellent and affectionate house dogs. They tend, however, to be a little surly and defensive of their home territory. They will also usually prove to be good guard dogs in these surroundings.

OTHER NAMES Picardy Shepherd.

large head with powerful muzzle

well-spaced, upright ears

tail slightly curled at tip

prominent chest

rough, tousled coat, never curly

muscular thighs

solid-boned legs

Color types

Height: 21½–26in (55–66cm)	Weight: 50–70lb (23–32kg)	Temperament: Lively, adaptable

| Place of origin: Germany | First use: Herding sheep | Origins: 1800s |

German Shepherd Dog

With a slightly elongated body and a strong, muscular build, the German Shepherd ranks among the most popular breeds in the world. A versatile and enthusiastic worker, it is used in many capacities, including search and rescue and guiding the blind. At one time, smooth-, long-, and wire-haired forms were recognized, but now only the short-haired form is accepted for show purposes. Occasionally, long-haired German Shepherds are still produced.

HISTORY Although its working ancestry dates a great deal further back, the modern German Shepherd was first exhibited at a show in Hanover, Germany, in 1882.
REMARK White coloration is not favored in this breed. White-coated individuals did, however, found the White Shepherd breed in North America, with a breed club being established there in 1969.
OTHER NAMES Deutscher Schäferhund, Alsatian.

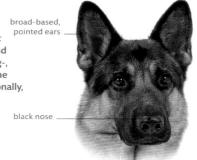

broad-based, pointed ears

black nose

muzzle is half the length of the head

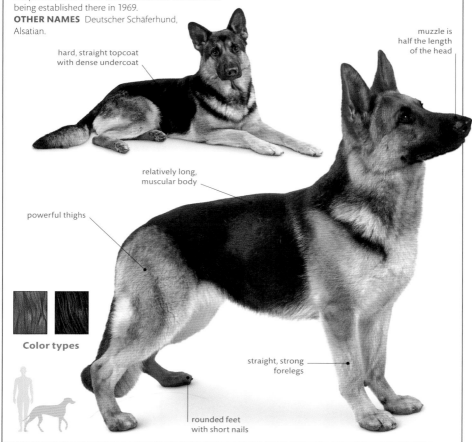

hard, straight topcoat with dense undercoat

relatively long, muscular body

powerful thighs

Color types

straight, strong forelegs

rounded feet with short nails

| Height: 23–25in (57–62cm) | Weight: 75–95lb (34–43kg) | Temperament: Intelligent, responsive |

Place of origin: Germany	First use: Guarding estates	Origins: 1200s

Hovawart

This breed has a long, thick, weatherproof coat, is lightly built, yet has a strong physique. In appearance, the breed is similar to the Flat-coated Retriever (see p.63), but there is no direct relationship between them. Indeed, the Hovawart is not a gundog but a traditional guardian of sheep and other domestic stock. It exhibits a highly developed protective nature and displays great loyalty.

Color types

HISTORY The development of the Hovawart is credited to the efforts of a German breeder, Kurt König. The breed was recognized by the German Kennel Club in 1936, and this dog was first seen in the US during the 1980s.
REMARK The name "Hovawart" comes from the German word, *hofewart*, meaning "guardian of the estate."

strong, straight back

tail extends past the hocks

feathering on back of forelegs

powerful hind legs

oval feet

color of claws matches that of coat

Height: 23–28in (58–70cm)	Weight: 55–90lb (25–41kg)	Temperament: Alert, protective

broad, convex forehead

color of nose
matches that of coat

pendulous ears

long topcoat with
straight or slightly
wavy undercoat

well-feathered tail, held
high when excited

dark, oval-
shaped eyes

slightly
sloping
pasterns

a few white hairs are
permissible at end of tail

| Place of origin: Germany | First use: Droving cattle | Origins: 1400s |

Giant Schnauzer

flat forehead

This is the largest of the three breeds of schnauzer and also the most recent addition to the group. The Giant Schnauzer is a powerful, muscular dog, whose height at the shoulders should match its body length, giving it a rather square shape when viewed in profile.

HISTORY It is likely that the Giant Schnauzer was developed from rough-coated cattle dogs that were mated with smaller schnauzers. The breed was first exhibited at a show in Munich, Germany, in 1909, under the name of the Russian Bear Schnauzer. It was also known as the Munich Schnauzer for a brief period during its early development.

REMARK The top coat of the Giant Schnauzer is especially important for show purposes. It must be harsh and wiry in texture, with no tendency toward softness. About twice a year, the coat needs to be stripped to remove dead hairs.

OTHER NAMES Riesenschnauzer.

round feet
with dark nails

chin whiskers
and stubby
moustache

deep chest

strong, rather
square profile

muscular forelegs

Color types

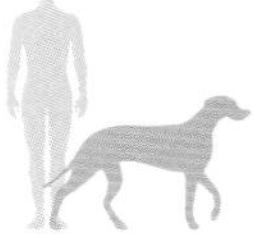

| Height: 23½–27½in (60–70cm) | Weight: 70–77lb (32–35kg) | Temperament: Loyal, protective |

Place of origin: Poland	First use: Herding sheep	Origins: 1500s

Polish Lowland Sheepdog

This breed looks a little like the Bearded Collie (see p.102), but it is smaller. It takes readily to training for a variety of purposes. Some are born tailless.

HISTORY After the Second World War, the breed was saved from extinction by a Polish veterinarian who had two dogs and six bitches that survived the war.

REMARK This dog is said to have an excellent memory.

OTHER NAMES Polski Owczarek Nizinny.

Color types

medium-size head

thick, shaggy coat

dark nose with wide nostrils

rectangular profile

Height: 16–20in (41–51cm)	Weight: 30–35lb (14–16kg)	Temperament: Alert, affectionate

Place of origin: Netherlands	First use: Herding sheep	Origins: 1700s

Schapendoes

The Schapendoes, a native of Holland, has a long, straight, powerful back. A dense, shaggy coat gives it a friendly appearance, although as a working dog, it is a hardy and fearless herder and guardian of its flock.

HISTORY It is believed to be a very old breed with a similar descent to that of the Briard (see p.113) and the Bergamasco (see p.131).

REMARK The decline in sheep herding has seen this dog's numbers fall.

OTHER NAMES Dutch Sheepdog.

broad skull

ears flat to head

tail raised when dog is alert

broad deep chest

Color types

Height: 17–20in (43–51cm)	Weight: 33lb (15kg)	Temperament: Active, friendly

Place of origin: Netherlands	First use: Herding stock	Origins: 1700s

Dutch Shepherd Dog

A keen, alert expression graces the finely chiseled face of this hardworking and agile herding dog. The Dutch Shepherd is officially recognized as having three distinctly different coat types: long-haired, rough-haired, and short-haired. It occurs in various shades of brindle, such as yellow, red, and blue, and its coloration lightens as it grows older.

HISTORY It is likely that this dog is descended from the Groenendael, one of the Belgian shepherd dog breeds (see p.122), and, apart from coloration, the two breeds are judged by the same standard.
REMARK Short-tailed pups often occur, but these are not acceptable for show purposes.
OTHER NAMES Hollandse Herdershond.

medium-length muzzle with prominent nostrils

triangular, erect ears, set high on head

slightly sloping rump

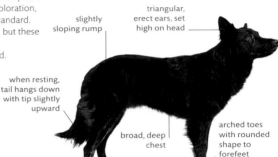

when resting, tail hangs down with tip slightly upward

broad, deep chest

arched toes with rounded shape to forefeet

Color types

Height: 23–25in (58–64cm)	Weight: 66lb (30kg)	Temperament: Alert, obedient

Place of origin: Switzerland	First use: Show/companion dogs	Origins: 1967

White Swiss Shepherd

Members of this attractive breed are closely related to the German Shepherd Dog (see p.115), as is very apparent from their physique. They may have long- or medium-length coats.

HISTORY When white German Shepherd Dogs were banned from the show ring, a Swiss breeder named Agatha Burch developed this lineage, now accepted as a breed in its own right.
REMARK Today these dogs are being used by the emergency services, including for search-and-rescue work.
OTHER NAMES Berger Blanc Suisse.

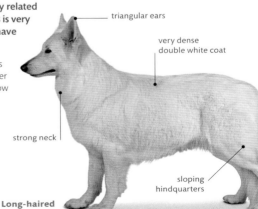

triangular ears

very dense double white coat

strong neck

sloping hindquarters

Long-haired

Height: 21–26in (53–66cm)	Weight: 55–88lb (25–40kg)	Temperament: Loyal, intelligent

Place of origin: Netherlands	First use: Improving dog stocks	Origins: 1900s

Saarloos Wolfdog

Unmistakably similar to a wolf in appearance, this dog still retains a strong pack instinct and needs suitable training as a result, due in particular to its large size and strong-willed nature.

HISTORY This powerful breed was developed in the Netherlands by Leendert Saarloos, who felt that contemporary dogs had become weakened with hip dysplasia and similar conditions. He resolved to rectify the situation and created this breed by crossing a German Shepherd Dog (see p.115) back to a wolf.
REMARK Saarloos died in 1969, just six years before his breed was accepted by the Dutch Kennel Club.

erect ears, broad at base and pointed at tips

almond-shaped, intelligent eyes

long, well-muscled back

ruff of longer hair may be evident around neck

slightly domed skull

prominent, dark nose

short and very dense coat

skull tapers down to nose, with only a slight stop

Color types

Height: 27½–29½in (70–75cm)	Weight: 79–90lb (36–41kg)	Temperament: Shy, independent

Place of origin: Belgium	First use: Herding stock	Origins: 1200s

Groenendael

Its characteristic black coat easily distinguishes the Groenendael from the other three breeds typically grouped under the general heading of Belgian shepherd dogs (see pp.122–125). These dogs are all of a similar type, differing only in terms of their coloration and coat length.

HISTORY The breeding of the Groenendael began by chance in about 1890. Nicholas Rose, owner of the Belgian Café du Groenendael, bred a black puppy and obtained another. This pair formed the basis of the breed.
REMARK In the US, the Groenendael is the only dog considered to be a Belgian shepherd: the Tervuren and Malinois are recognized as separate breeds under their own names.
OTHER NAMES Chien de Berger Belge.

long head

slightly elongated neck

round forefeet

moderately harsh, long, straight outercoat

ruff around neck

males have longer coats than females

thick, springy soles

strong, short pasterns

Height: 22–26in (56–66cm)	Weight: 62lb (28kg)	Temperament: Obedient, loyal

| Place of origin: Belgium | First use: Herding and guarding stock | Origins: 1200s |

Laekenois

This has always been the rarest of the Belgian shepherds, and it is still not widely recognized outside of its homeland. It can be immediately identified by its coat, which is rough and wiry, although not actually curly.

HISTORY This breed was the favorite of Queen Henrietta of Belgium and was named after the Château de Laeken where she lived. The breed was recognized in Belgium in 1897.
REMARK The Laekenois served not only to guard sheep but also linen. Linen-making was an important industry in the vicinity of Bloom, near Antwerp, where the breed originated, the linen being left in the fields to be bleached by the sun.
OTHER NAMES Lackense, Chien de Berger Belge.

dark shading on tail

Black shading on muzzle

erect, triangular-shaped ears

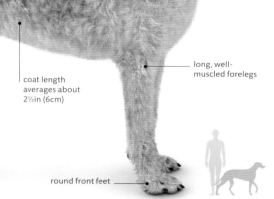

coat length averages about 2½in (6cm)

long, well-muscled forelegs

oval-shaped hind feet with arched toes

round front feet

| Height: 22–26in (56–66cm) | Weight: 62lb (28kg) | Temperament: Obedient, loyal |

Place of origin: Belgium	First use: Herding stock	Origins: 1890s

Tervuren

This member of the Belgian shepherd dog group is identical to the better-known Groenendael (see p.122) apart from its coat coloration. As a distinguishing feature, much emphasis is placed on the coloration—each of the Tervuren's hairs has a dark tip, creating an impression of blackening on the back, ribs, and shoulders, especially on a mature male. The bitch has a shorter coat than the dog.

HISTORY The Tervuren was developed under the guidance of Professor Reul at the Belgian School of Veterinary Science in 1891.
REMARK Sharing the same origins as all the Belgian shepherds, this robust breed's particularly close relationship with the Groenendael is demonstrated when the mating of two Groenendaels occasionally results in the birth of a Tervuren pup.
OTHER NAMES Belgian Tervuren, Chien de Berger Belge.

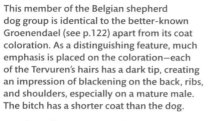

brownish eyes and black eyelids

scissor bite

hair shorter on face than on body

long, straight topcoat; dense undercoat

Color types

well-muscled, powerful hindquarters

long, well-muscled forelegs

Height: 22–26in (56–66cm)	Weight: 62lb (28kg)	Temperament: Obedient, loyal

| Place of origin: Belgium | First use: Herding stock | Origins: 1200s |

Malinois

The Malinois is the only Belgian shepherd dog with a short coat. It is also reputedly the oldest form, originating from the vicinity of Malines in Belgium.

HISTORY Rather ironically, it was only when the working value of this hardy dog declined, at the end of the 19th century, that interest was rekindled in it.
REMARK The breed obtains its full adult coloration by the time that it is 18 months old.
OTHER NAMES Belgian Malinois, Chien de Berger Belge.

slightly tapering muzzle

thicker hair on neck

neck broadens close to shoulders

black shading on ears and muzzle preferred

hindquarters fringed with longer hair

deep, low chest

short hair on lower legs

medium-length tail

front feet round in shape

Color types

| Height: 22–26in (56–66cm) | Weight: 62lb (28kg) | Temperament: Obedient, loyal |

Place of origin: Belgium	First use: Herding cattle	Origins: 1600s

Bouvier des Flandres

The protective nature of this breed is reflected in its formidable appearance and accentuated by its very impressive eyebrows, beard, and moustache. Despite this rugged appearance, the Bouvier des Flandres makes an excellent pet, being good with children and always vigilant. Although by no means indolent, this amiable giant is quite content with moderate exercise.

Color types

HISTORY The ancestry of this breed is unclear, but by the 1800s, several distinct types could be found on the Flanders plain. Three forms survived until 1965, when they were finally amalgamated under one standard. A breed club was founded in Belgium in 1922.

REMARK Renowned for their bravery and loyalty, this dog was in active service during the First World War, carrying messages and locating wounded servicemen.

OTHER NAMES Belgian Cattle Dog.

triangular-shaped ears

bushy eyebrows

harsh beard

coat length about 2½in (6cm), with unkempt appearance

short, round, compact feet

hair feels coarse to the touch and is dry and matt

Height: 23–27in (58–69cm)	Weight: 59½–88lb (27–40kg)	Temperament: Alert, responsive

large head

beard and
moustache

powerful neck
muscles

deep chest and
powerful body

large, powerful
thighs

hocks well
let down

Place of origin: Sweden	First use: Herding cows, ratting	Origins: 500s

Swedish Vallhund

Although small, the Swedish Vallhund is powerfully built with masses of energy. The breed bears a striking resemblance to the Welsh Corgis (see p.107), apart from its coat, which tends to be of more subdued coloration. In its native Sweden, the main role of the Vallhund is herding.

HISTORY The breed was recognized by the Swedish Kennel Club in 1948.
REMARK There is some argument about whether the Vallhund is the ancestor or the descendant of the corgi breeds.
OTHER NAMES Väsgötaspets.

erect ears

well-defined mask preferred

harsh, medium-length coat

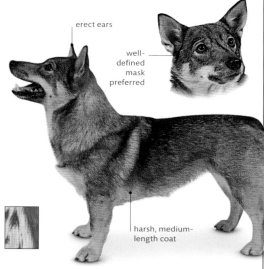

Color types

Height: 12–14in (31–35cm)	Weight: 25–35lb (11–15kg)	Temperament: Responsive, affectionate

Place of origin: Iceland	First use: Herding, pulling sleighs	Origins: 1800s

Iceland Dog

This small dog has an elongated muzzle and a thick, medium-length coat, and it carries its tail in a curve on its back. Although similar to other members of the spitz family, the Iceland Dog is more of a herder than a hunter.

HISTORY It is thought that the Iceland Dog was introduced to Iceland by Norwegians, who refer to the breed as the Friaar Dog. It may share common ancestry with the Greenland Dog (see p.240).
REMARK The breed came close to extinction at the turn of the 20th century, due to an epidemic of distemper. It was saved by the efforts of Icelandic and English breeders.
OTHER NAMES Icelandic Sheepdog, Friaar Dog.

black masking often present

widely spaced ears

slender legs

thick coat carried close to body

Color types

Height: 12–16in (31–41cm)	Weight: 20–30lb (9–14kg)	Temperament: Lively, tough

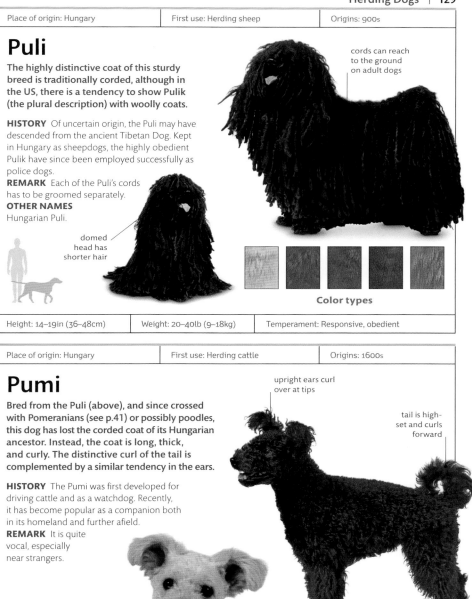

| Place of origin: Hungary | First use: Herding sheep | Origins: 900s |

Puli

The highly distinctive coat of this sturdy breed is traditionally corded, although in the US, there is a tendency to show Pulik (the plural description) with woolly coats.

HISTORY Of uncertain origin, the Puli may have descended from the ancient Tibetan Dog. Kept in Hungary as sheepdogs, the highly obedient Pulik have since been employed successfully as police dogs.

REMARK Each of the Puli's cords has to be groomed separately.

OTHER NAMES Hungarian Puli.

cords can reach to the ground on adult dogs

domed head has shorter hair

Color types

| Height: 14–19in (36–48cm) | Weight: 20–40lb (9–18kg) | Temperament: Responsive, obedient |

| Place of origin: Hungary | First use: Herding cattle | Origins: 1600s |

Pumi

Bred from the Puli (above), and since crossed with Pomeranians (see p.41) or possibly poodles, this dog has lost the corded coat of its Hungarian ancestor. Instead, the coat is long, thick, and curly. The distinctive curl of the tail is complemented by a similar tendency in the ears.

HISTORY The Pumi was first developed for driving cattle and as a watchdog. Recently, it has become popular as a companion both in its homeland and further afield.

REMARK It is quite vocal, especially near strangers.

upright ears curl over at tips

tail is high-set and curls forward

pointed nose, narrow at tip

long, tapering muzzle

Color types

| Height: 13–19in (33–48cm) | Weight: 18–29lb (8–13kg) | Temperament: Alert, energetic |

Place of origin: Slovenia	First use: Guarding flocks	Origins: 1600s

Karst Shepherd

The iron-gray coloration of this dog, offset with darker shadings, is quite striking. The coat itself is dense and harsh, offering good protection against the elements.

HISTORY Originating in Karst, in the north of Slovenia, this flock guardian is related to the Šarplaninac (below).
REMARK Although now scarce in its homeland, international interest in the breed started to develop in the late 1970s.
OTHER NAMES Karst Sheepdog, Krasky Ovcar, Istrian Sheepdog.

V-shaped ears lie flat to the head

tapering tail covered with hair

powerful chest

dark mask

straight back

compact, rounded feet

Height: 20–24in (51–61cm)	Weight: 58–88lb (26–40kg)	Temperament: Loyal, reserved

Place of origin: Macedonia and Serbia	First use: Guarding sheep	Origins: 1200s

Šarplaninac

The Šarplaninac shares the main physical characteristics of the Karst Shepherd (above), but it has more variation in coat coloration than its near relative.

HISTORY This breed was developed in Illyria, and is named after the Šar Mountains, which lie in the Balkans, having originated there centuries ago. Its thick, weatherproof coat reflects its outdoor life.
REMARK The Šarplaninac was first exported to the USA in 1975 and has proved to be popular.
OTHER NAMES Illyrian Sheepdog, Sar Planina.

pendent ears set high on head

Color types

dense, medium-length coat

bushy, scimitar-shaped tail

powerful, straight legs

powerful hind legs

feathering on underparts and legs

Height: 22–24in (56–61cm)	Weight: 55–80lb (25–37kg)	Temperament: Reserved, independent

Place of origin: Italy	First use: Guarding livestock	Origins: 100 BCE

Bergamasco

The distinctly corded coat of this sheepdog is not only effective protection against the elements, but it also made it harder for wolves to inflict injury in the days when such attacks were likely in its native Italy. Coloration may be all shades of gray, with white markings (if present) comprising no more than 20 percent of the entire coat area.

HISTORY This breed is named after the Bergamo region of Italy, where the stock is believed to have originated as a working sheepdog. Its precise ancestry is unknown, but it began to win major Italian dog shows in 1949 and has since become internationally popular.

REMARK A thick, naturally oily undercoat protects the skin.

OTHER NAMES Cane da Pastore Bergamasco.

broad skull, slightly domed between the ears

triangular ears

hair forms long, wavy, strong flocks

facial hair is finer textured

tail tapers to a point

natural parting in middle of back

well-muscled body

thick tail, carried low

oval-shaped feet with well-arched toes

Height: 22–24in (56–61cm)	Weight: 57–84lb (26–38kg)	Temperament: Loyal, intelligent

Place of origin: Spain	First use: Herding livestock	Origins: 1700s

Catalan Sheepdog

Bearing some similarity to the Bearded Collie (see p.102), the Catalan Sheepdog has a prominent beard and moustache and is about the same size as an English Springer Spaniel (see p.62). Developed in the region of Catalonia, in northeast Spain, two distinct forms arose, differing in coat length. The short-coated version, sometimes described as Gos d'Atura Cerdà, is now very scarce.

HISTORY The area in which the Catalan Sheepdog evolved has a strong French influence, and this suggests a possible relationship with French dog breeds. However, nothing certain has been recorded about its origins.

REMARK Dogs of this adaptable breed acted as messengers and guard dogs in the Spanish Civil War.

OTHER NAMES Gos d'Atura Català.

long hair extends from top of head down the face

broad rib cage emphasizes muscular body shape

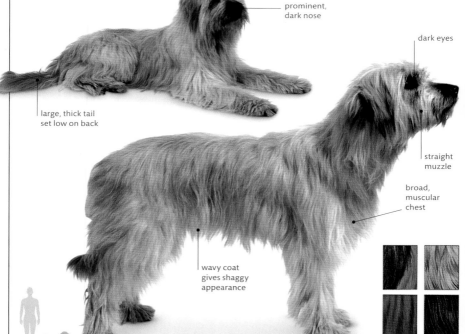

prominent, dark nose

large, thick tail set low on back

dark eyes

straight muzzle

broad, muscular chest

wavy coat gives shaggy appearance

Color types

Height: 18–20in (46–51cm)	Weight: 40lb (18kg)	Temperament: Brave, forceful

Place of origin: Portugal	First use: Herding	Origins: 1800s

Portuguese Sheepdog

This medium-size sheepdog can be variable in height, but the majority
are taller than 18in (45cm). Its similarity to the Briard (see p.113) is reflected
by the presence of the hind dew-claws and a similar coat, although the
Portuguese Sheepdog lacks an undercoat. Its facial expression has led to
it being called the "monkey dog" in its homeland. It not only works with
sheep but also guards horses, pigs, and other farm stock.

HISTORY Dogs of this general type have been used for working
purposes for many years, but only since 1930 has their appearance
become standardized. They may have originated from
crossings between Pyrenean Sheepdogs (see p.113) and
Briards (see p.113), or even Catalan Sheepdogs (see p.132).
REMARK With a reputation for intelligence and devotion
to duty, these dogs are well able to locate stock that has
strayed from the herd.
OTHER NAMES Cão da Serra de Aires.

well-defined
stop

dark nostrils

ears hang
straight down
sides of head

thick "eyebrows"
above dark eyes

broad head

long, slightly
wavy coat

beard and
moustache
of long hair

powerful,
prominent chest

Color types

Height: 16–22in (41–56cm)	Weight: 26–40lb (12–18kg)	Temperament: Active, independent

HOUNDS

ORIGINALLY BRED for hunting, these medium-size dogs usually have short, bi- or tricolored coats and an athletic build. Some are bred for stamina and others for pace. They may be divided broadly into sight hounds, such as the Afghan (see p.98), and scent hounds, such as the Bloodhound (see pp.162–63), depending on their hunting technique. Some breeds are still kept solely for working purposes and may be unknown outside their local area. Hounds do not always adjust well to an urban lifestyle and need plenty of space for exercise. They are friendly by nature, but their hunting instincts are so strong that training them to return can pose problems.

| Place of origin: US | First use: Hunting deer | Origins: 1700s |

Catahoula Leopard Dog

This compact, well-muscled, workman-like dog is used for a variety of purposes besides hunting. Its general appearance substantiates its affirmed hound ancestry. As a stock animal, it excels at rounding up and driving unruly cattle and pigs.

HISTORY Named after the Parish of Catahoula, Louisiana, its precise ancestry is not known. It is, however, highly valued for herding semi-wild cattle and pigs found in the region.
REMARK The Catahoula Leopard Dog was adopted as the state dog of Louisiana in 1979.
OTHER NAMES Catahoula Hog Dog.

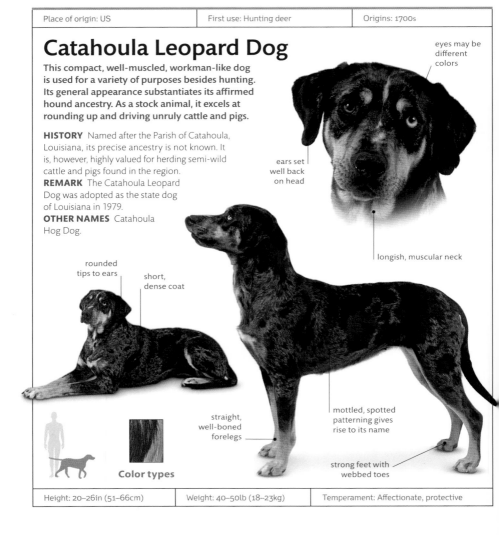

eyes may be different colors

ears set well back on head

longish, muscular neck

rounded tips to ears

short, dense coat

Color types

straight, well-boned forelegs

mottled, spotted patterning gives rise to its name

strong feet with webbed toes

| Height: 20–26in (51–66cm) | Weight: 40–50lb (18–23kg) | Temperament: Affectionate, protective |

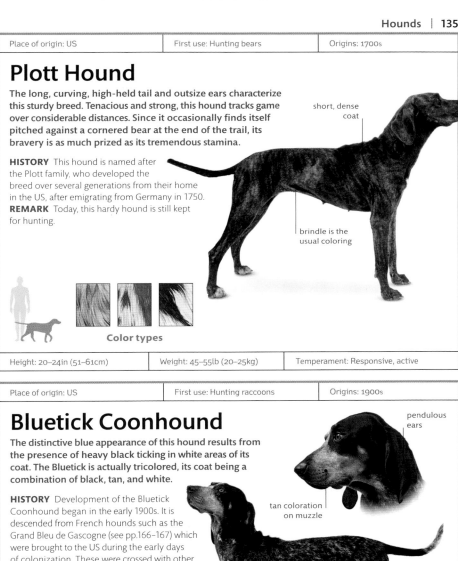

| Place of origin: US | First use: Hunting bears | Origins: 1700s |

Plott Hound

The long, curving, high-held tail and outsize ears characterize this sturdy breed. Tenacious and strong, this hound tracks game over considerable distances. Since it occasionally finds itself pitched against a cornered bear at the end of the trail, its bravery is as much prized as its tremendous stamina.

short, dense coat

HISTORY This hound is named after the Plott family, who developed the breed over several generations from their home in the US, after emigrating from Germany in 1750.
REMARK Today, this hardy hound is still kept for hunting.

brindle is the usual coloring

Color types

| Height: 20–24in (51–61cm) | Weight: 45–55lb (20–25kg) | Temperament: Responsive, active |

| Place of origin: US | First use: Hunting raccoons | Origins: 1900s |

Bluetick Coonhound

pendulous ears

The distinctive blue appearance of this hound results from the presence of heavy black ticking in white areas of its coat. The Bluetick is actually tricolored, its coat being a combination of black, tan, and white.

tan coloration on muzzle

HISTORY Development of the Bluetick Coonhound began in the early 1900s. It is descended from French hounds such as the Grand Bleu de Gascogne (see pp.166–167) which were brought to the US during the early days of colonization. These were crossed with other hunting breeds, such as the Bloodhound.
REMARK The Bluetick is described as having a "cold nose," referring to its ability to follow an old trail left by the animal being pursued.

dark blue ticking is characteristic

long legs

tan areas on legs

| Height: 20–27in (51–69cm) | Weight: 45–80lb (20–36kg) | Temperament: Active, alert |

Place of origin: US	First use: Hunting bears	Origins: 1800s

English Coonhound

This tenacious, medium-size hound has a hard, short coat that gives it some protection outdoors during cold weather and when it is hunting in undergrowth. The majority of English Coonhounds have a red and white coat, described as red tick, but other colors are also recognized. This hardy breed is used primarily for hunting raccoons, from which the description of "coonhound" originates. It may, however, pursue other creatures, including foxes and even bears.

HISTORY A number of divisions have occurred in coonhound breeds, with the English category coming into being by the early 1900s.
REMARK The English Coonhound is still kept primarily for hunting, and rarely just as a companion, even though it possesses a friendly nature.
OTHER NAMES Redtick Coonhound.

Color types

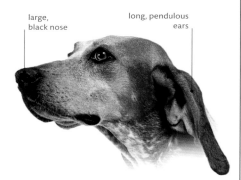

large, black nose

long, pendulous ears

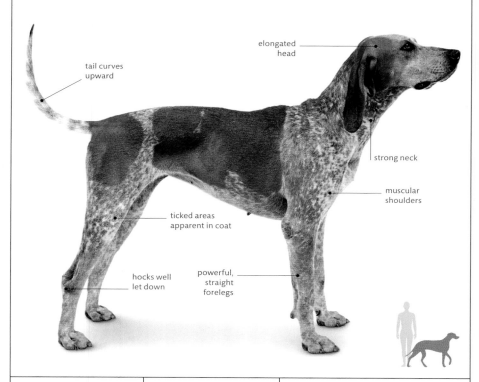

tail curves upward

elongated head

strong neck

muscular shoulders

ticked areas apparent in coat

hocks well let down

powerful, straight forelegs

Height: 21–27in (53–69cm)	Weight: 40–65lb (18–30kg)	Temperament: Active, lively

| Place of origin: US | First use: Hunting raccoons | Origins: 1700s |

Redbone Coonhound

Immediately distinguishable by its mainly red coat, this is the only solidly colored coonhound. Some individuals do have small traces of white, either on the feet or chest, but this is not penalized in show dogs. This good-natured, medium-size hound is becoming increasingly popular throughout the US and was recognised by the American Kennel Club during 2010.

HISTORY Hounds with this coloration have been documented in the US for more than 200 years. Earlier examples of this breed had larger areas of white on their coats than are seen in dogs today.

REMARK This type of hound was probably named after an early breeder, Peter Redbone, who lived in Tennessee.

Color types

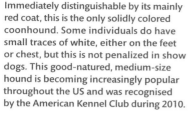

pendulous ears

light-colored iris

broad muzzle

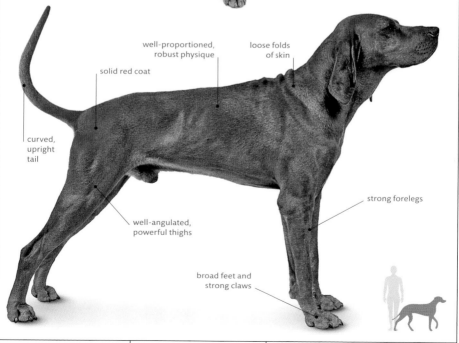

well-proportioned, robust physique

loose folds of skin

solid red coat

curved, upright tail

strong forelegs

well-angulated, powerful thighs

broad feet and strong claws

| Height: 21–26in (53–66cm) | Weight: 50–70lb (23–32kg) | Temperament: Determined, affectionate |

Place of origin: US	First use: Hunting raccoons	Origins: 1700s

Black and Tan Coonhound

This breed was developed from foxhound and, probably, bloodhound stock. It is predominantly black in color, with tan markings comprising 10 to 15 percent of the coat. Occasional white areas around the chest are also still seen. Although good-natured, the Black and Tan Coonhound is a tenacious tracker once it is on the scent. Hunters recognize their dogs by their individual calls.

long, drooping ears

HISTORY The origins of this dog lie in the US and can be traced back to the 1700s. In 1900, it was the first of the coonhounds to be recognized as a distinctive breed.

REMARK It is often referred to as a "treeing hound," since it forces the raccoon to take refuge in a tree.

OTHER NAMES American Black and Tan Coonhound.

small tan area above each eye, shaped like a pumpkin seed

skin fits loosely over body

powerful toes

black nails

Height: 23–27in (58–69cm)	Weight: 55–75lb (25–35kg)	Temperament: Determined, lively

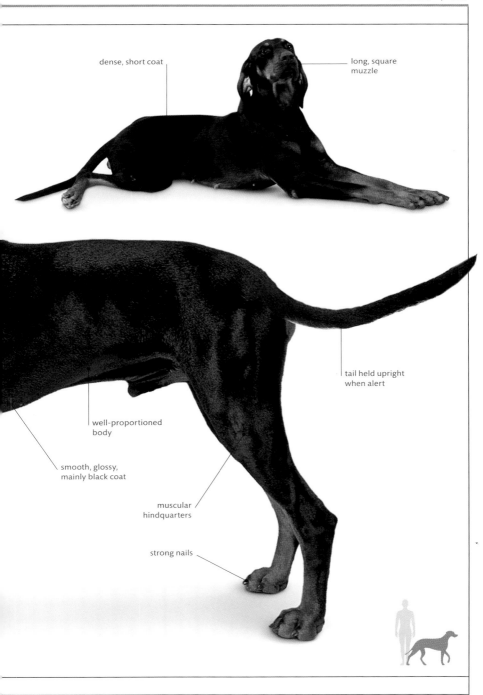

dense, short coat

long, square
muzzle

tail held upright
when alert

well-proportioned
body

smooth, glossy,
mainly black coat

muscular
hindquarters

strong nails

Place of origin: US	First use: Hunting raccoons	Origins: 1800s

Treeing Walker Coonhound

This coonhound is lighter and faster than other similar breeds. The tricolored dog is preferred, although bicolors do exist. Tan-and-white Treeing Walkers are not described as "red" to avoid confusion with the Redbone Coonhound (see p.137).

HISTORY Descended from English Foxhounds (see p.143), the development of this coonhound involved a dog stolen in the 1800s. This dog, named Tennessee Lead, added speed and treeing ability.

REMARK These coonhounds are still used for hunting raccoons and opossums.

Color types

broad ears hang down back of head

long, thin muzzle

tricolored patterning

very open nostrils

sleek, glossy, smooth coat

clearly defined areas of color

muscular hindquarters

straight forelegs

compact feet with thick pads

Height: 20–27in (51–69cm)	Weight: 50–70lb (23–32kg)	Temperament: Lively, intelligent

Place of origin: US	First use: Hunting foxes	Origins: 1700s

American Foxhound

Bred for greater pace, the American Foxhound has a finer build than its English relative (see p.143), is lighter in weight, and has a keener sense of smell. Its short coat is close and hard and is acceptable in any color combination, although the tricolored form is the one most often seen in the show ring.

Color types

HISTORY The ancestry of the American Foxhound can be traced back to English hounds imported to North America in 1650 by a Mr. Robert Brooke. A century later, these were crossed with French hounds sent by General Lafayette to George Washington.

REMARK The songlike voice of the American Foxhound has been recorded and incorporated into some popular music.

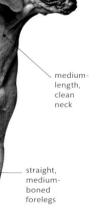

sloping, muscular shoulders

deep chest

medium-length ears, broad and straight

slightly domed skull

medium-length, clean neck

strongly muscled thighs

well-sprung ribs

straight, medium-boned forelegs

Height: 21–25in (53–64cm)	Weight: 65–75lb (30–34kg)	Temperament: Active, friendly

| Place of origin: Great Britain | First use: Hunting rabbits and hares | Origins: 1800s |

Basset Hound

The Basset Hound and bassets in general are characterized by their short legs. Relative to its size, however, the Basset Hound is the heaviest-boned dog of any breed. Both bi- and tricolor markings are acceptable.

HISTORY Ironically, whereas most basset breeds originated in France, the Basset Hound itself was developed in Britain toward the end of the last century.
REMARK The name is derived from the French word *bas*, meaning "low."

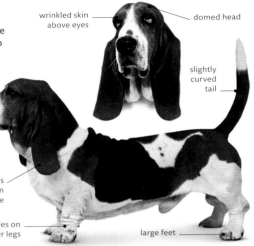

wrinkled skin above eyes

domed head

slightly curved tail

long ears extending down sides of face

wrinkles on lower legs

large feet

Color types

| Height: 13–15in (33–38cm) | Weight: 40–60lb (18–27kg) | Temperament: Independent, active |

| Place of origin: Great Britain | First use: Hunting rabbits and hares | Origins: 1300s |

Beagle

This sturdy and compact hound has medium-length legs and is traditionally used to hunt hares. Working in packs, it pursues its quarry by scent, and displays remarkable stamina and tenacity.

HISTORY The Beagle probably evolved from small foxhounds. Today it is still kept for hunting purposes, although it also makes an affectionate and playful pet.
REMARK A miniature form, the Pocket Beagle, standing about 10in (25cm) high, was popular up to the First World War.
OTHER NAMES English Beagle.

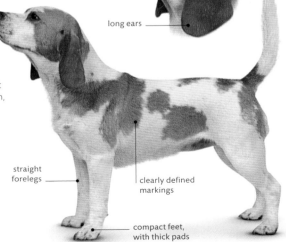

slightly domed skull

long ears

straight forelegs

clearly defined markings

compact feet, with thick pads

Color types

| Height: 13–16in (33–41cm) | Weight: 18–30lb (8–14kg) | Temperament: Lively, friendly |

| Place of origin: Great Britain | First use: Hunting foxes | Origins: 1700s |

Foxhound

The traditional Foxhound is a solid, well-built animal, with stamina an essential ingredient in its development. Foxhounds live in packs, the members of the pack always being counted in pairs, known as couples, rather than singly.

HISTORY This dog was bred from the St. Hubert Hound (see pp.162–163), originally brought to Great Britain by the Normans after the invasion of 1066. The records of the Association of Masters of Foxhounds reveal that in 1880 there were 140 packs and 7,000 Foxhounds in Great Britain.
REMARK Although kept in kennels, this breed is invariably friendly and affectionate.
OTHER NAMES English Foxhound.

broad skull

level back

color and markings highly variable between individuals

long, but never thick, neck

solid base to tail

deep girth giving plenty of room for heart

very powerful hindquarters

strong, straight forelegs

large space from end of ribs to hindquarters to give good stride length and pace

round, catlike feet with toes close together

Color types

| Height: 23–27in (58–69cm) | Weight: 55–75lb (25–34kg) | Temperament: Active, friendly |

Place of origin: Great Britain	First use: Hunting deer	Origins: 800s

Deerhound

Although similar to the Irish Wolfhound (see pp.158–159), the Deerhound is of a sleeker, lighter build, reflecting the contribution of greyhound stock to its ancestry. This is perhaps most obviously apparent in terms of its head shape, the muzzle clearly tapering along its length. Dark blue-gray tends to be the color most favored today, but one of the oldest colors still seen is sandy red, with black areas on both the muzzle and the ears.

HISTORY The Deerhound was originally developed in Scotland to hunt deer. However, the introduction of the gun for hunting led to a decline in numbers, but it is still valued today as a companion dog.
REMARK The Deerhound's shaggy coat offers excellent protection against the elements.
OTHER NAMES Scottish Deerhound.

dark eyes with black rims

head broadest at the ears

small ears preferred, kept folded back at rest

tapering muzzle

harsh, wiry, shaggy coat

ears have a soft, glossy appearance and feel like a mouse's coat

long, tapering tail almost reaching the ground

softer coat on underparts and head

Color types

Height: 28–30in (71–76cm)	Weight: 80–100lb (36–45kg)	Temperament: Gentle, active

| Place of origin: Great Britain | First use: Otter hunting | Origins: 1000s |

Otterhound

long, square muzzle

The coat, with its two distinct layers, is the chief feature of this breed. There is a rough outercoat, which feels hard to the touch, and a much shorter, woolly undercoat, which offers the dog protection when it enters the water.

HISTORY This ancient breed probably evolved from foxhounds and other pack hunting dogs. In fact, Otterhounds themselves used to hunt in packs.
REMARK Like its traditional quarry, the otter, the Otterhound has declined in numbers since the last half of the 19th century.

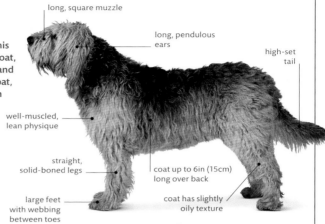

long, pendulous ears

high-set tail

well-muscled, lean physique

straight, solid-boned legs

coat up to 6in (15cm) long over back

large feet with webbing between toes

coat has slightly oily texture

large, hairy head

Color types

| Height: 23–27in (58–69cm) | Weight: 65–120lb (30–55kg) | Temperament: Athletic, independent |

| Place of origin: Northern India | First use: Hunting jackals | Origins: 1900s |

Rampur Greyhound

Named after the area in India where it was developed, this sighthound's ancestry combines the tenacity and toughness of the Afghan (see p.198) with the extra pace of the Greyhound (see p.146).

HISTORY This breed was created by Ahmad Ali Khan, the Nawab of Rampur, who was seeking a versatile hunting dog.
REMARK The Rampur Greyhound has declined in numbers over recent years and may be close to extinction.
OTHER NAMES North Indian Greyhound, Rampur Dog.

Color types

eye position offers wide field of vision

long, tapering tail curves upward to the tip

Deep chested, affording good lung capacity

short, smooth coat

straight, powerful forelegs

| Height: 22–30in (55–76cm) | Weight: 60–65lb (27–29.5kg) | Temperament: Sensitive, friendly |

| Place of origin: Great Britain | First use: Coursing hares | Origins: 3000 BCE |

Greyhound

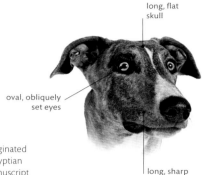

long, flat skull

oval, obliquely set eyes

long, sharp muzzle

The Greyhound kept for the show ring tends to be slightly larger and heavier than its well-known racing counterpart, but it is, nevertheless, still built for acceleration and speed. Both forms are muscular and athletic in build, with a deep chest which provides excellent lung capacity. Few other breeds today are available in such a wide range of coat colors, including parti-colored combinations.

HISTORY The best evidence is that Greyhound stock originated in the Middle East, for similar dogs are represented on Egyptian tombs dating back nearly 5,000 years. An early British manuscript confirms that the breed had reached Britain by 900 CE.
REMARK Although gentle dogs by nature, they do have a tendency to chase cats and small dogs, so they are best muzzled if allowed off the lead. They do not require a lot of exercise, with a short run off the leash being ideal.

long tail, carried low and slightly curved

long, muscular, arched neck

very deep chest

long, straight forelegs

compact, well-knuckled toes with solid pads

Color types

| Height: 27–30in (69–76cm) | Weight: 60–70lb (27–32kg) | Temperament: Lively, friendly |

Place of origin: Great Britain	First use: Racing	Origins: 1800s

Whippet

The Whippet has been purpose-bred for racing, and in the initial part of the race, it can outpace even a Greyhound (opposite). In many respects, the Whippet looks like a scaled-down version of a Greyhound.

HISTORY The ancestry of the Whippet is thought to lie in crossings between the Italian Greyhound (see p.46) and certain terrier breeds such as the Bedlington (see p.205).

REMARK Despite its rather delicate appearance, the Whippet is a robust and confident dog. Its great speed also makes it an excellent ratter.

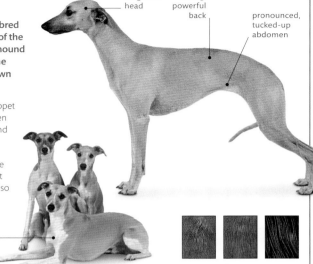

long, lean head

strong, powerful back

pronounced, tucked-up abdomen

long, muscular, well-arched neck

Color types

Height: 17–20in (43–51cm)	Weight: 28lb (13kg)	Temperament: Lively, affectionate

Place of origin: Great Britain	First use: Hunting hares	Origins: 1200s

Harrier

Tricolor markings are the most common coat configuration for the indefatigable Harrier. Numbers of this well-balanced, medium-size hound have been limited, mainly due to the popularity of its larger relative, the English Foxhound (see p.143).

HISTORY The ancestors of the Harrier are thought to include the Foxhound, Greyhound, and Fox Terrier.

REMARK The first pack of Harriers was established in Britain in 1260 and lasted for 500 years.

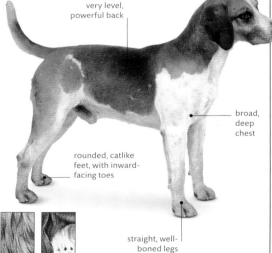

very level, powerful back

broad, deep chest

rounded, catlike feet, with inward-facing toes

straight, well-boned legs

Color types

Height: 18–22in (46–56cm)	Weight: 48–60lb (22–27kg)	Temperament: Active, friendly

Place of origin: Norway	First use: Hunting rabbits	Origins: 1800s

Dunker

This sleek, lightly built yet powerful hound has a poised, elegant appearance. Its thick, short coat is usually tan-colored with a unique blue-marbled or black splodgy saddle. It is an extremely hardy breed, able to withstand extremes of cold, and adapts well to any terrain.

HISTORY To create the Dunker, Norwegian breeder Wilhelm Dunker crossed a Russian Harlequin Hound with various reliable scent hounds, producing a dog that could hunt rabbits by scent rather than sight. It has yet to become popular outside of its homeland.

REMARK A merle gene from the Harlequin Hound gave the Dunker its distinctive mottled saddle marking.

OTHER NAMES Norwegian Hound.

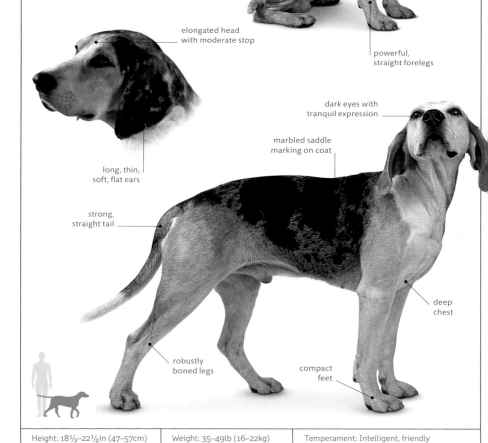

elongated head with moderate stop

powerful, straight forelegs

dark eyes with tranquil expression

marbled saddle marking on coat

long, thin, soft, flat ears

strong, straight tail

deep chest

robustly boned legs

compact feet

Height: 18½–22½in (47–57cm)	Weight: 35–49lb (16–22kg)	Temperament: Intelligent, friendly

Place of origin: Norway	First use: Tracking game	Origins: 1800s

Haldenstövare

This Norwegian scent hound has a distinctive tricolor coat that is predominantly white, with black and tan markings on particular areas of the body. It is the largest of the four recognized stövare breeds (see pp.151–153).

HISTORY Named after the city of Halden in southeastern Norway, not far from the Swedish border, it resulted from crossing local hounds with Swedish, German, and British hound stock.

REMARK Like other Norwegian hounds, it is not a pack dog and makes a fine pet.

OTHER NAMES Halden Hound.

pendent ears

straight muzzle with black nose

dome-shaped skull

long, thick tail carried low

long, curved neck

deep chest

oval-shaped feet with strong toes

Height: 20–25in (51–64cm)	Weight: 51–64lb (23–29kg)	Temperament: Active, affectionate

Place of origin: Norway	First use: Hunting small game	Origins: 1800s

Hygenhund

This solid breed is often described as being "short-coupled" because it has a relatively short, compact body. The Hygenhund has been bred in several coat colors, but the yellow variety with white markings tends to be most common.

HISTORY The Hygenhund was developed by a Norwegian enthusiast, F. Hygen, using Hölsteiner hounds from Germany crossed with various Scandinavian hounds.

REMARK Developed for stamina, the Hygenhund tends to hunt singly with its owner.

OTHER NAMES Hygenhound.

ears stand away from head

wedge-shaped head

pointed muzzle

deep chest

straight, dense coat

well-arched toes

Color types

Height: 18½–23in (47–58cm)	Weight: 44–53lb (20–24kg)	Temperament: Lively, cheerful

Place of origin: Finland	First use: Hunting small game	Origins: 1700s

Finnish Hound

This relatively large hound has an athletic build overall. It has a narrow head with a prominent nose and large, pendulous ears that give it a rather charming appearance. It is also an agile and very energetic hunter.

HISTORY This breed has a mixed ancestry. A variety of English, Swiss, German, and Scandinavian hounds have contributed to its development.

REMARK The Finnish Hound is a keen hunter in summer, but prefers the hearth in winter.

OTHER NAMES Suomenajokoira.

white facial blaze

large, pendulous ears

black saddle area

dense, coarse coat

white markings tend to be confined to lower parts of body

powerfully built limbs

long tail

tough, resilient pads

Height: 22–24½in (56–62cm)	Weight: 55lb (25kg)	Temperament: Friendly, active

Place of origin: Sweden	First use: Scenting and hunting game	Origins: 1900s

Drever

The long body and relatively short legs of the Drever give this breed a distinctly rectangular shape. White markings are an important feature and should be present on the face, neck, chest, and feet, as well as on the tip of the tail. The Drever can be recognized by its loud bark, which enables it to be tracked, even through woodland where its stature may conceal its presence.

HISTORY Crossings of Westphalian and Danish Dachsbrackes gave rise to the Drever.

REMARK These dogs have become popular in Canada.

OTHER NAMES Swedish Dachsbracke.

expressive, chestnut-colored eyes

white muzzle

short legs

Color types

Height: 11½–16in (29–41cm)	Weight: 33lb (15kg)	Temperament: Alert, affable

Place of origin: Sweden	First use: Hunting foxes and hares	Origins: 1200s

Schillerstövare

The light build of this hound gives it considerable pace, and it is regarded as the fastest of all Swedish breeds. The Schillerstövare has a thick undercoat that provides insulation, allowing it to work in deep snow, hunting foxes and snow hares.

HISTORY This breed was developed by Per Schiller from a combination of Swedish hounds and scent hounds from Switzerland, Germany, and Austria.

REMARK The Schillerstövare was represented at the first Swedish dog show, held in 1886.

OTHER NAMES Schiller Hound.

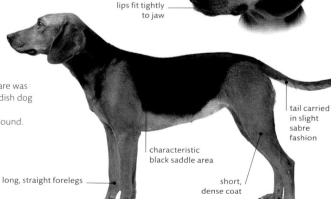

soft ears

chestnut-colored eyes

lips fit tightly to jaw

tail carried in slight sabre fashion

characteristic black saddle area

long, straight forelegs

short, dense coat

Height: 21–22in (53–57cm)	Weight: 40–53lb (18–24kg)	Temperament: Active, enthusiastic

| Place of origin: Sweden | First use: Tracking game | Origins: 1800s |

Hamiltonstövare

This well-built hound has plenty of stamina and will follow a scent with single-minded determination, no matter what the terrain or weather conditions. Well able to hunt in the thick snow of its native Sweden, the Hamiltonstövare's baying call indicates its position to the hunters when it is out of sight.

long, rectangular head

HISTORY A.P. Hamilton, founder of the Swedish Kennel Club, was responsible for the development of this hound. His breeding program was based on Foxhounds (see p.143) and Harriers (see p.147) from England, which were crossed with German hounds, including the now-extinct Holstein Hound, and Hanover Hounds.

REMARK When this sturdy breed was first introduced into Britain in 1968, it was initially referred to simply as the Swedish Foxhound.

OTHER NAMES Hamilton Hound.

black nose

short, dense, double coat

white tip to tail

ears lie flat against sides of head

powerful body

deep chest

tail carried low

white markings on feet, as well as on muzzle and chest

| Height: 20–24in (51–61cm) | Weight: 50–60lb (23–27kg) | Temperament: Courageous, active |

| Place of origin: Sweden | First use: Hunting foxes and hares | Origins: 1200s |

Smålandsstövare

blunt muzzle

This compact, fox- and hare-hunting dog is the shortest and most heavily built of all the Swedish stövare breeds. Many Smålandsstövares are born with tails that are unusually short for a hound. Coat color is invariably black with tan markings on the muzzle, eyebrows, and lower parts of the legs, and occasionally with white flashes on the tips of the tail and feet. The coat itself is thick, smooth, and glossy and needs very little attention in terms of grooming.

HISTORY Originating in Småland, central Sweden, this breed of hound was recognized by the Swedish Kennel Club in 1921. An early breeder, Baron von Essen, had a preference for the short-tailed individuals that were sometimes born and helped to establish this characteristic in the breed. The basic form of this dog may date back to the Middle Ages.

REMARK This dog requires lots of exercise.

OTHER NAMES Smålands Hound.

thick, smooth, glossy coat

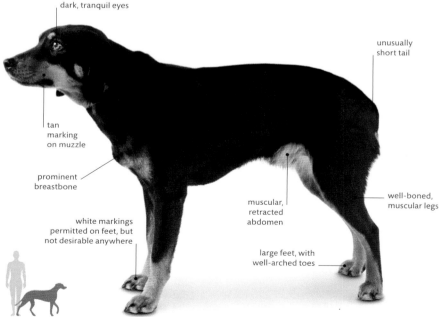

dark, tranquil eyes

unusually short tail

tan marking on muzzle

prominent breastbone

white markings permitted on feet, but not desirable anywhere

muscular, retracted abdomen

well-boned, muscular legs

large feet, with well-arched toes

| Height: 18–20in (46–50cm) | Weight: 33–40lb (15–18kg) | Temperament: Active, enthusiastic |

| Place of origin: Germany | First use: Flushing badgers | Origins: 1900s |

Miniature Dachshund

Noticeably smaller than its standard-sized counterparts, this breed is seen here in three different forms. The Smooth-haired Miniature has a short, dense coat lying close to the body. The Long-haired Miniature also has a flat coat, but it is much longer, with some feathering. The wire-haired form has a harsh-textured coat of even length all over its body.

HISTORY These miniatures, like the standard-sized version, are descended from the Teckel. The division between dachshund breeds was initially made on the basis of weight, and this still holds true today.

REMARK The Wire-haired Miniature form was the last of the dachshunds to receive official recognition in Britain, in 1959.

OTHER NAMES Zwergteckel.

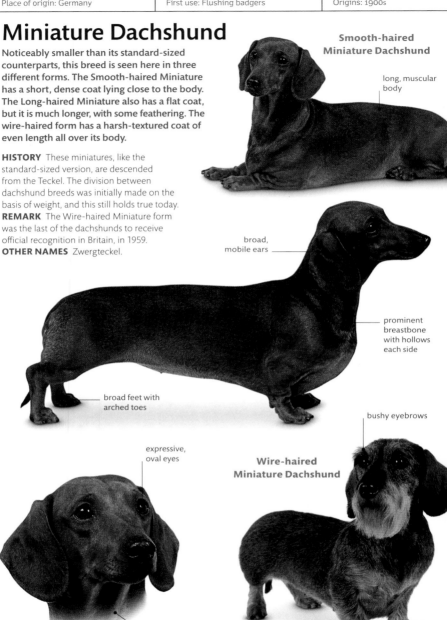

Smooth-haired Miniature Dachshund

long, muscular body

broad, mobile ears

prominent breastbone with hollows each side

broad feet with arched toes

bushy eyebrows

expressive, oval eyes

Wire-haired Miniature Dachshund

long, muscular neck

front feet directed slightly inward

| Height: 5–9in (13–23cm) | Weight: 9–10lb (4–5kg) | Temperament: Active, determined |

Long-haired Miniature Dachshund

Color types

coat longest on neck and underparts

feathering on tail

hind feet smaller than front feet

restricted amount of hair on feet

wide mouth opening behind level of eyes

relatively smooth hair on ears

rounded, broad rump

long neck

| Place of origin: Germany | First use: Tracking game | Origins: 1700s |

Hanoverian Mountain Hound

Relatively heavy in build, with short legs, this hound is often used to track an animal that has been wounded but not killed outright. It often sports a distinctive black mask.

HISTORY Developed by gamekeepers around Hanover in Germany, this breed descends from heavy tracking hounds crossed with lighter ones, such as the Haidbracke.
REMARK This breed is still mainly kept as a working dog, and is highly valued for its fine nose.
OTHER NAMES Hannoverscher Schweisshund.

very prominent nose with broad nostrils

dark mask is sometimes present

streaks of black create brindled effect

straight forelegs

Color types

| Height: 20–24in (51–61cm) | Weight: 84–99lb (38–44kg) | Temperament: Calm, loyal |

| Place of origin: Germany | First use: Tracking game | Origins: 1800s |

Bavarian Mountain Hound

Rather shorter and lighter in build than similar breeds (above), this hound is highly valued for its tracking ability. It will continue on the trail until a wounded animal is found.

HISTORY As its name suggests, this hound evolved in Bavaria in Germany, probably from crossings between Hanoverian and Tyrolean hounds.
REMARK The group to which this hound belongs is described as *schweisshunden*, meaning "bloodhounds."
OTHER NAMES Bayrischer Gebirgsschweisshund.

Color types

slightly domed skull

long, pendent ears set well back on head

short, straight forelegs

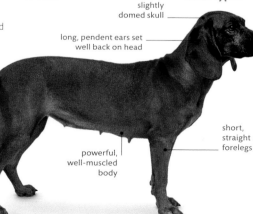

powerful, well-muscled body

| Height: 20in (51cm) | Weight: 55–77lb (25–35kg) | Temperament: Active, intelligent |

Place of origin: Poland	First use: Hunting large game	Origins: 1700s

Polish Hound

This large, heavy hound has a well-wrinkled face, a rectangular head, and powerful jaws. It is a dedicated tracker with a prominent nose and a fine voice.

HISTORY The breed's origins are unknown, but it is probably related to Austrian and German breeds. The Polish Hound declined in numbers during the Second World War but has since recovered.

REMARK There used to be a smaller version of the Polish Hound, known as the Gonczy Polski.

OTHER NAMES Ogar Polski.

noble, rectangular-shaped head

large ears hang down close to head

thick tail

deep, muscular chest

black saddle marking

wrinkles of skin on forehead

prominent black nose

Height: 22–26in (56–66cm)	Weight: 55–71lb (25–32kg)	Temperament: Determined, friendly

| Place of origin: Ireland | First use: Hunting wolves | Origins: 100 BCE |

Irish Wolfhound

A true giant, the Irish Wolfhound is the tallest dog in the world. It is somewhat similar in appearance to the Deerhound (see p.144), but it is larger in overall size. Despite its size, this is a graceful dog, with a rough, wiry coat and a muscular build. The long tail is surprisingly powerful and can cause havoc in the home when swinging back and forth. The Irish Wolfhound's temperament is excellent, but because of its size, it requires training from a young pup. Minimal grooming is needed.

HISTORY The Irish Wolfhound's ancestry dates back many centuries, originating from an ancient lineage of royal dogs. The extinction of the wolf in Ireland during the 1800s almost resulted in the loss of this breed. It was saved only through the efforts of a Scot, Captain George Graham.
REMARK An Irish Wolfhound pup should not be taken on long walks, as these can damage its joints. Instead, it should be encouraged to run and play at its own chosen pace.

long hair over eyes

long, slightly pointed muzzle

small ears

rough and hardy coat

coat longer and more wiry under jaw

| Height: 28–35in (71–90cm) | Weight: 90–120lb (40–55kg) | Temperament: Gentle, friendly |

Color types

long back

long, powerful,
well-arched neck

strong,
straight legs

slightly
curved tail

powerful
thighs

belly drawn
up tight

muscular
shoulders

arched toes with
curved nails

| Place of origin: Ireland | First use: Hunting hares | Origins: 1500s |

Kerry Beagle

Mostly black and tan in coloration, although mottled and tricolor forms are not unknown, the Kerry Beagle is a substantially larger animal than the Beagle (see p.142). This dashing hound is close-coated, has a deep muzzle, and medium-length, unfolded ears. Essentially a pack dog, the Kerry Beagle is as yet unrecognized as a breed in many countries in spite of its long history and unmistakable appearance.

HISTORY Although the ancestry of the Kerry Beagle is obscure, it is thought the breed descended from a larger, deer-hunting hound. Its appearance also suggests that its development could have involved the Bloodhound (see pp.162–163).
REMARK The breed is now used mainly for hunting small game and fowl.
OTHER NAMES Pocadan.

long, straight ears

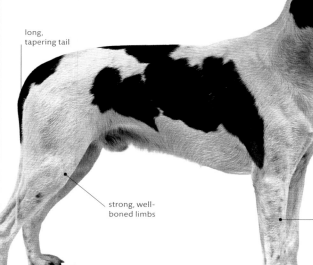

long, tapering tail

medium-length neck

strong, well-boned limbs

close-fitting coat

broad skull

Color types

heavy muzzle

| Height: 22–26in (56–66cm) | Weight: 45–60lb (20–27kg) | Temperament: Active, friendly |

Place of origin: Ireland	First use: Coursing hares	Origins: 1600s

Lurcher

There is considerable variation in the appearance of Lurchers, because they are not bred to conform to any standard. However, in general, the Lurcher has an athletic build and a wiry coat and is now usually the result of cross-breeding involving Deerhounds (see p.144).

HISTORY Traditionally, this dog has been bred for speed and responsiveness, often by Romany Gypsies in Ireland, who used collie and Greyhound (see p.146) crosses, as well as other breeds, for hunting purposes.
REMARK Lurchers combine the pace of their hound ancestor with the instinctive intelligence of a collie.

long, narrow head

ears tend to be small

very powerful hindquarters

long, muscular, arched neck

deep, strong chest

long body

strong hind legs

well-knuckled toes with strong pads

bright, intelligent eyes

Color types

Height: 27–30in (69–76cm)	Weight: 60–70lb (27–32kg)	Temperament: Responsive, quiet

Place of origin: Belgium	First use: Tracking scent	Origins: 800s

Bloodhound

The best-known scent hound in the world, the Bloodhound is also the largest. The folds of loose skin apparent on its face and neck create the famous mournful expression, which belies the breed's lively and active nature. In spite of its ferocious image, this dog is very friendly toward people. It has a very distinctive, melodious voice, which cannot be ignored.

HISTORY The likely ancestor of today's Bloodhound is the ancient St. Hubert's Hound, which was supposedly brought back to Europe by soldiers who had been fighting the Crusades.
REMARK This indomitable hound has incredible tracking skills. It has proved itself capable of following a trail over 14 days old and has been known to pursue a scent with its relentless, swinging stride for 138 miles (220 km). Evidence discovered by a Bloodhound has been used in courts of law.
OTHER NAMES St. Hubert Hound.

dark brown or hazel eyes

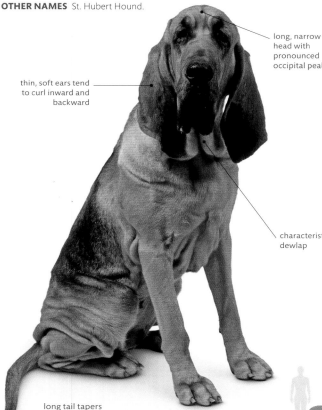

long, narrow head with pronounced occipital peak

thin, soft ears tend to curl inward and backward

characteristic dewlap

long tail tapers to a point

Color types

Height: 23–27in (58–69cm)	Weight: 80–90lb (36–41kg)	Temperament: Determined, responsive

waterproof coat

folds of loose skin
form wrinkles
above eyes

smooth,
short hair

powerful,
muscular body

thighs very
muscular

large, straight
forelegs

hocks well
let down

strong, well-
knuckled feet

Place of origin: France	First use: Tracking large game	Origins: 1800s

Billy

A large hound, with distinctive pale coloration, the Billy has a surprisingly musical call, which is often heard when packs are in pursuit of their quarry. The head is fine and lean, with a square muzzle and a prominent stop. Although not a heavy dog, a pack of Billys is nevertheless powerful enough for their favorite quarry, deer, and more than a match for wild boar, which they still track in France today.

HISTORY The Billy is named after the home of the breeder who created them—Monsieur Gaston Hublot de Rivault, who lived at the Château de Billy, in Poitou. He used mainly bicolored Céris hounds and the now-extinct Montemboeuf, another bicolored breed. Foxhounds and the Larye, with its expert nose, have also contributed to its lineage.

REMARK Just two Billys survived the Second World War. These were used by the son of the breed's founder to save these hounds from extinction.

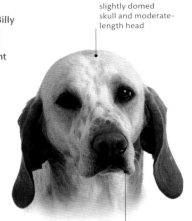

slightly domed skull and moderate-length head

upper lip extends down over lower jaw

short coat, hard to the touch

long, powerful tail, sometimes showing traces of feathering

long, sloping shoulders

very deep, narrow chest

strong, well-boned forelegs

coat is white with orange or lemon, but no black or red

strong, tight, rounded feet

Height: 24–26in (61–66cm)	Weight: 55–66lb (25–30kg)	Temperament: Intelligent, active

Place of origin: France	First use: Hunting small game	Origins: 1800s

Basset Fauve de Bretagne

Overall, the body shape of the Basset Fauve de Bretagne is typical of basset breeds—long, relative to its height, with slightly crooked legs and a long face. The coat, however, is quite different, having neither the rough texture of the Basset Griffon-Vendéen (see p.171), nor the smoothness of the Basset Artésian Normand (see p.169).

HISTORY This breed was developed from the larger Griffon Fauve de Bretagne crossed with other bassets. It retains the solid coloration of its relative, sometimes with a single white spot on the chest or neck, although this is not encouraged.

REMARK Traditionally, these dogs hunted small game in packs of four.

OTHER NAMES Tawny Brittany Basset.

dark, open nose

shortish, muscular neck

oval-shaped ears set level with eyes and pleated at base

any white mark on chest to be discouraged

lively eyes

shortish, flat coat, hard and coarse

thick tail, tapering toward point

prominent breastbone

typical, slightly crooked legs but can be straight

Color types

Height: 13–15in (33–38cm)	Weight: 36–40lb (16–18kg)	Temperament: Lively, friendly

| Place of origin: France | First use: Hunting deer and wild boar | Origins: 1300s |

Grand Bleu de Gascogne

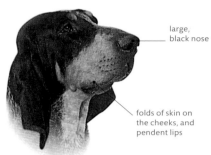

large, black nose

Considered by many hound enthusiasts to be the most majestic and aristocratic of the French breeds, the Grand Bleu de Gascogne is large and powerful. Developed in the dry and hot Midi region in the southwest of France, it is not especially quick in terms of pace, but it displays prodigious stamina. Its characteristic mottled appearance is shared with other hounds from the area.

folds of skin on the cheeks, and pendent lips

HISTORY The origins of the Grand Bleu de Gascogne are not known for sure, but it is certainly an ancient breed. It was developed in the old French provinces of Guyenne and Gascony and was originally used to hunt wolves, a task it performed until the latter years of the 19th century. The breed first appeared in the US in the late 1700s.

REMARK This hound is found in the US more often than anywhere else in the world, including France itself.

OTHER NAMES Large Blue Gascony Hound.

prominent and well-muscled thighs

long ears positioned low on head

long, oval, well-knuckled feet

| Height: 25–28in (64–71cm) | Weight: 71–77lb (32–35kg) | Temperament: Active, friendly |

light tan markings above both eyes, creating a "four-eyed" impression

elongated head with convex skull

ears curl inward

long, powerful forelegs

slightly sloping pasterns

dense mottling on weather-resistant coat

strong, black claws

Place of origin: France	First use: Hunting rabbits	Origins: 1500s

Petit Bleu de Gascogne

In spite of its name, the Petit Bleu de Gascogne is a relatively large breed of hound. Although a relative of the Petit Griffon Bleu de Gascogne (opposite), it can be distinguished by its ears, which are folded rather than flattish, and larger in size. It is also slightly taller in the leg and of a heavier build and has a smoother, shorter coat.

HISTORY Selective breeding, essentially from the Grand Bleu de Gascogne (see pp.166–167), which led to a reduction in its size, underlies the development of this breed of dog. It originated in the province of Gascony, close to the Pyrenees, in the southwest of France.
REMARK The Petit Bleu de Gascogne is highly prized in its homeland for its ability to hunt rabbits and hares.

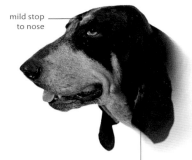

mild stop to nose

long, folded ears set well back below eye level

refined, narrow head

characteristic tan markings above eyes

tail tapers along its length, finishing in a point

straight, well-muscled back

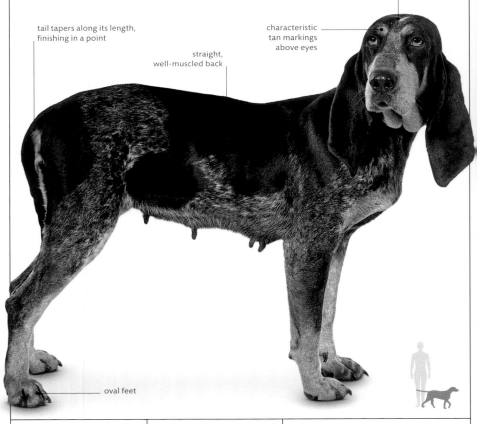

oval feet

Height: 19–23in (48–58cm)	Weight: 40–46lb (18–21kg)	Temperament: Proud, tenacious

Place of origin: France	First use: Hunting hares	Origins: 1700s

Petit Griffon Bleu de Gascogne

The rough, wiry nature of the coat of this breed sets it apart from the other Bleu de Gascogne breeds. However, it still retains the characteristic coloration of the group, with the tan areas confined essentially to the head, as is the solid black coloration. The rest of the body should ideally appear bluish, resulting from the roaning of black and white hairs in the coat.

HISTORY Of uncertain origin, the Petit Griffon Bleu de Gascogne is described as having a "rustic appearance," which reflects the involvement of the Petit Bleu de Gascogne (opposite) and wire-haired griffons in its ancestry.
REMARK This good-natured breed is considered to rank among the rarest of all of today's French hounds.

eyebrows must not obscure eyes

long ears lying unfolded, close to face

long, straight back

close, harsh coat—never curly or woolly

coat denser on thighs

oval feet with firm toes

Height: 17–21in (43–52cm)	Weight: 40–42lb (18–19kg)	Temperament: Diligent, friendly

| Place of origin: France | First use: Hunting hares | Origins: 1500s |

Chien d'Artois

This small, well-muscled, tricolored scent hound is one of the original breeds of French hunting dog. It is the forerunner of many of the later breeds of hound still seen today.

HISTORY This dog is named after the French province of Artois, where it was developed by crossing hounds and pointing breeds. Later infusions of British gundog blood almost resulted in the original breed's total disappearance. However, the numbers of pure Chien d'Artois are now slowly recovering in France.
REMARK This breed specializes in small game animals such as hares.
OTHER NAMES Briquet.

broad skull

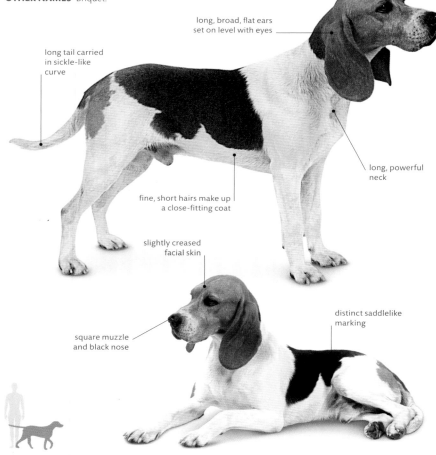

long, broad, flat ears set on level with eyes

long tail carried in sickle-like curve

long, powerful neck

fine, short hairs make up a close-fitting coat

slightly creased facial skin

square muzzle and black nose

distinct saddlelike marking

| Height: 20½–23in (52–58cm) | Weight: 40–53lb (18–24kg) | Temperament: Lively, friendly |

| Place of origin: France | First use: Hunting dog | Origins: 1600s |

Basset Bleu de Gascogne

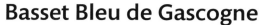

domed skull

This smallest member of the Bleu de Gascogne group retains the distinctive coloration of its larger relatives. It is a tricolored dog, being mostly white with black spots on its head and body, with tan markings on its head.

HISTORY This basset is essentially a re-creation, by M. Alain Bourbon, of the original breed, which had died out by 1911.
REMARK An enthusiastic hunting dog, the Basset Bleu de Gascogne is also a charming pet.
OTHER NAMES
Blue Gascony Basset.

relatively
long tail

dark
brown eyes

strong, oval-
shaped feet

| Height: 12–14in (30–36cm) | Weight: 35–40lb (16–18kg) | Temperament: Friendly, active |

| Place of origin: France | First use: Hunting dog | Origins: 1600s |

Basset Artésian Normand

Although smaller in stature, this breed is sometimes confused with the Basset Hound (see p.142). The tricolored form, with black predominating, is preferred. Areas of white tend to be confined to the extremities.

wide,
black nose

ears set
below level
of eyes

HISTORY This is the survivor of breeds from Artois and Normandy.
REMARK There is a curled area of hair over each hip joint.
OTHER NAMES Artesian Norman Basset.

short,
well-boned legs

| Height: 10–14in (25–36cm) | Weight: 33lb (15kg) | Temperament: Active, gentle |

| Place of origin: France | First use: Hunting roe deer | Origins: 1800s |

Grand Gascon-Saintongeois

Compared with many other breeds of hound, the Grand Gascon-Saintongeois is a large dog, with exaggeratedly long ears. It has loose folds of skin around the head and neck. Ticking is evident in its fine, short, white coat. This dog has a black mask and head, with black often extending down on to its shoulders. A smaller version of this breed, the Petit Gascon-Saintongeois, is identical in all respects except height.

HISTORY This breed was created by Baron Joseph de Carayon-LaTour of Château Virelade as a result of crossing the Gascon Bleu, Saintongeois, and Ariègeois breeds.
REMARK Although a popular pack hound in France, the breed is very uncommon in other countries.
OTHER NAMES Virelade.

very pronounced occipital peak

clear tan markings restricted to head

long, conical, pendulous ears

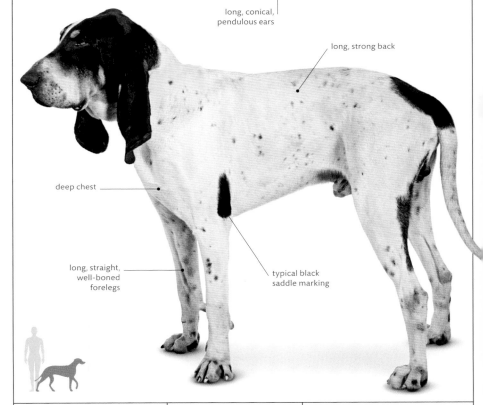

long, strong back

deep chest

long, straight, well-boned forelegs

typical black saddle marking

| Height: 25–28in (63–71cm) | Weight: 66–71lb (30–32kg) | Temperament: Affectionate, gentle |

Place of origin: France	First use: Coursing hares	Origins: 1700s

Grand Basset Griffon Vendéen

ears attach below eye level

This form of the Basset Griffon Vendéen differs from its smaller Petit relative only in size. White is often the predominant color in bi- and tricolor forms. It is an active dog and is valued for hunting rabbits and hares.

HISTORY Both basset forms are descended from the Grand Griffon Vendéen (see p.174).

REMARK The Grand Basset Griffon Vendéen can be very affectionate yet has an independent nature.

OTHER NAMES
Large Vendéen Griffon.

Petit Basset Griffon Vendéen

Grand Basset Griffon Vendéen

solid-boned forelegs

tail tapers along its length

wide, deep chest with rounded ribs

legs straighter than most bassets

large, powerful feet

Color types

Height: 15–16½in (38–42cm)	Weight: 40–44lb (18–20kg)	Temperament: Affectionate, independent

| Place of origin: France | First use: Hunting boars | Origins: 1400s |

Grand Griffon Vendéen

The Grand Griffon Vendéen is either white or wheaten, with various other color markings. This dog adapts well to land or water, having a rough, wiry outercoat and a thick undercoat. Its head is slightly elongated and its nose is well developed. It has a moustache of longer hair above its lips.

HISTORY Originating in the district of Vendée in France, its ancestors are the St. Hubert Hound (see pp.180–181), the Bracco Italiano (see p.97), and the Griffon Nivernais (opposite).
REMARK Like many hounds, this breed has a friendly nature with a good disposition, but possesses high energy levels, meaning that it requires plenty of exercise. They do have an independent side to their nature.
OTHER NAMES Large Vendéen Griffon.

large, dark eyes

tail carried in a sabrelike curve

straight, well-muscled back

large black nose and moustache

ears shaped like an elongated oval

strong chest

firm, well-boned legs

wiry coat must never be woolly

Color types

long hair covers feet

| Height: 23½–26in (60–66cm) | Weight: 66–77lb (30–35kg) | Temperament: Lively, friendly |

Place of origin: France	First use: Hunting small game	Origins: 1600s

Briquet Griffon Vendéen

This smaller relative of the Grand Griffon Vendéen (opposite) has a short head and low-set ears. It has a dense, bushy double coat, in solid or mixed colors.

Color types

HISTORY This hound shares a common ancestry with the Grand Griffon Vendéen but, instead of hunting boars and wolves, the Briquet's more likely quarry will be rabbits.

REMARK This breed works either in a pack or as a solitary hunter.

OTHER NAMES Medium Vendéen Griffon.

large, black nose with facial whiskers

narrow, pendulous ears

solid bone structure

thick-soled feet

Height: 19–22in (48–56cm)	Weight: 53lb (24kg)	Temperament: Energetic, lively

---

Place of origin: France	First use: Hunting large game	Origins: 1200s

Griffon Nivernais

The Griffon Nivernais is a tall, light-framed dog, not unlike the Spinone (see p.96) and the Otterhound (see p.145). It has a bushy, slightly unkempt appearance. The coat hair is long and hard and usually gray or fawn in color.

long, slightly conical ears

HISTORY This is an ancient breed descended from the now-extinct Chien Gris de St. Louis.

REMARK This hound was developed specifically to hunt wild boar and bears.

OTHER NAMES Chien de Pays.

shaggy, coarse-textured coat

long hair covering legs

broad, prominent muzzle

Color types

Height: 21–24in (53–62cm)	Weight: 50–55lb (23–25kg)	Temperament: Active, lively

| Place of origin: France | First use: Hunting small game | Origins: 1600s |

Anglo-Français de Petite Vénerie

This is the smallest of the three Anglo-Français breeds. Generally, this scent hound's coat is colored tan and white, black and white, or a combination of white, black, and tan. Although compact, it has an athletic, well-muscled body, a head that is slightly small in relation to its body size, low-set ears, and a well-developed nose.

HISTORY This hound was developed in France and is the result of cross-breeding between English and French scent hounds, several hundred years ago. A preliminary standard was first drawn up in 1978.

REMARK Of all the Anglo-Français breeds, the Petite makes the best house dog. It is not particularly small in size though—the description of 'petite' in this case refers to the game that it was bred to hunt, such as rabbits and hares.

OTHER NAMES Small French-English Hound.

slightly domed skull

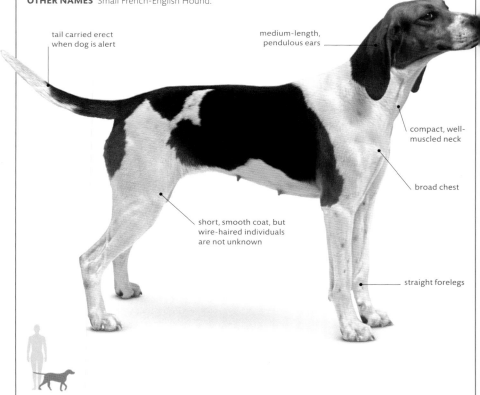

tail carried erect when dog is alert

medium-length, pendulous ears

compact, well-muscled neck

broad chest

short, smooth coat, but wire-haired individuals are not unknown

straight forelegs

| Height: 18–22in (46–56cm) | Weight: 35–44lb (16–20kg) | Temperament: Reserved, willing |

Place of origin: France	First use: Hunting wolves	Origins: 1200s

Griffon Fauve de Bretagne

The Griffon Fauve de Bretagne is mainly distinguished by its coat, which is very coarse-textured without being too long. Coloration varies through shades of fawn to brownish red; black is not a permitted color. This well-muscled dog has a slightly elongated muzzle, either a black or a brown nose, and long, pendulous ears terminating in a point. This is an excellent pack hound, which is becoming better known outside its native France.

HISTORY This ancient breed of hound was very well known during the Middle Ages in France. It reached its peak of popularity during the 1800s.
REMARK The popularity of this breed as a household companion has grown over recent years, but it is generally not as commonly seen as the Basset form.
OTHER NAMES Tawny Brittany Griffon.

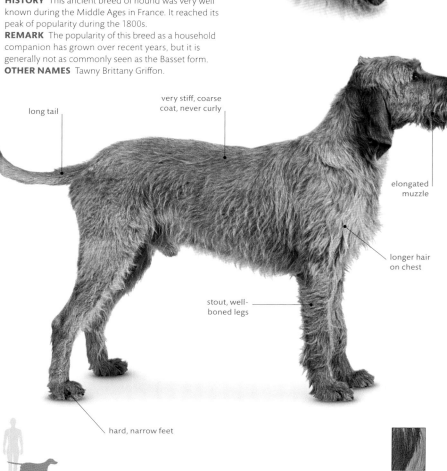

narrow skull

very stiff, coarse coat, never curly

long tail

elongated muzzle

longer hair on chest

stout, well-boned legs

hard, narrow feet

Color types

Height: 20–22in (51–56cm)	Weight: 44lb (20kg)	Temperament: Active, courageous

| Place of origin: France | First use: Hunting deer and hares | Origins: 1600s |

Porcelaine

The magnificent white coat of the Porcelaine is the inspiration for this breed's name, which in French means literally "porcelain." It is a solid white coat consisting of very short, fine-textured hairs, although orange-colored markings may be present, especially on the ears. Its head is finely formed, its ears are long, and its build is light but well muscled.

HISTORY This is thought to be the oldest of the French scent hounds, evolved from the now-extinct Montaimboeuf. The breed died out during the French Revolution but was recreated in the mid-1800s by Swiss enthusiasts.

REMARK The Porcelaine has an excellent sense of smell and a fine, musical voice.

OTHER NAMES Chien de Franche-Comte.

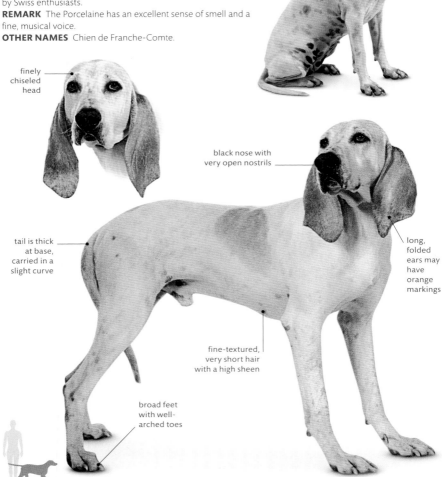

long, slender neck

finely chiseled head

black nose with very open nostrils

tail is thick at base, carried in a slight curve

long, folded ears may have orange markings

fine-textured, very short hair with a high sheen

broad feet with well-arched toes

| Height: 22–23in (56–58cm) | Weight: 55–62lb (25–28kg) | Temperament: Active, friendly |

| Place of origin: Switzerland | First use: Hunting small game | Origins: 1500s |

Jura Laufhund: Bruno

This hound, from the Jura region of western Switzerland close to the French border, is characterized by the absence of white markings in its coat. Otherwise, the Bruno Jura is similar to laufhunds from other regions. It can be distinguished immediately from the St. Hubert form (see pp.180–181) by its less massive head and generally more refined appearance.

Color types

HISTORY The laufhund is thought to descend from the old, heavier, French breeds, of which only smooth-haired forms survive.
REMARK This breed retains a strong hunting instinct and requires plenty of exercise in order to remain in good condition.
OTHER NAMES Jura Hound.

broad, round skull

large, black nose with broad nostrils

long, broad back

large, black, saddle-shaped marking on back

ears set low on head and folded

rounded feet with hard pads

| Height: 18–23in (46–58cm) | Weight: 34–44lb (15–20kg) | Temperament: Lively, determined |

Place of origin: Switzerland	First use: Hunting game	Origins: 1500s

Jura Laufhund: St. Hubert

heavy, massive, domed skull

Although the black-and-tan coloration of this hound suggests a close affinity with the Bruno Jura Laufhund (see p.179), it is somewhat different in appearance. It tends to be of heavier build, with wrinkled skin on its forehead, reminiscent of a Bloodhound (see pp.162–163). The black markings may take the form of a saddle over the back, or they may be more widespread, typically on the head and legs, contrasting with tan areas.

HISTORY The St. Hubert is thought to have a close relationship with the now-extinct St. Hubert Hound of France. The Swiss breed seemingly has distinct similarities with this particular ancient breed.

REMARK The word *laufhund* means "walking dog." A keen tracker, it bays loudly when following a scent. This laufhund has plenty of stamina and is used to hunt a variety of game, ranging from small hares and foxes to larger animals such as deer.

OTHER NAMES Jura Hound.

pronounced dewlap

tail carried high, without a marked curve

powerful thighs

deep rib cage

strong, straight forelegs

Height: 18–23in (46–58cm)	Weight: 34–44lb (15–20kg)	Temperament: Active, friendly

folds of loose
skin evident
on back

wrinkled skin on
forehead

prominent black nose
with wide nostrils

long, pendent
ears

relatively long,
straight back

rounded feet

strong, dark nails

| Place of origin: Hungary | First use: Hunting small game | Origins: 800s |

Hungarian Greyhound

This breed of greyhound is long-legged, lean, and elegant and closely resembles the Greyhound proper (see p.146), although it is somewhat smaller in stature. The head and muzzle are wide for a dog that relies on sight rather than scenting ability. Its coat is short and coarse, and solid colors and brindles are acceptable.

HISTORY This is an ancient breed that accompanied the fierce Magyar people into central Europe in the 10th century.
REMARK This breed is not well known outside its native Hungary and is rarely seen at shows.
OTHER NAMES Magyar Agár.

ears folded back

elongated head

wide muzzle

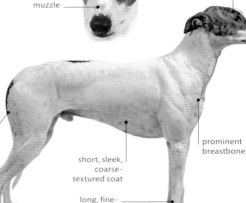

long, thin tail, curled at end

short, sleek, coarse-textured coat

prominent breastbone

long, fine-boned limbs

Color types

| Height: 25–27½in (64–70cm) | Weight: 49–68lb (22–31kg) | Temperament: Active, affectionate |

| Place of origin: Switzerland | First use: Hunting in Alpine regions | Origins: 1000s |

Berner Laufhund

This breed of hound has a narrow head and long, folded ears. Its body is long but not heavy, with strong, well-boned legs. The Berner Laufhund's soft undercoat is covered with a harder, tricolored outercoat.

HISTORY These hounds have been used by Swiss Alpine hunters for about 900 years.
REMARK The formation of the Swiss Hound Club in 1931 is largely responsible for the preservation of this breed.
OTHER NAMES Bernese Hound.

strong muzzle

black and white body markings

tan markings on face

long, conical ears

thick, powerful neck

soft undercoat, abundant outercoat

well-boned legs may show tan markings

| Height: 18–23in (46–58cm) | Weight: 34–44lb (15–20kg) | Temperament: Active, responsive |

| Place of origin: Switzerland | First use: Hunting small game | Origins: 1500s |

Schweizer Laufhund

The bicolored appearance of this hound serves to distinguish it from other related Swiss breeds. White predominates in the coat, offset against yellowish orange, orange, or even red markings, which are large in extent, although occasional small spots of color are not penalized in the show ring. The Schweizer Laufhund is a talented tracker and has a powerful voice, which is invariably heard whenever a scent trail is located.

HISTORY This breed originated close to the Franco-Swiss border and is related to the French breeds found in that region.
REMARK The shorter-legged version of this breed, known as the Schweizer Neiderlaufhund, has identical coat coloration.
OTHER NAMES Swiss Hound.

well-defined stop

large, black nose with broad nostrils

long ears set well back on head

coat either short and smooth or doubled with rough-haired appearance

long muzzle and powerful jaws

rounded feet with tough pads and hard nails

bridge of nose slightly arched

characteristic coloration

pointed tip to tail, carried either horizontally or slightly curved

straight forelegs

Short-haired form

powefully boned legs

Color types

| Height: 18–23in (46–58cm) | Weight: 34–44lb (15–20kg) | Temperament: Active, friendly |

Place of origin: Switzerland	First use: Hunting large game	Origins: 1500s

Luzerner Laufhund

The Luzerner Laufhund is generally similar to the other four breeds of laufhund that have been developed in Switzerland. This breed, however, is characterized by a distinctive tricolored appearance. The pronounced black ticking over the white areas of the coat gives rise to an impression of blue coloration. There is a short-legged form of this breed, known as the Luzerner Neiderlaufhund, which stands no more than 16½in (42cm) tall.

HISTORY The similarity between the Luzerner and French breeds, as well as their geographical proximity, indicates a close ancestral relationship. Its precise origins are, however, unknown.

REMARK This breed has excellent tracking abilities, and it gives voice with a very distinctive bark whenever a fresh scent is located.

OTHER NAMES Lucernese Hound.

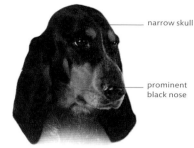

narrow skull

prominent black nose

long, pendulous, folded ears

heavy ticking in coat, offset against black and tan areas

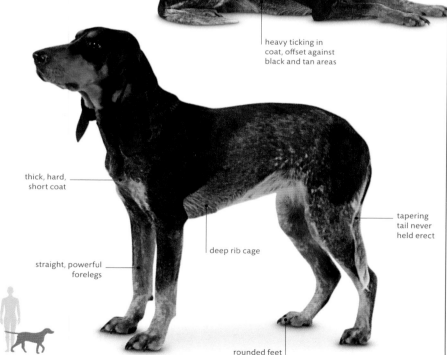

thick, hard, short coat

straight, powerful forelegs

deep rib cage

tapering tail never held erect

rounded feet

Height: 18–23in (46–58cm)	Weight: 34–44lb (15–20kg)	Temperament: Active, friendly

| Place of origin: Serbia | First use: Tracking and hunting game | Origins: 1000 BCE |

Serbian Hound

This obedient hound is black and tan, typically with a distinctive black saddle, flat head, and black marks over the eyes. It is particularly muscular in the shoulders and limbs. A diligent, determined hunter, the Serbian Hound works in packs, and is used to hunt game ranging from hares to wild boars.

HISTORY The Serbian Hound's ancestors are thought to have been brought to the Balkan region from Egypt by Phoenicians in about 1000 BCE.
REMARK Despite its undoubted tracking skills in many different terrains, the Serbian Hound is still not widely known.
OTHER NAMES Balkanski Gonic, Balkan Hound.

rounded, pendulous ears

flat top to skull and relatively long head

distinctive markings

rounded, powerful feet with dark nails

| Height: 17–21in (43–53cm) | Weight: 44lb (20kg) | Temperament: Active, responsive |

| Place of origin: Croatia | First use: Hunting small game | Origins: 1700s |

Posavac Hound

The coat of this stocky hound tends to be predominantly red in color. Other colors, such as yellow and fawn, are less common.

HISTORY The Posavac probably shares a common origin with other similar breeds that have originated in parts of the former Yugoslavia, their ancestors having been introduced via the ports of the Adriatic coast.
REMARK Exercise is absolutely essential for this active hound.
OTHER NAMES Posavski Gonic.

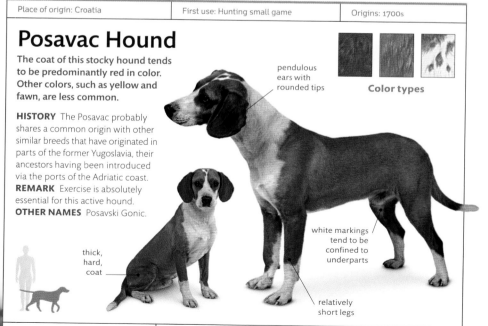

pendulous ears with rounded tips

Color types

thick, hard, coat

white markings tend to be confined to underparts

relatively short legs

| Height: 17–23in (43–59cm) | Weight: 35–45lb (16–20kg) | Temperament: Active, alert |

| Place of origin: Montenegro | First use: Hunting | Origins: 1700s |

Montenegrin Mountain Hound

This particular breed of hound, of the many breeds that have originated within the borders of Montenegro, can be recognized by its black-and-tan coloration. The Montenegrin Mountain Hound has a smooth, coarse-textured, thick outercoat and a very full undercoat, making it ideal for the harsh mountain terrain and thick bushland in which it normally hunts.

HISTORY This is certainly an old breed, whose ancestors may have been brought to the Adriatic by the Phoenicians. Selective breeding in different parts of the region has given rise to the diversity of hound breeds seen there today.

REMARK A keen sense of smell, an athletic build, and a good voice make this an excellent hunting dog.

OTHER NAMES Jugoslavenski Planinski Gonic, Yugoslavian Mountain Hound.

broad head

powerful muzzle

long, tapering tail

long, pendulous ears with rounded tips

relatively long body creates rectangular profile

clearly defined areas of black and tan

strong, relatively short legs

flat, coarse, thick outercoat

| Height: 18–22in (46–56cm) | Weight: 44–55lb (20–25kg) | Temperament: Active, friendly |

| Place of origin: Serbia | First use: Hunting small game | Origins: 1800s |

Serbian Tricolored Hound

The coloration of this short-haired breed of hound distinguishes it from the Montenegrin Mountain Hound (opposite). Tan markings are prominent here, offset against black; a white area is evident at the front of the dog, sometimes extending down to its underparts. This rare breed is very localized in its distribution, and is most common in the southern parts of Serbia.

HISTORY A combination of sight and scent hound stock, as has been used in other Balkan hounds, underlies this dog's breeding history.

REMARK Although a devoted hunter, this breed is very adaptable and enjoys human companionship.

OTHER NAMES Jugoslavenski Tribarvni Gonic, Yugoslavian Tricolored Hound.

white facial blaze

prominent black nose

muscular ears hang down sides of face

black tends to dominate in coat

white tip on tail

prominent white area on front

white areas on feet and legs

powerful thighs

solid, thick pads

| Height: 18–22in (46–56cm) | Weight: 44–55lb (20–25kg) | Temperament: Active, obedient |

| Place of origin: Italy | First use: Hunting game | Origins: 100s |

Italian Hound

Strong and powerfully built, this hound has a long, tapering muzzle, which is convex when seen in profile, sloping downward to the nose. Its lips are black at the edges.

HISTORY This breed is descended from the early sight hounds, which were probably introduced to Italy by the Phoenicians, and scent hounds from Europe. During the Renaissance, it was a popular hunting dog and later underwent a further revival in Italy.

REMARK A rough-coated form, known as Segugio Italiano a Pelo Forte, is identical in all respects other than coat type.

OTHER NAMES Segugio Italiano.

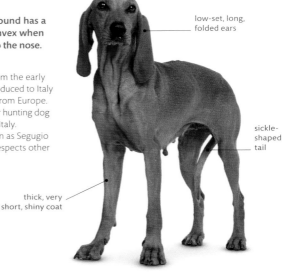

low-set, long, folded ears

sickle-shaped tail

thick, very short, shiny coat

Color types

| Height: 20½–23in (52–58cm) | Weight: 40–62lb (18–28kg) | Temperament: Docile, active |

| Place of origin: Italy | First use: Hunting small game | Origins: 1000 BCE |

Cirneco dell'Etna

This elegant, athletic Sicilian sight hound also hunts by scent. It is smaller than similar Mediterranean island breeds.

HISTORY The Cirneco dell'Etna is probably descended from ancestral sight-hound stock acquired in Egypt and traded in the Mediterranean by the Phoenicians.

REMARK Surprisingly, this breed is internationally less well known than either the similar Ibizan Hound (see p.190) or the Pharaoh Hound (opposite).

OTHER NAMES Sicilian Greyhound.

broad, stiff, triangular ears

long, straight forelegs

short, smooth coat

white marking permitted

| Height: 16½–19½in (42–50cm) | Weight: 18–26lb (8–12kg) | Temperament: Friendly, alert |

| Place of origin: Malta | First use: Hunting rabbits | Origins: 1000 BCE |

Pharaoh Hound

The large, upright ears and the tan coloration of this hound immediately attract attention. It bears a striking likeness to depictions of the Egyptian god Anubis, whose task it was to act as guide for the souls of the dead. Although it is a sight hound, it also tracks its quarry by scent.

HISTORY Ancestors of the Pharaoh Hound are thought to have been brought to Malta by Phoenician traders. Here they remained in a relatively pure state, first attracting attention overseas only during the late 1960s.
REMARK Without adequate exercise, these dogs rapidly become overweight.
OTHER NAMES Kelb Tal-fenek.

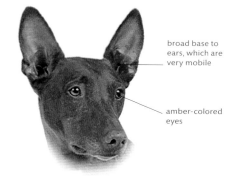

broad base to ears, which are very mobile

amber-colored eyes

long, lean face

slightly arched, long, muscular neck

white area on chest, called "the star"

white-tipped, tapering tail, reaching to just below hocks

short, glossy coat

white markings may be present on feet

firm, well-knuckled feet

| Height: 21–25in (53–64cm) | Weight: 45–55lb (20–25kg) | Temperament: Affectionate, intelligent |

| Place of origin: Spain | First use: Hunting rabbits | Origins: 3000 BCE |

Ibizan Hound

Using large ears, this hound hunts by means of sound as well as sight. It is quite tall and, compared with other fast-paced hunting dogs, relatively stocky. Variable coloration helps distinguish it from Pharaoh Hounds (see p.189).

HISTORY Images of hounds similar to the Ibizan have been found in Egypt, and date back some 5,000 years. Some were probably taken from there to the island of Ibiza.
REMARK This is a sensitive and loyal dog.
OTHER NAMES Podenco Ibicenco.

ears erect
when alert

long, slightly
arched neck

base of ears
level with eyes

back slopes
slightly to rump

thin tail set
low on back

deep chest and
flat rib cage

long, straight
legs

powerful
hindquarters

Color types

| Height: 22½–27½in (57–70cm) | Weight: 42–55lb (19–25kg) | Temperament: Alert, adaptable |

| Place of origin: Spain | First use: Tracking game | Origins: 500s |

Sabueso Español

The similarity in appearance of the Sabueso Español and the mastiff breeds indicates that this is an ancient dog. There are two forms of this breed: the de Monte (shown here) weighs about 55lb (25kg), stands 22in (56cm) high, and has a hard, white coat with red or black patches; the Lebrero form is smaller, standing no more than 20in (51cm) high, and is usually of a more uniform red color.

HISTORY Thought to have been introduced to the region by the Phoenicians, this breed has changed little within the confines of the Iberian Peninsula.
REMARK This is still primarily a hunting dog and does not generally make a good house pet.
OTHER NAMES Spanish Hound.

prominent, pigmented nose

large dewlap

fine, glossy coat and loose, flexible skin

tail extends below level of hocks

legs are short in relation to body

clearly defined colored markings

large, convex-shaped skull

very long, soft, folded ears

Color types

| Height: 18–22in (46–56cm) | Weight: 45–55lb (20–25kg) | Temperament: Energetic, loyal |

Place of origin: Spain	First use: Haunting game, racing	Origins: 600 BCE

Spanish Greyhound

With the unmistakable outline of a greyhound, this dog is built for speed. It is a little smaller than the Greyhound (see p.146) itself, which it otherwise resembles in appearance. The stop is also more pronounced and its build generally sturdier. Crosses with Greyhounds have occurred to produce a breed known locally in Spain as the Galgo Inglés-Español, which is used for racing.

HISTORY The early origins of the Spanish Greyhound are not clear, but it is of ancient lineage and was documented in Roman times.

REMARK As a racing dog, this breed is not as swift as the Greyhound itself.

OTHER NAMES Galgo Español.

dark, expressive, oval eyes

Smooth-haired form

rose ears falling backward

Wire-haired form

long, narrow head

long, muscular, elegantly arched neck

slightly arched, powerful loin

Color types

well-bent stifles

tall, straight forelegs

very long, relatively slender tail carried low

Height: 26–28in (66–71cm)	Weight: 60–66lb (27–30kg)	Temperament: Active, friendly

| Place of origin: Portugal | First use: Flushing game, ratting | Origins: 1800s |

Podengo Portugueses Pequeño

The Pequeño is sometimes described as resembling a sturdy Chihuahua (see p.37), but there seems to be no ancestral link between the two breeds. The Pequeño is in fact a miniature sight hound, a well-proportioned little dog, with a body longer than it is tall, a convex skull, a straight muzzle, and a lively, intelligent expression.

HISTORY It appears that this breed was derived from the Podengo Portugueses Medio (see p.194), and it, too, is bred in both wire- and smooth-haired forms.

REMARK This enthusiastic breed sometimes works with its larger cousins. It enters warrens and flushes out rabbits, leaving them to be captured by the other dogs. It is also a very talented ratter and an affectionate and popular house pet.

OTHER NAMES
Small Portuguese Hound.

triangular, mobile ears

short, coarse coat

tail carried erect when dog is alert

convex skull

Smooth-haired form

medium-length, shaggy coat

straight muzzle

Wire-haired form

Color types

| Height: 8–12in (20–31cm) | Weight: 11–13lb (5–6kg) | Temperament: Lively, affectionate |

| Place of origin: Portugal | First use: Hunting small game | Origins: 1600s |

Podengo Portugueses Medio

Both smooth- and wire-haired forms of the Medio are bred, with fawn and white coloration tending to predominate, although yellow and black forms with white markings are also seen. This medium-size hound is powerful for its size, muscular, agile, and an extremely efficient hunter of small game, either singly or working in conjunction with other dogs.

Wired-haired form

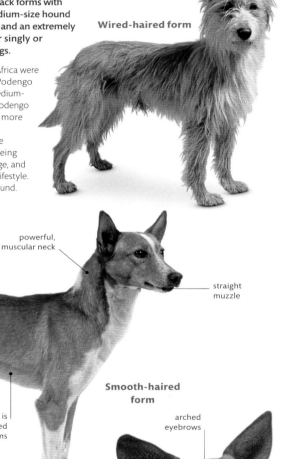

HISTORY The sight hounds of northern Africa were probably used in the development of the Podengo breeds, although it is thought that this medium-size version descended directly from the Podengo Portugueses Grande and is, therefore, of more recent origin.

REMARK Of all the Podengo breeds, the Medio is the most popular in Portugal, being thought of as neither too small nor too large, and able to adapt readily to a softer, domestic lifestyle.

OTHER NAMES Medium Portuguese Hound.

powerful, muscular neck

tail erect when dog is alert

straight muzzle

coat is coarse-textured in both forms

Smooth-haired form

arched eyebrows

Color types

| Height: 15–22in (39–56cm) | Weight: 35–44lb (16–20kg) | Temperament: Lively, alert |

Place of origin: Iran	First use: Hunting gazelle	Origins: 3000 BCE

Saluki

In terms of appearance, the Saluki is unmistakable – slim, high-stepping, and elegant. It has a relatively short coat with significantly longer hair on both its ears and tail. Feathering is also present on the thighs and at the back of the legs. For all its elegance, the Saluki possesses impressive acceleration, which, in its homeland, enables it to outpace gazelles, one of the fastest of all antelopes.

HISTORY Images of dogs similar to the contemporary Saluki have been found on ancient Egyptian tombs dating back more than 5,000 years, but the breed's name is thought to derive from the village of Saluk, which is now part of Iranian territory.
REMARK Care should be taken when exercising these hounds in areas where they could encounter cats or small dogs.
OTHER NAMES Gazelle Hound.

long, narrow head

long, mobile ears hang close to sides of head

smooth, silky coat

black or liver-colored nose

powerful hips

long, naturally curved tail

long, muscular and supple neck

well-boned, straight forelegs

feathering present on backs of legs

inner toes longer than outer toes

Color types

Height: 22–28in (56–71cm)	Weight: 44–66lb (20–30kg)	Temperament: Active, friendly

Place of origin: Russia	First use: Hunting wolves	Origins: 1200s

Borzoi

Built on lines of speed and grace, this beautiful sight hound was traditionally used to course wolves. This required not only pace but also intelligence and considerable bravery on the part of the dog. These qualities are clearly reflected in the Borzoi's proud, aristocratic bearing. Sensitive and aloof in temperament, it is, nevertheless, faithful and protective toward its owner.

HISTORY The ancestry of the Borzoi is inextricably linked with Russian royalty. Popular as gifts, they were sent to Britain's Princess Alexandra in 1842, and were exhibited at the first Crufts Dog Show in 1891.
REMARK The name "Borzoi" derives from the Russian word *borzii*, meaning swift.
OTHER NAMES Russian Wolfhound.

long, powerful jaws

hair is longer over chest, neck, and thighs

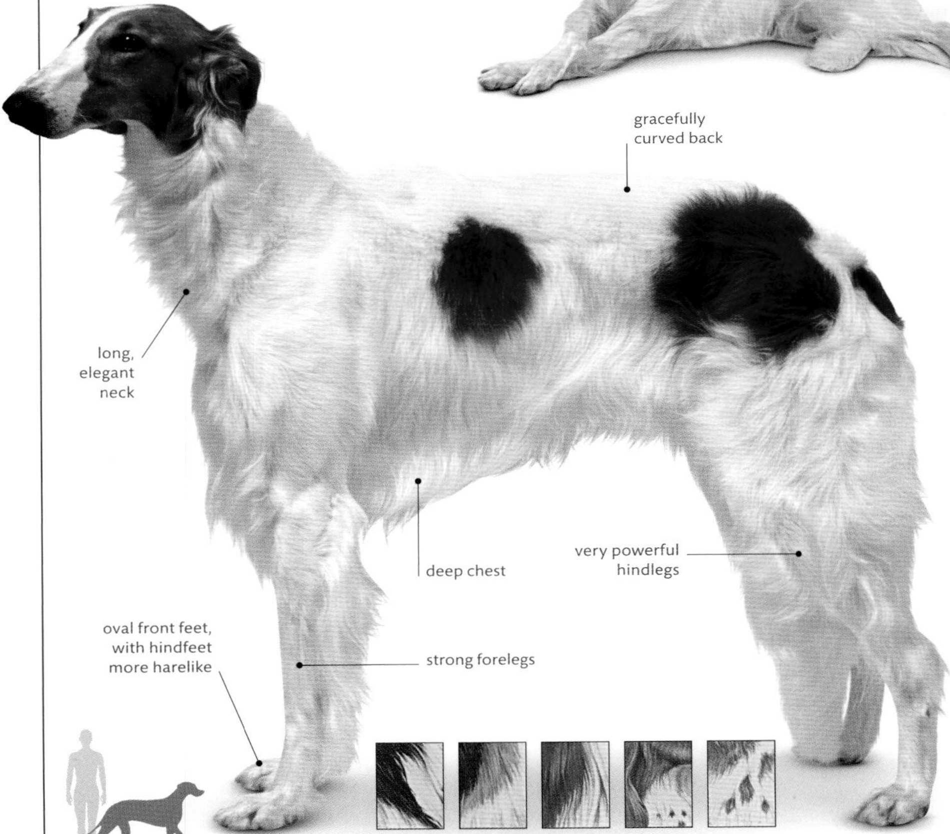

gracefully curved back

long, elegant neck

deep chest

very powerful hindlegs

oval front feet, with hindfeet more harelike

strong forelegs

Color types

Height: 27–31in (69–79cm)	Weight: 75–105lb (35–48kg)	Temperament: Active, intelligent

Place of origin: Mali	First use: Hunting gazelles	Origins: 1000s

Azawakh

With an exceedingly athletic appearance, the Azawakh is exceptionally fast, being able to reach speeds of 40mph (64km/h), and displays considerable stamina. The breed's slender head is characterized by the presence of distinctive swellings on the sides of its face.

HISTORY The Azawakh was developed by the Tuareg people of the southern Sahara to slow down gazelles and other game animals, thus allowing riders to overtake and kill them.
REMARK This breed is slowly finding homes in other countries throughout the world.
OTHER NAMES Tuareg Sloughi.

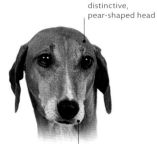

distinctive, pear-shaped head

strong jaws

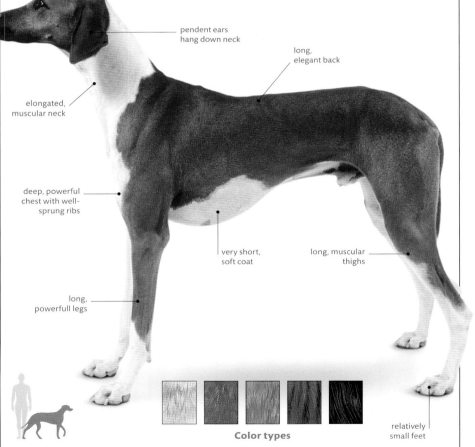

pendent ears hang down neck

long, elegant back

elongated, muscular neck

deep, powerful chest with well-sprung ribs

very short, soft coat

long, muscular thighs

long, powerfull legs

relatively small feet

Color types

Height: 23–29in (58–74cm)	Weight: 37–55lb (17–25kg)	Temperament: Independent, alert

Place of origin: Afghanistan	First use: Hunting gazelles and wolves	Origins: 1600s

Afghan Hound

The elegant appearance of the Afghan, with its long, silky coat, has attracted many people to this breed. Such styling, however, is possible only by dedicated grooming. The length of the coat has been greatly developed by selective breeding over about the last 50 years. In motion, the Afghan Hound is high-stepping, giving the impression of springing over the ground with its coat flowing behind.

HISTORY This hound was first seen in Europe in the late 1800s, when it was brought back by soldiers returning from the Afghan War. At that time, there were a number of localized forms—some were larger, for example—but such distinctions have disappeared in contemporary bloodlines.

REMARK This athletic sight hound requires plenty of exercise. It may tend to run off too readily—perhaps a reflection of its hunting past.

OTHER NAMES Tazi.

Color types

long skull

long, silky hair covering eyes

prominent hip bones

long, straight legs

dense covering of long hair on feet

large, strong forefeet

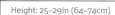

Height: 25–29in (64–74cm)	Weight: 50–60lb (23–27kg)	Temperament: Lively, active

| Place of origin: Morocco | First use: Guarding flocks | Origins: 6000 BCE |

Sloughi

The build of the Sloughi has led to debate that it is merely a smooth-coated form of Saluki (see p.195), modified by crossings with other similar breeds. That aside, the Sloughi is a striking dog, slenderly built, with fine, well-defined musculature and rather sad, dark eyes.

HISTORY This breed's origins lie in North Africa where ancient drawings and carvings depict similar dogs. Earlier, its ancestors probably came from the region of present-day Saudi Arabia.
REMARK Although used as a flock guardian and hunter in its homeland, it can be seen in the show ring in Britain and the US, being recognized by the American Kennel Club in 2016.
OTHER NAMES Arabian Greyhound.

large, dark eyes

well-defined bone structure

medium-length, pendent ears, with slightly rounded tips

long, lean neck with folds of skin at the throat

hard, smooth coat consisting of tough, fine hair

very straight, well-boned forelegs

abdomen is well tucked up

long, thin tail with slight curve at end

| Height: 24–28½in (61–72cm) | Weight: 45–60lb (20–27kg) | Temperament: Active, friendly |

| Place of origin: Japan | First use: Hunting boar and deer | Origins: 1700s |

Kai Dog

The fiercely loyal Kai Dog is a powerfully built breed with strong legs that makes it well suited to hunting in its mountainous Japanese homeland. It is invariably brindled in coloration. The red form is known as Aka-Tora, the medium is called Chu-Tora, and the black brindle form is Kuro-Tora.

HISTORY The name of this breed originates from a part of central Japan that is now in the prefecture of Yamanashi. The Kai was first seen in the US in 1951, but it did not become established here at this stage.

REMARK Kai Dog pups are usually born solid black in color. Their distinctive brindle coloring develops only as they grow and mature.

OTHER NAMES Tora Dog.

ears are larger than on other medium-size Japanese breeds

thick tail set high and curled over the back

thick, muscular neck

harsh, straight outercoat with soft, thick undercoat

deep, muscular chest

triangular, pricked ears directed slightly forward

straight, well-muscled forelegs

small, dark brown eyes

well-arched, tightly closed toes

Color types

| Height: 18–23in (46–58cm) | Weight: 35–40lb (16–18kg) | Temperament: Determined, independent |

| Place of origin: Japan | First use: Hunting wild boar and deer | Origins: 1700s |

Shikoku

This breed makes an energetic and lively companion and takes its name from the mountainous Japanese island where it was first bred.

HISTORY Recognized as one of Japan's National Treasures in 1937, the Shikoku is not commonly seen, even today.

REMARK It is considered one of the world's purest dog breeds, having been kept on its native island in isolation for centuries.

OTHER NAMES Kōchi-ken.

wedge-shaped head

pricked ears

tail curls forward over the back

white often present on the feet and legs

relatively square-shaped body

Color types

| Height: 18½–20in (47–51cm) | Weight: 31–51lb (14–23kg) | Temperament: Independent, alert |

| Place of origin: South Africa | First use: Hunting lions | Origins: 1800s |

Rhodesian Ridgeback

Dignified and formidable, the Ridgeback derives its name from the distinctive ridge of hair that grows, contrary to the direction of the rest of the coat, in a tapering line along the middle of its back. It shares the color as well as the heart of the lion, which was once its quarry.

HISTORY Developed by the Boers in the late 19th century, its standard was fixed in Rhodesia (now Zimbabwe) in 1922. In the hunt for lions, it was renowned for its great stamina and surprising agility. Nowadays, it is used as a guard dog and makes a loyal and affectionate family pet.

REMARK The breed's unique ridge of hair is thought to have been inherited from the now extinct Hottentot Dog.

OTHER NAMES African Lion Hound.

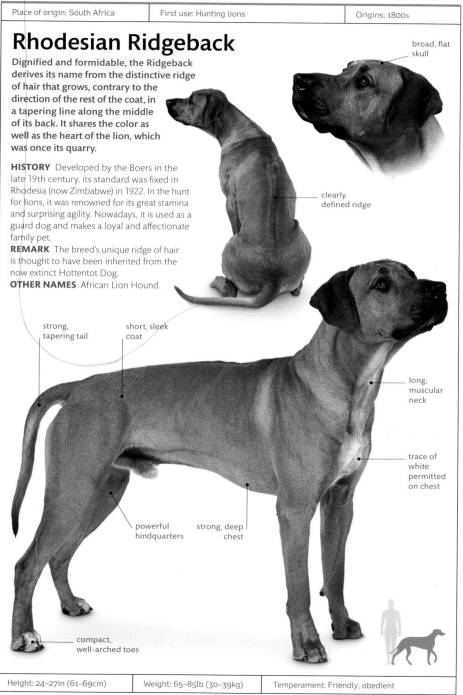

broad, flat skull

clearly defined ridge

strong, tapering tail

short, sleek coat

long, muscular neck

trace of white permitted on chest

powerful hindquarters

strong, deep chest

compact, well-arched toes

| Height: 24–27in (61–69cm) | Weight: 65–85lb (30–39kg) | Temperament: Friendly, obedient |

TERRIERS

MOST OF THE DOGS in this group are relatively small in size, but, despite this, they can be quite spirited and independent. Although many terriers were originally kept on farms, often as rat catchers, they have made the transition to household pets quite readily, to the extent that a number of them are among the best-known breeds in the world. Their alert and curious nature, and their tendency to explore underground, mean that they are more inclined to dig than other breeds and have an alarming tendency to disappear down rabbit holes when out for a walk. As a result, they are not true lap dogs, although they do make loyal companions. Terriers are usually lively, alert, and extremely plucky. They do not always get on well together, however, and enjoy every opportunity to run about on their own.

Place of origin: US	First use: Hunting rats	Origins: 1930s

Toy Fox Terrier

This small, attractive terrier shows a clear relationship to the Smooth Fox Terrier (see p.212). The tricolored form with white predominating in the coat is favored in the show ring. A popularizing feature is the American Toy Terrier's smooth, short coat, which is extremely easy to care for and groom.

HISTORY The American Kennel Club recognized this breed in 1936. Crosses with English Toy Terriers (see p.206) and Chihuahuas (see p.37) have refined its features.
REMARK These terriers have been trained to assist handicapped people around the home.
OTHER NAMES Toy Fox Terrier, Amertoy.

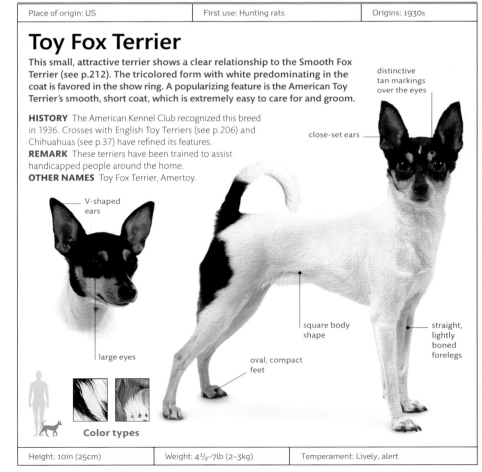

distinctive tan markings over the eyes

close-set ears

V-shaped ears

large eyes

square body shape

oval, compact feet

straight, lightly boned forelegs

Color types

Height: 10in (25cm)	Weight: 4½–7lb (2–3kg)	Temperament: Lively, alert

Place of origin: US	First use: Hunting rats	Origins: 1970s

Rat Terrier

This terrier has yet to establish an international following but is standardized in its homeland now for show purposes. It occurs in both miniature and standard versions. There is also a hairless form of this terrier, with its coloration evident in the skin.

HISTORY These lively dogs were originally seen on farms and have been developed from working stock.
REMARK They are very active and retain strong hunting instincts.
OTHER NAMES American Rat Terrier, Ratting Terrier.

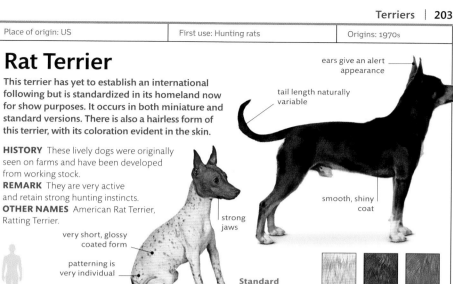

ears give an alert appearance

tail length naturally variable

strong jaws

smooth, shiny coat

very short, glossy coated form

patterning is very individual

Standard

Color types

Height: 13–18in (33–46cm)	Weight: 10–25lb (4.5–11kg)	Temperament: Strong-willed, active

Place of origin: US	First use: Dogfighting	Origins: 1800s

American Pit Bull Terrier

The growing popularity of these very powerful dogs triggered fears over their aggression and a range of breed-specific legislation in many countries toward the end of the 20th century. This terrier exudes power, with a broad, slablike head, very powerful jaws, plus a thickly muscled neck and body.

HISTORY Originally, these dogs were used on farms for various tasks, including rounding up stray livestock. Their ancestry is based on Staffordshire Bull Terriers (see p.208) crossed with bulldogs.
REMARK In recent times, this terrier has been bred for illegal dogfighting reflecting a brave and stoic side to its nature.
OTHER NAMES Pit Bull Terrier, American Pit Bull.

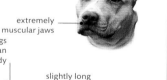

wide face

thick-boned, slablike head

extremely muscular jaws

white markings typically cover less than 80 percent of body

small ears

slightly long back in relation to height

powerful hindquarters

round, often black, eyes

very broad, muscular chest

thick, hard, short coat

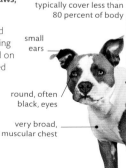

Height: 18–22in (46–56cm)	Weight: 50–80lb (23–36kg)	Temperament: Tenacious, fearless

Place of origin: US	First use: Baiting bulls	Origins: 1800s

American Staffordshire Terrier

This breed resembles its English ancestor, the Staffordshire Bull Terrier (see p.208), although it is taller, heavier, and generally more substantial. This dog is very powerful but not usually ill-disposed toward people.

Color types

HISTORY The American Kennel Club first granted recognition of the American Staffordshire Terrier as a separate breed in 1936.
REMARK It is bold and intelligent and makes a loyal family pet.

tail appears short in relation to body

smooth, short coat

broad head with powerful jaw muscles

Height: 17–19in (43–48cm)	Weight: 40–50lb (18–23kg)	Temperament: Intelligent, determined

Place of origin: US	First use: Baiting bulls, ratting	Origins: 1800s

Boston Terrier

Although descended from bull-baiting dogs, the Boston Terrier today, with its broad, flat head without wrinkles, large, round eyes, and sweet expression, is a well-tempered and patient companion dog. Brindle and white are the preferred coat colors. The breed is grouped into three categories depending on weight.

small, thin ears set at corners of skull

large, round, dark, intelligent eyes

HISTORY The Boston Terrier can be traced back to crosses involving bulldogs and terriers in the city of Boston some time in the 1800s.
REMARK The broad head of this dog can lead to problems, pups sometimes becoming trapped in the birth canal.

small, rounded feet with well-arched toes

Color types

Height: 15–17in (38–43cm)	Weight: 10–25lb (4.5–11.5kg)	Temperament: Intelligent, lively

Place of origin: Great Britain   First use: Hunting badgers and otters   Origins: 1800s

Airedale Terrier

The largest of all the terriers, the Airedale is a distinctive combination of black and tan in color. Its wiry coat is dense and waterproof.

long, flat skull

tops of ears extend above line of skull

HISTORY This hardy breed evolved in southern Yorkshire, England. It is descended from an old type of terrier crossed with an Otterhound (see p.145).
REMARK The coat is shed twice a year and should be stripped on these occasions.
OTHER NAMES Waterside Terrier, Bingley Terrier.

deep chest

black saddle extends over top of tail and neck

small, rounded feet

Height: 22–24in (56–61cm)   Weight: 44–50lb (20–23kg)   Temperament: Intelligent, responsive

Place of origin: Great Britain   First use: Hunting badgers and rats   Origins: 1800s

Bedlington Terrier

Lithe and graceful, with a lamblike appearance, the Bedlington Terrier is unlikely to be confused with any other breed. In spite of its gentle appearance, however, it is tough and hardy.

Color types

HISTORY Wire-coated terriers crossed with Whippets (see p.147) and Dandie Dinmonts (see p.209) laid the foundations for the breed.
REMARK The coat requires regular trimming. Bedlingtons should be tested for a potentially fatal genetic condition that causes copper to build up in the liver.
OTHER NAMES Rothbury Terrier.

roached (sloping) back

silky "top-knot"

long, harelike feet

Height: 15–17in (38–43cm)   Weight: 17–23lb (8–10kg)   Temperament: Alert, affectionate

| Place of origin: Great Britain | First use: Ratting and rabbiting | Origins: 1800s |

English Toy Terrier

A miniature form of the Manchester Terrier (below), it can be distinguished primarily by its size and the erect carriage of the ears. Coloration is a vital feature of this breed, comprising jet-black and rich chestnut markings. Thin black lines, described as "penciling," are present on the toes and pasterns.

HISTORY This compact breed was developed from crossing-breeding the Black and Tan Terrier (below) with the Italian Greyhound (see p.46).

REMARK It bonds with its owner and makes a good watchdog.

OTHER NAMES Toy Manchester Terrier.

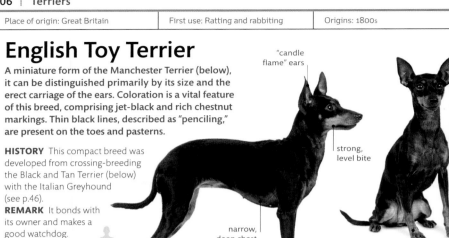

"candle flame" ears

strong, level bite

narrow, deep chest

dainty, arched feet

| Height: 10–12in (25–30cm) | Weight: 6–8lb (3–4kg) | Temperament: Lively, alert |

| Place of origin: Great Britain | First use: Ratting and rabbiting | Origins: 1500s |

Manchester Terrier

Evidence of Whippet (see p.147) is visible in this breed's elegant, roach back and the relatively straight shape of the nose.

HISTORY The Manchester Terrier used to show great variation in size, and miniature versions became popular in the latter part of the 19th century, when the breed was first introduced to North America.

REMARK These terriers became very popular in England during the 19th century as cities grew rapidly in size, being valued for controlling the rat population.

OTHER NAMES Black and Tan Terrier.

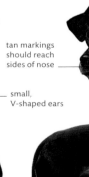

tan spots above eyes

tan markings should reach sides of nose

small, V-shaped ears

sleek coat

forelegs set well under dog

well-arched toes

tan markings on legs

| Height: 15–16in (38–41cm) | Weight: 12–22lb (5–10kg) | Temperament: Lively, attentive |

Place of origin: Great Britain	First use: Hunting rats	Origins: 1700s

Border Terrier

The Border is one of the most popular terrier breeds as a pet. In spite of its small size, it is still able to keep up with horses when out fox-hunting, while its narrow body allows it to go to earth without difficulty. Its coat is durable enough to withstand the weather on the borders between Scotland and England, which is the area where it was first developed, hence its name.

HISTORY There is evidence of dogs similar to the Border Terrier in the 18th century, and the name is thought to come from the then-famous Border Hunt.
REMARK A Border Terrier Club was established in 1921 and the breed is now widely distributed throughout the world.

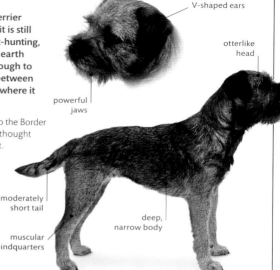

small, V-shaped ears

otterlike head

powerful jaws

moderately short tail

muscular hindquarters

deep, narrow body

Color types

Height: 10in (25cm)	Weight: 11½–15½lb (5–7kg)	Temperament: Plucky, alert

Place of origin: Great Britain	First use: Hunting rats	Origins: 1800s

Norwich Terrier

This is one of the native terrier breeds of Norfolk, England, a region traditionally rich in game. The Norwich is readily distinguishable from the Norfolk Terrier (see p.210) by its alert, pricked ears. The coat is generally short and smooth on the head and ears. For its size it is a powerful dog, with a tight-lipped mouth and a scissor bite.

HISTORY In the 19th century, the Norwich Terrier was the mascot of the students at Cambridge University, England.
REMARK It is a playful breed and loves to chase after balls.

erect, pointed ears

strong neck

slightly rounded, wide skull

short, powerful legs and rounded feet

Color types

Height: 10in (25cm)	Weight: 11–12lb (5–5.5kg)	Temperament: Alert, friendly

Place of origin: Great Britain	First use: Baiting bulls, ratting	Origins: 1800s

Miniature Bull Terrier

This breed is the smallest surviving version of the Bull Terrier (see p.235) and is still a strong reminder of its larger relative. The head is almost flat at the top of the skull and curves down to the tip of its powerful muzzle.

HISTORY Common during the 1800s, its popularity waned until the end of the 20th century.

REMARK The Miniature Bull Terrier delights in human company, but tends to be less tolerant toward other dogs.

small, thin ears

muscular neck

powerful hind legs

short, flat, glossy coat

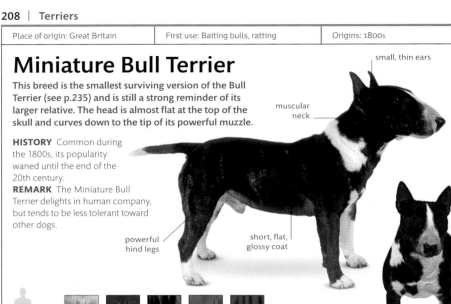

Color types

Height: 10–14in (25–35cm)	Weight: 24–33lb (11–15kg)	Temperament: Fearless, determined

Place of origin: Great Britain	First use: Dogfighting, ratting	Origins: 1800s

Staffordshire Bull Terrier

This smooth-coated breed gives the appearance of power and strength coupled with agility and athleticism. Coat coloration is very varied.

HISTORY This powerful terrier originates from the county of Staffordshire, England, and its ancestry displays crossings with the Bulldog (see p.39) and a variety of terrier breeds.

REMARK Although bred originally for dogfighting, its loyalty and devotion is legendary.

rose, or half-pricked, ears

well-sprung ribs

deep chest

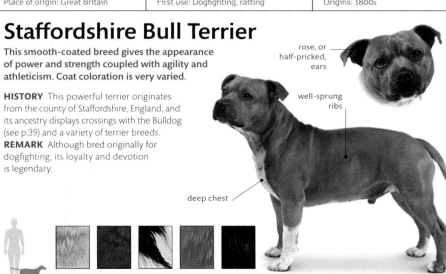

Color types

Height: 14–16in (36–41cm)	Weight: 24–38lb (11–17kg)	Temperament: Plucky, strong-willed

| Place of origin: Great Britain | First use: Hunting badgers and rats | Origins: 1600s |

Dandie Dinmont Terrier

Distinguished by its "top-knot" of hair, this small terrier also has an unusual texture to its coat. This occurs because of a combination of hard and soft hair, which creates a crisp texture over much of the body. The underparts, however, are predominantly soft-haired.

HISTORY This very old breed was probably developed by crossing Scottish and Skye Terriers (see p.213).

REMARK It is named after a character in Sir Walter Scott's book *Guy Mannering*, making it the only dog breed named after a fictional character.

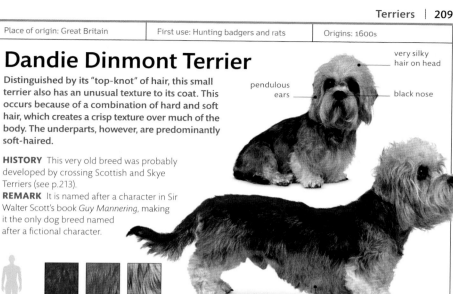

very silky hair on head

pendulous ears

black nose

long, low body

Color types

| Height: 8–11in (20–28cm) | Weight: 18–24lb (8–11kg) | Temperament: Independent, lively |

| Place of origin: Great Britain | First use: Hunting foxes and rats | Origins: 1500s |

Cairn Terrier

Lively and fearless, this shaggy terrier is well adapted to working outdoors and possesses a dense, double-layered, water-resistant coat. The head of a Cairn is broader and not as long as that of other terrier breeds, and the jaw is surprisingly powerful for a dog of this size.

HISTORY The breed name was changed to Cairn Terrier only after 1909, before which it was called the Short-haired Skye Terrier. Cairn Terriers were originally used to drive foxes and other animals from rocky retreats. The breed was introduced into the US in 1913.

REMARK The Cairn Terrier is an excellent swimmer.

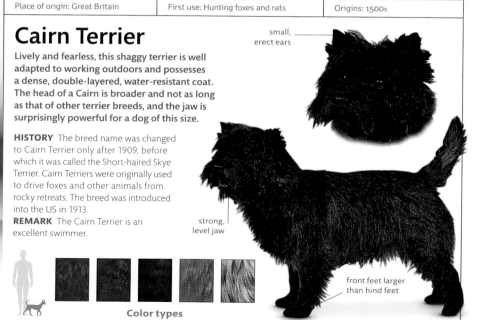

small, erect ears

strong, level jaw

front feet larger than hind feet

Color types

| Height: 10–12in (25–30cm) | Weight: 13–16lb (6–7.5kg) | Temperament: Bold, alert |

| Place of origin: Great Britain | First use: Ratting, killing vermin | Origins: 1700s |

Lakeland Terrier

Square-framed and solidly built, with a wiry, waterproof double coat, this sturdy terrier is equally content on the slopes of its Lake District ancestral home, in the north of England, as it is in the family home.

HISTORY There used to be several strains of this terrier, known under a variety of names. They were grouped in 1912.

REMARK Stingray of Derrybach, a Lakeland Terrier, was best in show at Crufts in 1967, and at the National Westminster Show, New York, in 1968.

small, V-shaped ears

tail set high

broad muzzle

straight, well-boned forelegs

relatively narrow chest

Color types

| Height: 13–15in (33–38cm) | Weight: 15–17lb (7–8kg) | Temperament: Brave, hardy |

| Place of origin: Great Britain | First use: Ratting | Origins: 1800s |

Norfolk Terrier

The Norfolk is distinguishable from its close relative, the Norwich Terrier (see p.207), by its drop ears, which are folded forward. Its outercoat is hard and wiry and there is a thick undercoat beneath. White markings on the coat are considered an undesirable feature.

HISTORY The Norfolk and Norwich Terrier breeds were inextricably linked until 1964, when the two breeds finally received separate recognition. They both seem to have developed as farm terriers in their East Anglian homeland in England.

REMARK It makes a good guard dog or companion for families with older children.

broad, and slightly rounded skull

ears drop forward close to cheeks

wedge-shaped, strong muzzle

rougher and longer coat at shoulders

Color types

| Height: 10–10¼in (25–26cm) | Weight: 11–12lb (5–5.5kg) | Temperament: Alert, friendly |

| Place of origin: Great Britain | First use: Going to ground and ratting | Origins: 1800s |

Parson Jack Russell Terrier

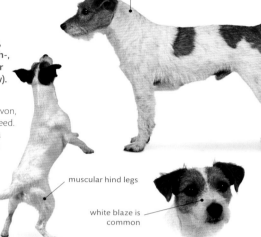

strong neck

This active, robust, and well-known terrier has a predominantly white coat, which can occur in three forms: smooth-, broken-, and rough-coated. It is similar in appearance to the Fox Terrier (below).

HISTORY The Reverend Jack Russell (nicknamed "the Hunting Parson"), from Devon, England, is credited with developing this breed. **REMARK** The Jack Russell Terrier makes a very personable companion and can form a close bond with family members.

Color types

muscular hind legs

white blaze is common

| Height: 9–15in (23–38cm) | Weight: 12–18lb (5–8kg) | Temperament: Alert, lively |

| Place of origin: Great Britain | First use: Hunting foxes | Origins: 1700s |

Wire Fox Terrier

short, level back

Similar to the smooth-coated breed (see p.212) in all but coat type, the Wire Fox Terrier should have a coat with a dense and wiry texture, without any traces of curls. It is actually double-layered, with a softer undercoat.

HISTORY Breeds of terrier that are now extinct, notably the Wire-haired Terrier, contributed to the development of this dog. **REMARK** It takes considerable time to prepare the coat for show purposes.

dark, round eyes

straight front legs

ears fold forward toward cheeks

Color types

| Height: 15½in (39cm) | Weight: 16–18lb (7–8kg) | Temperament: Alert, determined |

Place of origin: Great Britain	First use: Flushing foxes	Origins: 1700s

Smooth Fox Terrier

Less well-known than its wire-haired relative (see p.211), the Smooth Fox Terrier is an easily recognized breed, with its short back and long, tapering muzzle. Its distinctive, short tail is set high and carried gaily. This dog is lively and alert, and will take any amount of exercise.

HISTORY The origins of this terrier are not clear, although it was first recorded about 20 years after the appearance of the wire-haired form. The breed standard has not altered significantly in terms of type since 1876, except that today's dogs are somewhat lighter than their ancestors.

REMARK White coloring should always predominate in the coat of this terrier.

tail set high and held upright

long, sloping shoulders

deep chest

small, dark, circular eyes

long muzzle

Color types

Height: 15½in (39cm)	Weight: 16–18lb (7–8kg)	Temperament: Alert, determined

Place of origin: Great Britain	First use: Hunting rats	Origins: 1800s

Welsh Terrier

Often confused with the Lakeland Terrier (see p.210), the Welsh Terrier can be distinguished by its broader head and distinctive coloration. Black and tan is preferred, but black, grizzle, and tan is also permitted, provided there is no black penciling on the toes.

HISTORY The old Black and Tan Terrier contributed to the ancestry of this breed. It was first recognized by the Kennel Club in Britain in 1886 and was introduced to the US two years later.

REMARK It needs hand-stripping twice a year for show purposes.

small ears

hard, wiry, thick coat

flat top to head

small, catlike feet

long, sloping shoulders

powerful, muscular thighs

Color types

Height: 14–15½in (36–39cm)	Weight: 20–21lb (9–10kg)	Temperament: Active, playful

| Place of origin: Great Britain | First use: Going to ground | Origins: 1800s |

Scottish Terrier

This energetic terrier has a distinctive appearance because of its elongated head shape. In addition, it has longer hair on its forehead, creating the impression of eyebrows.

HISTORY Although the Scottish Terrier breed dates back many years, it was not until 1882 that an official standard was drawn up.

REMARK The coat of this terrier lies close to the ground. Mud sticking to it can be brushed out quite easily once it has dried.

OTHER NAMES Aberdeen Terrier.

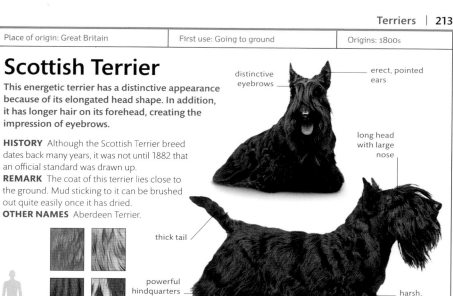

distinctive eyebrows

erect, pointed ears

long head with large nose

thick tail

powerful hindquarters

harsh, wiry, dense outercoat

Color types

| Height: 10–11in (25–28cm) | Weight: 19–23lb (8.5–10.5kg) | Temperament: Active, assertive |

| Place of origin: Great Britain | First use: Hunting foxes and badgers | Origins: 1600s |

Skye Terrier

The long, trailing coat of the Skye Terrier needs plenty of grooming to stay immaculate. The hair covering the head is shorter and softer than elsewhere on the body and forms a veil over the forehead and eyes. The front feet, when visible, are large and point directly forward. A small white area on the chest may be noticeable on some individuals.

HISTORY Bred in the isolation of the Scottish Isle of Skye, in the Inner Hebrides, these terriers were developed to hunt foxes and badgers.

REMARK It may take up to three years for the coat of a young Skye Terrier to develop to its full extent.

long, powerful head

ears are usually pricked but can be dropped

Adult and puppies

strong hindquarters

long, level back

softer, shorter hair on head

Color types

| Height: 9–10in (23–25cm) | Weight: 19–23lb (8.5–10.5kg) | Temperament: Loyal, lively |

Place of origin: Great Britain	First use: Hunting rabbits	Origins: 1700s

Patterdale Terrier

Although small in size, the Patterdale Terrier is a brave and tenacious working dog, with a short, coarse, weatherproof coat of black, black-and-tan, brown, or red coloration. This stocky, well-built dog retains the terrier's love of hunting.

HISTORY Originating in the north of England, the breed is named after the Cumbrian village of Patterdale, where it was popular.
REMARK These lively dogs need plenty of exercise.
OTHER NAMES Black Fell Terrier.

triangular, folded ears

sturdy hindquarters

broad chest

short, coarse coat

straight back

small feet

Color types

Height: 12in (30cm)	Weight: 11–13lb (5–6kg)	Temperament: Brave, enthusiastic

Place of origin: Great Britain	First use: Hunting rats	Origins: 1800s

West Highland White Terrier

As its name implies, this terrier from the Western Highlands of Scotland is pure white in coloration. Its face is a little foxlike in appearance, and there is a pronounced stop to the nose.

HISTORY It is likely that all the Scottish terriers descended from a common ancestry in what was then a sparsely populated part of Great Britain. The dogs were first shown as Poltalloch Terriers—bred in a village of this name for more than 60 years by a Colonel Malcolm.
REMARK The thick coat needs a lot of attention.

naturally short tail

slightly domed skull

very pointed, small, erect ears

powerful muzzle

hind feet smaller than forefeet

Height: 10–11in (25–28cm)	Weight: 15–22lb (7–10kg)	Temperament: Active, assertive

Place of origin: Great Britain	First use: Hunting rats	Origins: 1800s

Yorkshire Terrier

Apart from its diminutive size, the most distinctive feature of this active little terrier is its coat, which is steely blue in coloration with areas of golden tan on the head, silky in texture, and sufficiently long to reach the ground. When seen walking, the Yorkshire Terrier can give the impression of being mounted on wheels since its feet may not be visible.

HISTORY Developed by the miners of the West Riding area of Yorkshire, this terrier is the result of relatively recent crosses of the Skye (see p.213), Dandie Dinmont (see p.209), and Maltese (see p.53) Terriers.
REMARK Newborn Yorkshire Terriers are black in color.
OTHER NAMES Broken-haired Scottish Terrier.

medium-length muzzle

very long hair on muzzle

straight limbs

dark, sparkling eyes

short, level back

rich, bright tan-colored hair on chest

Height: 23cm (9in)	Weight: Less than 3kg (7lb)	Temperament: Intelligent, confident

Place of origin: Great Britain	First use: Hunting rats	Origins: 1990s

Sporting Lucas Terrier

This friendly terrier is derived from the Lucas Terrier, which had a Sealyham (see p.216) and Norfolk (see p.210) Terrier ancestry. In the 1990s, Plummer and Fell Terriers were then crossed with Lucas Terriers to create this taller breed.

HISTORY The Lucas Terrier was created by Sir Jocelyn Lucas in Scotland during the 1940s. He felt the Sealyham Terrier was becoming too large.
REMARK The Sporting Lucas Terrier tends not to bark a lot, compared with many terriers.

pronounced stop

tail carried vertically

straight back

powerful jaws

wide head

strong, compact body

double-coated with a stiff topcoat

Color types

Height: 10–13in (25–33cm)	Weight: 11–18lb (5–8kg)	Temperament: Affectionate, athletic

Place of origin: Great Britain	First use: Hunting badgers and otters	Origins: 1850s

Sealyham Terrier

Although small, no more than 12in (30cm) high, the Sealyham has powerful jaws, a muscular neck, and strong legs. Its coat is long and coarse, usually white or yellowish-white in color, and it must be stripped by hand every six months to remove dead hair.

HISTORY This strong, determined terrier is named after the village of Sealyham, Wales, where it originated. The first breed club was established there in 1908.
REMARK Having been bred to hunt badgers, the Sealyham has kept its bold disposition and active temperament.

long, powerful head

erect tail

deep, broad chest

rounded, catlike feet

Color types

Height: 10–12in (25–30cm)	Weight: 18–20lb (8–9kg)	Temperament: Strong-willed, active

---

Place of origin: Australia	First use: Working on farms	Origins: 1800s

Australian Terrier

This terrier used to be only blue and tan in coloration, but shades of red were introduced following crosses with Cairn Terriers (see p.209).

HISTORY Descended from British terriers, it was originally known as the Broken-coated Toy Terrier. It was recognized by the Kennel Club in 1936.
REMARK Among the smallest of the working breeds, it is still tough enough to tackle snakes.

distinctive ruff

small ears

long body for its height

hard, straight hair

Color types

Height: 10in (25.5cm)	Weight: 12–14lb (4–7kg)	Temperament: Feisty, dutiful

Place of origin: Australia	First use: Companion	Origins: 1800s

Australian Silky Terrier

A compact and lightly built dog, the Australian Silky has typical terrier characteristics. Straight, silky body hair forms a natural parting along its moderately long, level back, and the ears are pricked and alert.

HISTORY The Australian Silky was developed during the 1800s from British terriers, notably the Yorkshire Terrier (see p.215), and also the Australian Terrier (opposite).
REMARK This dog was developed strictly as a companion dog.
OTHER NAMES Silky Terrier, Sydney Silky.

hair parts naturally, even down over the head and face

wedge-shaped skull

silky hair may be 6in (15cm) long on the back

erect ears

skull broad between the ears

small catlike feet

Height: 9in (23cm)	Weight: 8–11lb (4–5kg)	Temperament: Spirited, friendly

Place of origin: Germany	First use: Hunting rats and small game	Origins: 1800s

German Hunting Terrier

The cheeks of this relatively large terrier are full, the jaw powerful, and the teeth strong. Its dense coat is usually black or chocolate with tan markings, or it may be pure red. Both wire-haired and smooth-haired forms are found.

HISTORY Despite being developed in Bavaria, its ancestry consists entirely of British terrier breeds, including Welsh (see p.212) and Fox Terriers.
REMARK This breed is still primarily a working dog, renowned for its fine nose.
OTHER NAMES Deutscher Jagdterrier.

short, thick tail

triangular, folded ears

well-muscled legs

powerful jaws and muzzle

large feet

Color types

Height: 16in (41cm)	Weight: 20–22lb (9–10kg)	Temperament: Keen, tenacious

Place of origin: Gemany	First use: Hunting rats	Origins: 1800s

German Pinscher

Often bearing the black-and-tan markings of its relative, the Doberman Pinscher (see pp.246–247), the German, or Standard, Pinscher is, however, also seen in dark brown and various shades of fawn. It has the same elegance of bearing and cleanness of line as the Doberman Pinscher, albeit without that dog's musculature and aura of barely restrained power.

Color types

natural, folded position of ears

HISTORY This native of Germany may be related to the Manchester Terrier (see p.206), as are the Doberman and Miniature (opposite) Pinschers, although it has never achieved the international popularity of the other two breeds.

REMARK This breed is large for a terrier and so is most often used as a general farm hand.

OTHER NAMES Standard Pinscher.

well-muscled neck

deep chest

well-defined color markings

well-boned forelegs

well-arched toes

Height: 16–19in (41–48cm)	Weight: 25–35lb (11–16kg)	Temperament: Alert, intelligent

| Place of origin: Germany | First use: Hunting rodents | Origins: 1600s |

Affenpinscher

A foreshortened muzzle, pronounced stop, large round eyes, erect ears, domed forehead, and facial hair all combine to give this little terrier a unique, rather impish appearance. The coat is variable in length, being longer on some parts of the body than others.

HISTORY There is no precise record of the Affenpinscher's ancestry, although it contributed to the development of the better-known Brussels Griffon (see p.225).
REMARK Although small, this breed makes an excellent watch dog.

domed skull

blunt, short muzzle

straight, well-boned forelegs

distinct moustache

rough, harsh-textured coat

| Height: 10in (25cm) | Weight: 7–8lb (3–3.5kg) | Temperament: Alert, quiet |

| Place of origin: Germany | First use: Hunting rats | Origins: 1800s |

Miniature Pinscher

This square-shaped, high-spirited terrier is sturdy and athletic and able to outjump dogs far larger than itself. One of its most distinctive features is its hackney gait (characterized by pronounced flexion of the knee).

HISTORY This ancient breed descended from traditional native German terriers. The German Pinscher Club was established in 1895 and the breed became standardized.
REMARK This breed was known as the Reh Pinscher because of its resemblance to small roe deer (*reh* in German) living in German forests.
OTHER NAMES Reh Pinscher, Zwergpinscher.

large, erect ears

narrow, tapering muzzle

very dark eyes

powerful hindquarters

short, smooth coat, hard to the touch

| Height: 10–12in (25–30cm) | Weight: 8–10lb (4–5kg) | Temperament: Lively, alert |

Place of origin: Germany	First use: Ratting	Origins: 1400s

Miniature Schnauzer

This dog has the general appearance and all the appealing features of its full-sized brethren (see p.118)—bushy eyebrows, bristly, stubby moustache, and chin whiskers. It is very nearly square in profile, with a straight and level back and well-developed thighs.

HISTORY This miniature form of schnauzer is thought to have evolved from crossings of the Standard Schnauzer and Affenpinschers (see p.219). The breed was first seen in Britain in 1928. Its diminutive size makes it an excellent ratter.
REMARK The coat of this terrier must be stripped at least twice a year and regularly groomed to remove dead hairs. Its whiskers and longer hair should be combed every day.
OTHER NAMES Zwergschnauzer.

V-shaped ears, high on head, hanging forward to temples

prominent black nose and wide nostrils

strong, straight back, slightly higher at shoulders than hindquarters

dark, oval eyes set beneath bushy eyebrows

forelegs appear straight from every angle

Color types

Height: 13–14in (33–36cm)	Weight: 13–15lb (6–7kg)	Temperament: Lively, very friendly

Place of origin: Germany	First use: Watchdog, companion	Origins: 1945

Kromfohrländer

Of powerful build, this attractive terrier has been bred in a wire-coated form, which is the most common, and in a less popular, straight-haired form. Coloration is a significant feature, being a combination of white and tan in various shades. There is often a tan area on the head and another on the back that forms a saddle-type patch.

HISTORY At the end of the Second World War, American soldiers entering the town of Siegen in Westphalia, Germany, brought with them a tawny-colored dog of griffon type. They gave it to a local resident named Frau Schleifenbaum, and it mated with a terrier. Frau Schleifenbaum decided to form a breed from the resulting puppies.
REMARK The Kromfohrländer was first recognized by the German Kennel Club in 1953.

balanced markings are desirable

muzzle tapers along its length

Straight-haired form

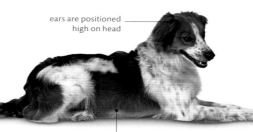

ears are positioned high on head

medium-length coat

dark, oval-shaped eyes

wedge-shaped head

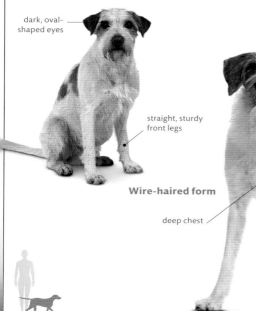

straight, sturdy front legs

Wire-haired form

deep chest

strong hind legs

Height: 15–17in (38–43cm)	Weight: 26lb (12kg)	Temperament: Affectionate, alert

| Place of origin: Ireland | First use: Watchdog | Origins: 1700s |

Irish Terrier

Of unmistakable terrier appearance, with a harsh coat, the long-legged Irish Terrier is somewhat reminiscent of the larger Airedale (see p.205). It has an active, lively nature. Good-tempered toward people, it is not generally well disposed toward other dogs.

HISTORY Crossings involving the old Black and Tan and Wheaten Terriers may have laid the foundations of this breed, which originated in County Cork, Ireland. Standardization occurred only in 1879 when a breed club was established.

REMARK Hand clipping of the coat is required to maintain the graceful outline of these terriers.

OTHER NAMES Irish Red Terrier.

long head, and stop visible only in profile

long, powerful, muscular jaws

small, V-shaped ears falling close to cheeks

moderately long neck widening toward shoulders

deep, muscular chest

perfectly straight forelegs

small, dark eyes

arched toes with black nails

dense, crisp hair on legs

| Height: 18–19in (46–48cm) | Weight: 25–27lb (11–12kg) | Temperament: Determined, friendly |

Place of origin: Ireland	First use: Herding cattle, ratting	Origins: 1700s

Soft-coated Wheaten Terrier

This terrier has a distinctive coat, which is not shed. It needs thorough grooming daily to prevent matting. The coat color is described as "wheaten," because it should match the color of ripening wheat. Whitish or reddish tones are not acceptable. Pups may have darker markings on their coats, however, which should disappear by two years of age. The adult coat hangs either in loose waves or in large, light curls.

HISTORY This is believed to be the oldest terrier breed in Ireland, most common in the vicinity of Kerry (where it gave rise to the Kerry Blue Terrier, see p.224) and Cork, but its precise origins are unknown. When working, the Soft-coated Wheaten Terrier is an adept badger and otter hunter.

REMARK Training requires a little effort, but the results are worth it.

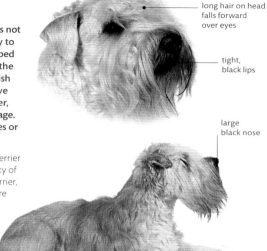

long hair on head falls forward over eyes

tight, black lips

large black nose

V-shaped, folded ears

moderately long, strong, muscular neck

upright tail, set high on back

square-shaped muzzle with strong jaws

strong, muscular thighs

powerful feet with black toenails

deep chest

Height: 18–19in (46–48cm)	Weight: 35–45lb (16–20kg)	Temperament: Lively, loyal, energetic

| Place of origin: Ireland | First use: Hunting vermin | Origins: 1700s |

Glen of Imaal Terrier

The body of this terrier is relatively long compared with its height, and its coat is of medium length. It is both agile and silent when working, factors that allow it to strike its quarry unexpectedly.

HISTORY This dog is named after the Glen of Imaal in County Wicklow, Ireland, where it was first recognized in 1933.

REMARK This is a hardy, working terrier breed, traditionally used to hunt badgers in the past, as well as the more typical terrier fare, such as rats.

round, brown eyes

harsh outercoat

ears back when relaxed

strong feet with rounded pads

front feet turn out slightly

| Height: 14in (36cm) | Weight: 35lb (16kg) | Temperament: Determined, brave |

| Place of origin: Ireland | First use: Hunting vermin | Origins: 1800s |

Kerry Blue Terrier

The appearance of pups of this breed differs greatly from that of adult dogs because they are born with black coats. It can take up to 18 months before young dogs acquire the characteristic blue adult coloration. Dark points may also be seen in adult dogs.

HISTORY Originating in County Kerry, in the southwest of Ireland, this terrier is thought to be descended from Welsh (see p.212), Bedlington (see p.205), and Soft-coated Wheaten (see p.223) Terrier stock.

REMARK The silky coat of these terriers is not shed and needs daily attention.

V-shaped ears hang forward on head

tail set high and carried erect

long, lean head with powerful jaws

straight forelegs

small, rounded feet with black nails

| Height: 18–19in (46–48cm) | Weight: 33–37lb (15–17kg) | Temperament: Determined, friendly |

Place of origin: Belgium	First use: Hunting vermin	Origins: 1800s

Griffon Bruxellois

There is considerable confusion over the nomenclature of this dog, which is shown as one breed in North America and the UK but separated into three types in Europe. The Brussels Griffon can be distinguished from the Belgian Griffon by its red coloration, although both have long coats. In contrast, the Petit Brabancon has a short coat.

HISTORY It is thought that the Affenpinscher (see p.219) may have been involved in the ancestry of this dog. Other breeds, such as the Pug (see p.49), may also have played a part in its development.

REMARK This breed is affectionate and enjoys a good walk.

OTHER NAMES Griffon Belge.

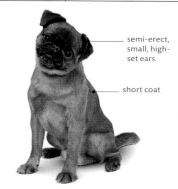

semi-erect, small, high-set ears

short coat

Petit Brabancon

tail set high

slight arch to neck

very dark, large, round eyes

Belgian Griffon

short, tight coat

straight, medium-length legs

head is large in relation to body

harsh, wiry coat with no hint of a curl

Brussels Griffon

Color types

Height: 7–8in (18–20cm)	Weight: 6–12lb (2.5–5.5kg)	Temperament: Lively, obedient

Place of origin: Austria	First use: Ratting, watchdog	Origins: 1800s

Austrian Pinscher

This small dog displays typical pinscher characteristics. Seen from the front, it has a very broad chest, suggesting greater width than height.

HISTORY Although related to other European terrier breeds, it has never been particularly common outside Austria.

REMARK The Austrian Pinscher proves to be an alert and noisy guardian but is often given to persistent barking.

OTHER NAMES Österreichischer Kurzhaariger Pinscher.

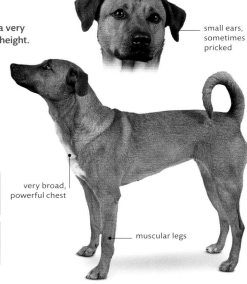

small ears, sometimes pricked

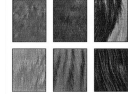

very broad, powerful chest

muscular legs

Color types

Height: 14–20in (36–51cm)	Weight: 26–40lb (12–18kg)	Temperament: Bold, alert

Place of origin: Czech Republic	First use: Watchdog	Origins: 1940s

Cesky Terrier

Sporting a distinctive, silky coat and a fine beard and eyebrows, this graceful little terrier is robust and agile. It has a long head with a large nose.

HISTORY This loyal breed was developed by the Czech geneticist, Dr. F. Horàk. It was officially recognized in 1963.

REMARK The Cesky is good with children and makes a fine watchdog.

OTHER NAMES Czesky, Bohemian Terrier.

long head

coat is clipped

sturdy legs

silky coat

profuse beard

Color types

Height: 10–14in (25–36cm)	Weight: 12–18lb (5.5–8kg)	Temperament: Good-natured, obedient

WORKING DOGS

THE DIVERSITY IN APPEARANCE of the many breeds of working dogs reflects the variety of tasks they have performed throughout history. For thousands of years, humans have exploited the dog's powerful territorial instinct to protect their own property from intruders. This basic function was mythologized by the Ancient Greeks in the form of Cerberus, the fearsome guardian at the gates of Hades. But the dog has other, more specialized, functions: seeing for those who are blind; hearing for those who are deaf; rescuing the injured; transporting people and cargo across Arctic terrain. As humans made ready to enter the Space Age, it was the dog that was sent ahead to prepare the way.

Place of origin: US	First use: Guarding farms, fighting	Origins: 1700s

American Bulldog

This powerful dog is thought to be similar to the old form of 16th-century British bulldog, a breed used for bullbaiting. The head of the American Bulldog is large, and the neck and shoulders hugely muscled.

HISTORY Settlers brought the original bulldog stock from Britain, and their versatility as hunters and farm dogs ensured their popularity in the US.
REMARK The American Bulldog has grown in popularity over recent years and so there is a wider variation in height and weight than there is with its British counterpart (see p.39), which has become a companion and show breed.
OTHER NAMES Old Country Bulldog.

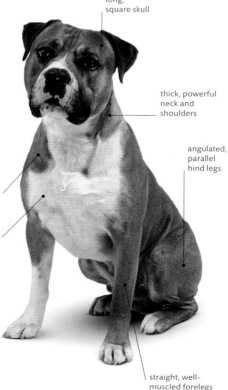

long, square skull

thick, powerful neck and shoulders

angulated, parallel hind legs

short, shiny, hard coat

more than half of the coat should be white, with patches of color

straight, well-muscled forelegs

very powerful jaws

Color types

Height: 19–28in (48–71cm)	Weight: 65–130lb (30–58kg)	Temperament: Bold, lively

| Place of origin: US | First use: Baiting bulls, guard dog | Origins: 1900s |

Olde English Bulldogge

This powerfully built, medium-size, mastiff-type dog is the result of American breeders' attempts to produce a traditional image of the old-style English Bulldog, while eliminating breed weaknesses such as breathing difficulties.

HISTORY This form of dog is said to be the result of a breeding program carried out by David Leavitt in Pennsylvania, involving Bullmastiffs (see p.234), the Bulldog (see p.39) itself, American Bulldogs (see p.227), and American Pit Bull Terriers (see p.203).

REMARK Although a large, fierce-looking dog, the aim of the breeding program has been to produce a determined and courageous dog yet one that is not aggressive.

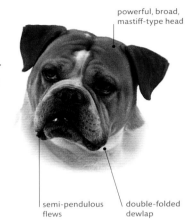

powerful, broad, mastiff-type head

semi-pendulous flews

double-folded dewlap

short, broad muzzle with prominent stop

thick, powerful neck

rose or button-style ears

well-boned, straight forelegs

short, close coat

Color types

| Height: 20–25in (51–64cm) | Weight: 65–105lb (29.5–48kg) | Temperament: Bold, friendly |

Place of origin: US	First use: Pulling sledges	Origins: 1900s

Chinook

The tawny coloration is characteristic of this breed. Seen from the side, it has a square profile, emphasizing its great strength. The thick, double coat of the Chinook becomes thinner during the hot summer months.

HISTORY Developed as a sledge dog by breeder Arthur Walden, the Chinook was derived from crossings involving Eskimo Dogs (see p.235), smooth-coated St. Bernards (see p.269), and Belgian shepherd dogs (see pp.122–125).
REMARK Around 800 known individuals of this breed exist today, with about 100 puppies being born annually.

pendent ears are preferred

heavily muscled hindquarters

broad, deep, strong chest

thickly cushioned pads on feet

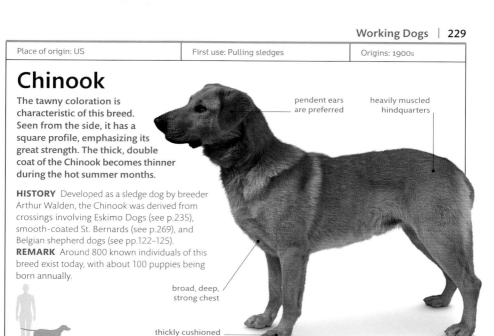

Height: 21–26in (53–66cm)	Weight: 65–90lb (29.5–41kg)	Temperament: Strong, determined

Place of origin: US	First use: Herding, hunting	Origins: 1000 BCE

Carolina Dog

This dog is similar in appearance to other pariah-type dogs, such as the Dingo, seen in other parts of the world. The Carolina Dog has a dense, yellowish gold coat and a strong, prominently boned head and face.

HISTORY This breed could be similar to the earliest types of dog seen in North America. Formerly kept by Native Americans, the Carolina Dog is now best known in the southern states of the US.
REMARK Some Carolina Dogs are semi-wild, but pups can easily be trained to herd stock or hunt small prey.

large, triangular-shaped ears

thick neck and broad chest

straight forelegs

tail reaches to level of hocks

Height: 22in (56cm)	Weight: 30–40lb (13.5–18kg)	Temperament: Active, reserved

| Place of origin: US | First use: Pulling sledges | Origins: 3000 BCE |

Alaskan Malamute

Powerful and strong, this northern dog has been developed for stamina rather than speed, unlike some of the smaller breeds from this part of the world. Its dense, double-layered coat affords excellent protection from the often severe elements, having coarse outer guard hairs over a thick, oily, woolly undercoat. The length of the guard hairs varies, becoming longest over the shoulders and in the vicinity of the neck, as well as down the back. The color ranges from light gray to intermediate shades to black, or from gold to shades of red to liver, in combination with white.

HISTORY The breed is named after the Malhemut Eskimos (now called the Kuuvangmiut or Kobuk people), who lived in the northwest of Alaska. They were nomadic, and the dogs were used to haul their possessions between locations.

REMARK Due to its size and considerable strength, firm training from an early age is essential. It still retains something of a pack instinct, which may lead to outbreaks of aggressive behavior when it is in the company of other dogs. However, by nature it is friendly and affectionate to people.

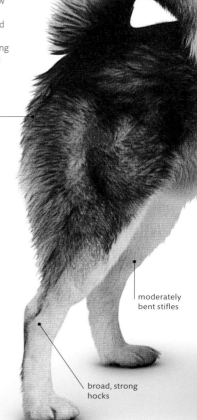

powerful hindquarters

large, prominent muzzle

weather-resistant double coat

moderately bent stifles

broad, strong hocks

tough, thick pads

| Height: 23–28in (58–71cm) | Weight: 85–125lb (39–57kg) | Temperament: Active, exuberant |

ears are small in relation to size of head

brown, almond-shaped eyes which may be lighter in red or white dogs

powerful neck

body is somewhat longer than dog's height

broad jaws with large teeth

longer guard hairs around shoulders and neck

white coloration dominates lower part of body

strong, deep chest

Color types

large, compact feet

| Place of origin: Great Britain | First use: Guard dog | Origins: 1000 BCE |

Mastiff

This grand, ancient breed is powerfully built, well boned, and extremely muscular. The Mastiff is renowned for its great courage and guarding instincts. Its massive size is an important feature of this dog, combined with a symmetrical, well-knit frame. The head should appear square when viewed from any angle. In spite of its ferocious appearance, the Mastiff is responsive and docile in temperament, although it is a reliable guardian that does not take kindly to intruders.

HISTORY Mastiffs were documented in Britain at the time of the Roman invasion: Julius Caesar acknowledged their bravery in battle. Later, at the Battle of Agincourt in 1415, Sir Peers Legh's body was guarded by his Mastiff as the battle raged. On returning to England, it reputedly started the famous Lyme Hall bloodline. Mastiffs nearly died out during the Second World War but have since recovered in number.

REMARK Renowned for its intelligence, this breed requires plenty of human contact. Potential owners should, therefore, have a great deal of time for their dog. The Mastiff also requires lots of space and exercise.

black hair extends over the muzzle, nose, and around the eyes, irrespective of the dog's coloration

high-set tail, wide at base and tapering along length

ears positioned at highest point on sides of skull

square head

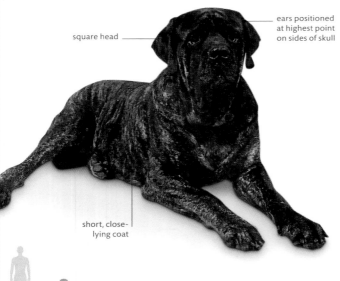

short, close-lying coat

| Height: 27½–30in (70–76cm) | Weight: 175–190lb (79–86kg) | Temperament: Loyal, alert |

broad skull with flat forehead

very powerful hindquarters

forehead wrinkles when attention is excited

large, rounded feet

ears lying flat and close to cheeks

very muscular and slightly arched neck

great depth in the flanks, emphasizing the powerful build

strong, straight legs

| Place of origin: Great Britain | First use: Guarding estates | Origins: 1800s |

Bullmastiff

The powerful, active Bullmastiff can easily be distinguished from the Mastiff (see pp.232–33) by its smaller size and its more compact face. The American Bullmastiff tends to be more Mastiff-like than its British counterpart. Originally, dark-colored brindle was the favoured coloration, but today fawns and reds are popular.

HISTORY Crossings between Mastiffs and bulldogs gave rise to the Bullmastiff, which is sometimes known as "the gamekeeper's dog." It was bred specifically to accompany gamekeepers on their rounds, being able to track well and having sufficient size and strength to tackle and overpower a poacher.

REMARK As is the case with other large breeds, pups may seem clumsy and uncoordinated when very young. Once mature, there should be no evidence of awkwardness in the way they move.

large, square-shaped skull

short muzzle

short, hard coat lying close against body

muscular shoulders

black muzzle is essential

short, straight back

wide, deep chest

tail is set high on back and tapers along its length

well-spaced, powerful legs

well-arched, rounded toes

Color types

| Height: 25–27in (64–69cm) | Weight: 90–130lb (41–59kg) | Temperament: Loyal, fearless |

| Place of origin: Great Britain | First use: Bullbaiting | Origins: 1800s |

Bull Terrier

The most obvious features of this powerful breed are its very long, oval-shaped head with no stop; small, triangular eyes; thin, erect ears; and tight-fitting coat over a large-boned and muscular physique.

HISTORY The Bull Terrier was developed from crosses with the bulldog and Old English Terrier.

REMARK It may not get on well with other dogs.

OTHER NAMES English Bull Terrier.

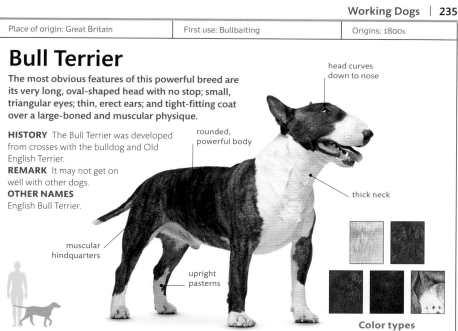

head curves down to nose

rounded, powerful body

thick neck

muscular hindquarters

upright pasterns

Color types

| Height: 21–22in (53–56cm) | Weight: 52–62lb (24–28kg) | Temperature: Fearless, determined |

| Place of origin: Canada | First use: Hunting, pulling sledges | Origins: 1000 BCE |

Eskimo Dog

This dog originated in the lands of the Arctic. It is seen in a variety of colors, with upright ears and a long tail that curls down over its back. Its dense coat affords it some protection in temperatures that fall far below freezing.

HISTORY This breed provided a vital lifeline for Arctic peoples before mechanized transportation.

REMARK Firm training is essential for this dog.

OTHER NAMES Husky, Esquimaux.

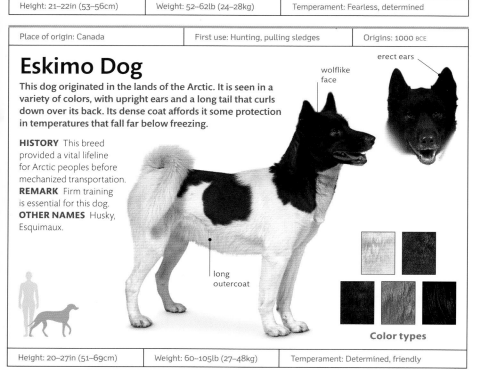

erect ears

wolflike face

long outercoat

Color types

| Height: 20–27in (51–69cm) | Weight: 60–105lb (27–48kg) | Temperature: Determined, friendly |

| Place of origin: Canada | First use: Helping fishermen | Origins: 1700s |

Newfoundland

This massive, imposing dog looks rather like a bear cub as a puppy. In spite of its size, the adult Newfoundland is usually gentle and affectionate. However, it can prove to be a loyal household guard if necessary. Its distinctive, oily coat is highly water-resistant and falls back naturally into place if groomed against the lie of the fur.

HISTORY The earliest Newfoundland originated in northeastern Canada. It is thought to be descended from dogs brought by European colonists, although Native Americans may have had mastiff-type dogs.
REMARK It was originally used to help fishermen haul in nets.

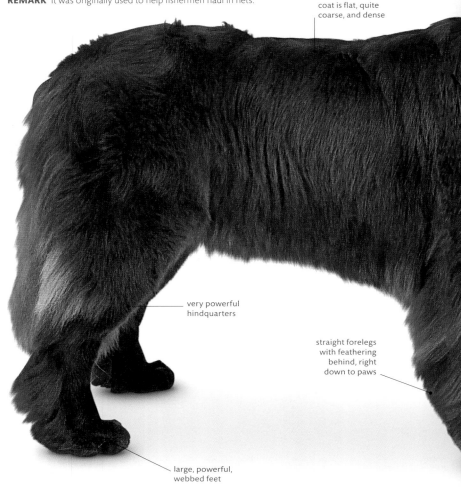

coat is flat, quite coarse, and dense

very powerful hindquarters

straight forelegs with feathering behind, right down to paws

large, powerful, webbed feet

| Height: 26–28in (66–71cm) | Weight: 110–150lb (50–68kg) | Temperament: Responsive, docile |

small, dark brown, wide-set eyes

dark brown coloration

short, square muzzle

broad and massive skull

small, close-lying ears

strong neck

Color types

Place of origin: Argentina	First use: Hunting pumas and jaguars	Origins: 1920s

Dogo Argentino

One of the few breeds developed in South America, the Dogo Argentino is a powerful dog, invariably white in color. It has a strong, square-shaped head, indicative of mastiff origins. Notorious for its aggressive, fearless nature, it was originally used to pursue big cats in its homeland. It is, nevertheless, reputedly trustworthy with people and is exceptionally loyal.

HISTORY The breed is descended from the Old Fighting Dog, which originated in Spain. Crosses with other breeds, most notably the Boxer (see p.251), took place under the guidance of the breed's founder, Dr. Antonio Martinez, to produce a more biddable temperament.
REMARK Like white Boxers, this breed may suffer deafness in one or both ears.
OTHER NAMES Argentinian Mastiff.

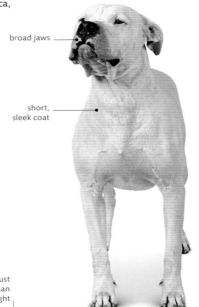

broad jaws

short, sleek coat

length of the body just slightly greater than breed's height

relatively long tail

long, straight forelegs

traces of pigment on skin may be visible through hair

powerful hind legs

Height: 24–27in (61–69cm)	Weight: 80–100lb (36–45kg)	Temperament: Bold, brave

| Place of origin: Brazil | First use: Pursuing jaguars | Origins: 1800s |

Fila Brasileiro

The result of the combination of powerful mastiff stock with the Bloodhound (see pp.162–163), the Fila Brasileiro displays distinctive folds of skin on its huge head, which extend on to the neck. Further links with the Bloodhound can be detected from its unerring sense of smell and elongated muzzle.

HISTORY This breed was used for hunting down cattle that had strayed and is descended from European stock.
REMARK Confident and determined, the Fila Brasileiro does not fear intruders of any kind.
OTHER NAMES Brazilian Mastiff.

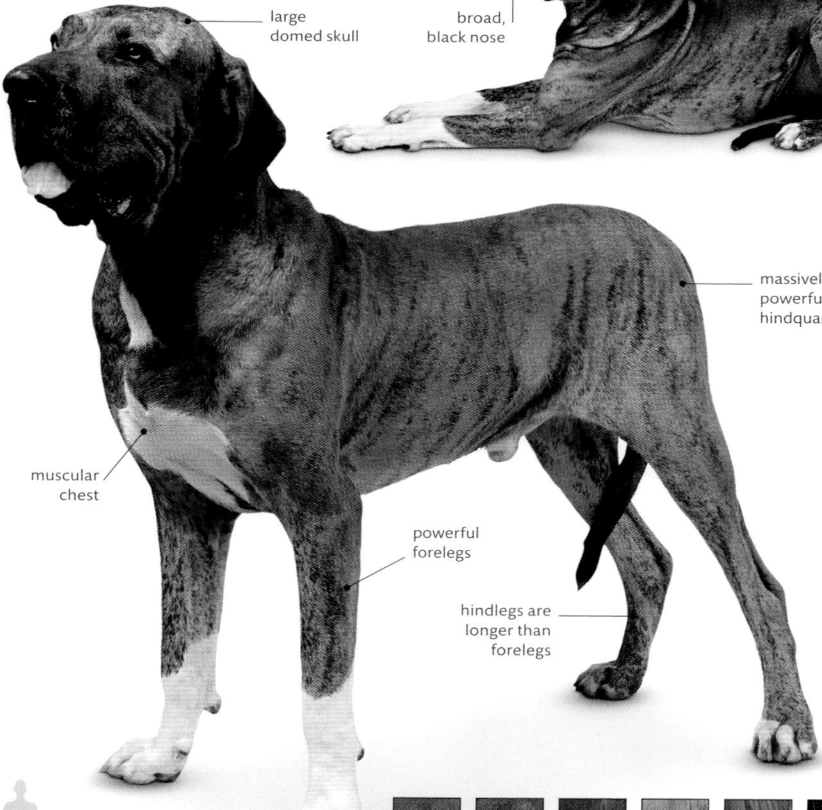

prominent dewlap

large domed skull

broad, black nose

massively powerful hindquarters

muscular chest

powerful forelegs

hindlegs are longer than forelegs

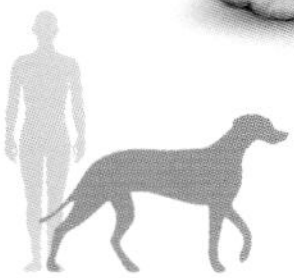

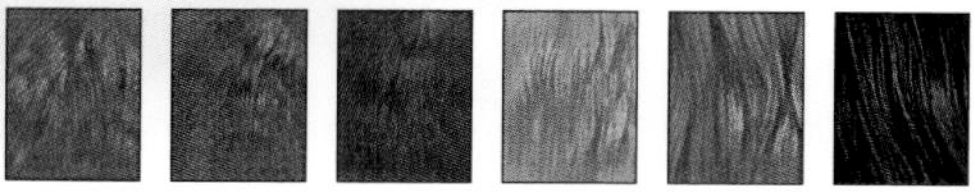

Color types

| Height: 24–30in (61–76cm) | Weight: 90–110lb (41–50kg) | Temperament: Bold, aggressive |

Place of origin: Greenland	First use: Pulling sledges	Origins: 1500s

Greenland Dog

The Greenland Dog is generally taller than the Eskimo Dog (see p.235) but slightly lighter and shorter in the back. So close is the relationship between these breeds, however, that they are judged to the same standard in some countries.

HISTORY Thought by some to be descended from Arctic wolves, this dog is superbly adapted to survival in the harsh conditions found in that region. Many local forms of this type of dog were bred in the Arctic regions before mechanized transportation was introduced. **REMARK** As a hunter, the Greenland Dog can track the breathing holes of seals in the ice. **OTHER NAMES** Grønlandshund, Grünlandshund.

broad wedge-shaped head

strong jaws

small, triangular-shaped ears

large, well-spread feet

large, bushy tail curls to one side over back

broad chest

color is highly variable between individuals

straight, powerful forelegs

Color types

Height: 22–25in (56–64cm)	Weight: 66–70lb (30–32kg)	Temperament: Affectionate, independent

| Place of origin: Norway | First use: Hunting elk | Origins: 1000s |

Norwegian Elkhound

Bred as a specialist hunter of elk, this dog is large and powerfully built. Its heavily muscled body is compact, giving it a rather stocky appearance, an impression that is reinforced by a dense covering of gray hair. A black form also exists (below).

HISTORY Skeletons of Stone Age dogs closely resembling Elkhounds have been unearthed in Scandinavia.
REMARK This is a very friendly dog and makes an excellent companion.
OTHER NAMES Norsk Elghund (Grå), Elkhound.

tightly curled tail

gray coat with black tips

large, dark eyes

powerful hindquarters

darker hair on muzzle

well-boned legs

| Height: 19–21in (49–52cm) | Weight: 44–50lb (20–23kg) | Temperament: Alert, friendly |

| Place of origin: Norway | First use: Hunting elk | Origins: 1000s |

Black Norwegian Elkhound

This dog is the black form of the more common gray Norwegian Elkhound (above). Apart from its comparative rarity, it is essentially the same dog, except a little smaller and lighter.

HISTORY The Norwegian Elkhounds are thought to have changed little since they first became human companions over a thousand years ago.
REMARK It can scent an elk over a distance of several miles.
OTHER NAMES Norsk Elghund (Sort).

pointed, mobile ears

glossy black coat

conical head

thick, coarse hair

straight forelegs

strong jaws

| Height: 18–20in (46–51cm) | Weight: 40lb (18kg) | Temperament: Alert, friendly |

Place of origin: Norway	First use: Hunting puffins	Origins: 1500s

Lundehund

A neat, compact build characterizes this strong and industrious breed. Its specialized breeding has resulted in well-developed feet, additional toes, and extra joints to aid it in its traditional job of scaling cliff faces in search of puffins. This very agile dog can bend its head horizontally backward almost to touch its back.

HISTORY The breed was used for centuries along the coasts of Norway. The Lundehund went into decline, however, along with the popularity of puffin hunting, and at one point, there were only 50 individuals known to exist.
REMARK The Lundehund can close its ears to keep out water.
OTHER NAMES Norwegian Puffin Dog.

shortish, rough coat

at least six toes on each foot

Color types

Height: 12–15½in (31–39cm)	Weight: 13–14lb (6kg)	Temperament: Lively, alert

Place of origin: Norway	First use: Herding stock	Origins: 800s

Norwegian Buhund

This dog shows typical spitz characteristics, as do many northern European breeds. It has erect, pointed ears, a powerful, stocky body, and a tail curling up and forward over its body.

HISTORY The Buhund was developed primarily for farm work, undertaking a variety of tasks. Its herding instinct is so ingrained that it will even round up chickens.
REMARK The name comes from the Norwegian word *bu*, meaning "shed" or "stall."
OTHER NAMES Norsk Buhund.

tail set high on back

deep chest

short, dense outercoat

quite small, oval feet

Color types

Height: 17–18in (43–46cm)	Weight: 53–58lb (24–26kg)	Temperament: Brave, companionable

| Place of origin: Finland | First use: Hunting birds and game | Origins: 1800s |

Finnish Spitz

An alert, pointed face and a reddish brown or red-gold coloration give this member of the spitz family a distinctly foxlike appearance.

HISTORY A standard for the Finnish Spitz was established in 1812. Originally the dog was used for hunting birds and small game.

REMARK In contests, dogs bark to indicate the presence of game and are marked on the number of barks per minute, which can be as many as 160.

OTHER NAMES Suomenpystykorva, Finsk Spets.

dark, almond-shaped eyes

plumed tail curves forward and around the thigh

outercoat is longer and coarser on shoulders

deep chest and strong, straight forequarters

round feet

| Height: 15–20in (38–51cm) | Weight: 31–35lb (14–16kg) | Temperament: Lively, vocal |

| Place of origin: Finland | First use: Hunting large game | Origins: 1600s |

Karelian Bear Dog

Robust and lively, this breed has a very distinctive coloration—predominantly black with white markings on its face, neck, chest, abdomen, feet, and tail.

HISTORY This breed was named after the Karelia province of Finland. It was first recognized by the Finnish Kennel Club in 1935.

REMARK This breed works quietly, barking only when it has located its quarry.

OTHER NAMES Björnhund, Karjalankarhukoira.

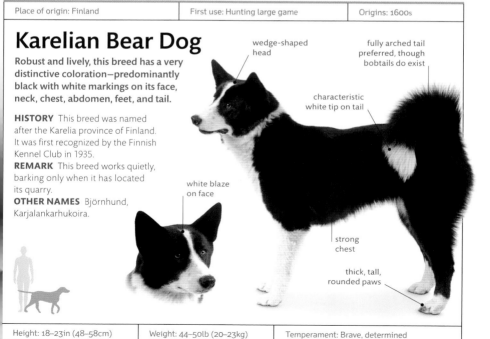

wedge-shaped head

fully arched tail preferred, though bobtails do exist

characteristic white tip on tail

white blaze on face

strong chest

thick, tall, rounded paws

| Height: 18–23in (48–58cm) | Weight: 44–50lb (20–23kg) | Temperament: Brave, determined |

Place of origin: Sweden	First use: Hunting elk	Origins: 1000s

Swedish Elkhound

This is the largest and most powerful of the elkhound-type breeds native to Scandinavia. The Swedish Elkhound has an elongated, rather narrow head, and this, combined with a straight muzzle, gives it a slightly foxlike appearance. The coat of this breed consists of a long, hard outercoat and a dense, woolly, much softer undercoat.

HISTORY The forebears of the Swedish Elkhound may have accompanied Stone Age people in the Scandinavian region of the world. Certainly this specific breed has been known for centuries, even though it was not officially recognized by the Swedish Kennel Club until 1946.

REMARK Best known in the Jämtland area of Sweden, the Swedish Elkhound is well-adapted to living in cold climates.

OTHER NAMES Jämthund.

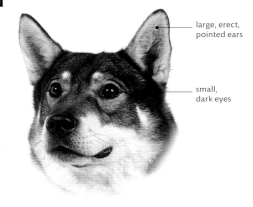

large, erect, pointed ears

small, dark eyes

tail curls tightly over back and rests on one side

broad, muscular shoulders

heavily muscled hind legs

deep, powerful chest

hard, long outercoat over woolly undercoat

Height: 23–25in (58–64cm)	Weight: 66lb (30kg)	Temperament: Friendly, alert

| Place of origin: Sweden | First use: Herding reindeer | Origins: 1800s |

Swedish Lapphund

This medium-size dog shows typical spitz characteristics in terms of its foxlike facial appearance and dramatically curving tail. It is protected from the cold of its homeland by a dense, woolly, double coat.

HISTORY The ancestors of this breed were kept by the Sámi to herd reindeer, although they have since been adapted to working sheep. The breed was officially recognized in Sweden in 1944.

REMARK This dog tends to be solid in color, although individuals with white markings are seen and not penalized.

OTHER NAMES Lapplandska Spets.

short, erect ears

dark, chestnut-colored eyes

plumed tail hangs forward

Color types

harsh, thick coat

feathering on legs and body

| Height: 17½–19½in (44–49cm) | Weight: 44lb (20kg) | Temperament: Lively, alert |

| Place of origin: Sweden | First use: Hunting birds | Origins: 1600s |

Norrbottenspets

The Norrbottenspets is one of the smaller spitz breeds, distinguishable from other spitzes by its relatively short coat, which is dense and stands away from the body. Its ears are pointed and erect, its muzzle is pointed, and its eyes are alert and lively.

HISTORY The breed was close to extinction in 1948, but enthusiasts sought out the last few remaining dogs and bitches and started a successful breeding program.

REMARK The Norrbottenspets was once widely kept in Sweden as a hunting dog.

OTHER NAMES Pohjanpystykorva, Nordic Spitz.

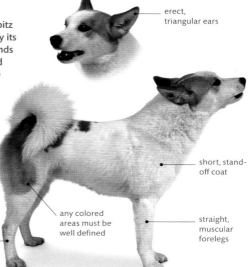

erect, triangular ears

short, stand-off coat

straight, muscular forelegs

any colored areas must be well defined

Color types

white is the dominant color

| Height: 16–17in (41–43cm) | Weight: 26–33lb (12–15kg) | Temperament: Quiet, affectionate |

| Place of origin: Germany | First use: Guard dog | Origins: 1800s |

Doberman Pinscher

This medium-size mastiff breed has a sculpted, elegant appearance. It is sleek, well muscled, and powerful and is usually black and tan in coloration. The Doberman Pinscher is a bold, alert dog with a great deal of stamina.

HISTORY This breed of dog was developed by a German tax collector, Ludwig Dobermann, to act as a deterrent against thieves and muggers, as well as aggrieved taxpayers. He used a variety of breeds, including the German Shepherd Dog (see p.115), Rottweiler (see p.256), German Pinscher (see p.218), and Manchester Terrier (see p.206).

REMARK The Doberman Pinscher once had a particular reputation for aggression. Although this has now been curbed to a great extent, firm training is still necessary from puppyhood.

OTHER NAMES Dobermann.

flat top to skull

lean, relatively long neck

almond-shaped eyes, no lighter than coat color

powerful jaws and well-filled face

Color types

| Height: 25½–27in (65–69cm) | Weight: 66–88lb (30–40kg) | Temperament: Bold, fearless |

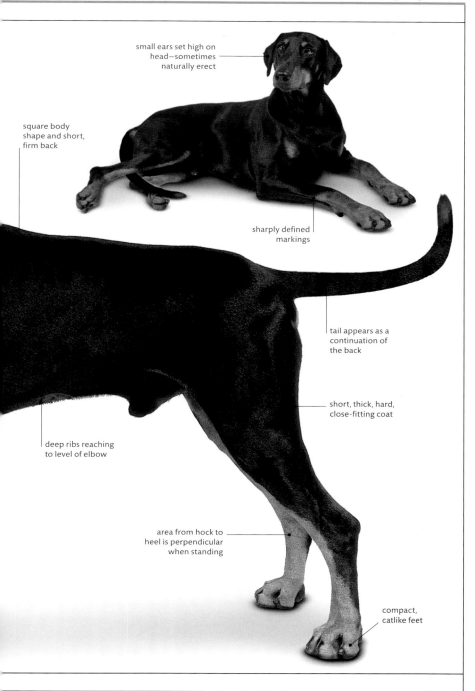

small ears set high on head—sometimes naturally erect

square body shape and short, firm back

sharply defined markings

tail appears as a continuation of the back

short, thick, hard, close-fitting coat

deep ribs reaching to level of elbow

area from hock to heel is perpendicular when standing

compact, catlike feet

Place of origin: Germany	First use: Hunting large game	Origins: 2000 BCE

Great Dane

A gentle giant, the Great Dane combines enormous size and strength with equal proportions of dignity and elegance. It has a long, well-chiseled face with a distinctive, intelligent expression. It comes in a variety of colors, including black, blue, brindle, fawn, and a striking harlequin. The breed has a naturally affectionate disposition.

HISTORY Of ancient origin, the Great Dane was developed in Germany and is believed to have inherited its grace and agility from crossings with greyhounds.
REMARK Renowned for its tolerance toward children, clean in its habits, and easy to groom, the Great Dane makes an excellent family pet for those who have the space and can afford to pay for this gigantic dog's equally huge food bill.
OTHER NAMES Deutsche Dogge.

wide, blunt nose with characteristic ridge

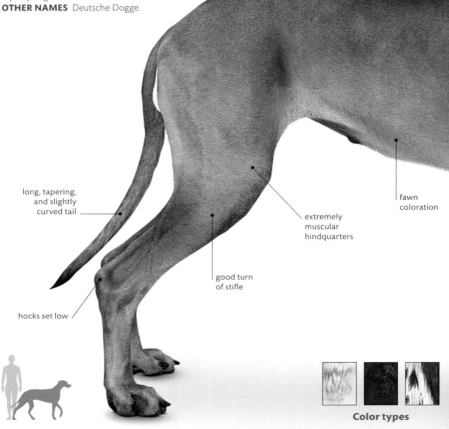

long, tapering, and slightly curved tail

fawn coloration

extremely muscular hindquarters

good turn of stifle

hocks set low

Color types

Height: 30–32in (76–81cm)	Weight: 100–120lb (45–55kg)	Temperament: Alert, lively

long, flat skull

round, fairly
deep-set eyes

ears set high
and folded
forward

very deep chest with
well-sprung ribs

short coat
is dense
and sleek

harlequin
coloration

Place of origin: Germany	First use: Retrieving from water	Origins: 1400s

Standard Poodle

This is the largest of the three breeds of poodle. An elegantly proportioned, squarely built dog, the Standard Poodle is a highly regarded retriever of game from rivers and marshland. The hair is clipped (as shown here), to provide warmth around its ankle joints, while the mane improves buoyancy.

HISTORY Originating in Germany, the modern poodle is likely to have descended from the now rare French water dog, the Barbet (see p.91).
REMARK As a working dog, its profuse coat used to hinder movement in the water, hence the need for clipping.
OTHER NAMES Barbone, Caniche.

moderately rounded skull

tight-fitting lips

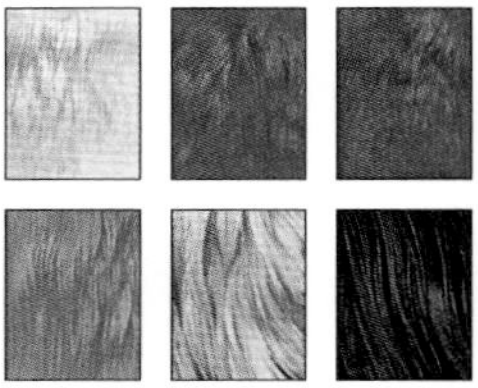

long, straight muzzle

Color types

coat color must be solid

coat texture can vary between individuals, being softer in some cases than others

tail is set high and carried erect

strong, well-proportioned neck

muscular hind legs

straight, parallel forelegs

deep chest with well-sprung ribs

Height: 15in (38cm)	Weight: 45–70lb (20.5–32kg)	Temperament: Intelligent, lively

| Place of origin: Germany | First use: Baiting bulls, guard dog | Origins: 1800s |

Boxer

This statuesque, mastiff-type dog has a boisterous and exuberant personality. However, the Boxer has a more refined appearance than many other mastiff breeds, with a less massive head and a leaner, more agile body.

HISTORY The Boxer is the result of crossings between Bullenbeisser mastiffs and bulldogs in Munich, Germany, in the 1850s. It was first seen in Britain in the 1930s.

REMARK Despite its powerful appearance and lively nature, it is responsive enough to be used as a guide dog in various countries.

mask confined to muzzle

strong, muscular neck without dewlap

short, straight, muscular back

well-arched ribs

strong, straight, firmly muscled forelegs

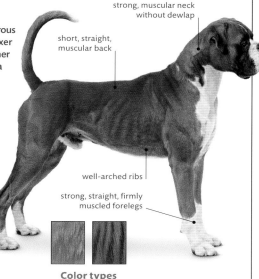

Color types

| Height: 21–25in (53–63cm) | Weight: 66–70lb (25–32kg) | Temperament: Playful, affectionate |

| Place of origin: Germany | First use: Pulling sledges | Origins: 1940s |

Eurasier

This medium-size, spitz-type dog has a heavy, profuse coat of medium length. Though the hair is dense, it still allows the dog's underlying form to be readily distinguished.

HISTORY This creation is the work of Julius Wipfel of Weinheim, Germany, and is descended from Chow Chow (see p.284), German Wolfspitz, and Samoyed (see p.283) bloodlines. It was recognized by the German Kennel Club in the 1960s.

REMARK The Eurasier is sensitive and responds best to gentle training.

OTHER NAMES Eurasian.

pointed, erect ears

darker mask on muzzle

slightly tapering muzzle

ruff of longer hair

profuse stand-off coat

only solid colors are recognized

Color types

| Height: 19–24in (48–61cm) | Weight: 40–70lb (18–32kg) | Temperament: Determined, alert |

Place of origin: Germany	First use: Helping fishermen	Origins: 1800s

Landseer

This dog closely resembles the Newfoundland (see pp.236–237), but differs most notably in its coloration. Black areas should be prominent on the back and rump, as well as the head, where only a small white blaze is present. In some countries, including Great Britain and the US, it is registered only as a color form of the Newfoundland.

HISTORY In the early 1800s, Newfoundlands varied a great deal in appearance. Gradually, two types evolved in mainland Europe. The traditional form is larger, with a short muzzle and a predominantly black coat. The taller Landseer is lighter, has a longer head, and a distinctive, slightly curly coat.

REMARK The artist Sir Edwin Landseer (1802–1873) gave his name to the new breed. Portraying contemporary Newfoundland dogs in his painting *Off to the Rescue*, he established the accepted appearance of the Landseer.

massive head

strong, powerful neck

short hair on face

narrow, white blaze

huge, powerful jaws

large feet for swimming

medium-length, dense coat

Height: 26–28in (66–71cm)	Weight: 110–150lb (50–68kg)	Temperament: Alert, friendly

even, black
markings on body

tail hangs
down and
curves slightly
upward
when dog
stands quietly

well-boned
limbs

Place of origin: Germany	First use: Symbolic mascot	Origins: 1800s

Leonberger

black mask on
face is preferred

This large, friendly dog displays many of the characteristics
of the breeds that contributed to its ancestry, most
notably the Newfoundland (see pp.236–237), from
whom it inherited its love of water, and the St. Bernard
(see p.269). Other breeds, such as the Great Swiss
Mountain Dog (see p.268), were probably involved
as well. Only very restricted areas of white are
presently permitted in the Leonberger.

HISTORY In the 1840s, Heinrich Essig, the Mayor of Leonberg,
Germany, set out to create a breed of dog that resembled
the dog featured on the town's crest. Not surprisingly, it was
named the Leonberger.
REMARK This breed has a natural love of water and has proved
outstanding as a water rescue dog. Its coat is waterproof and it
has webs between its toes.

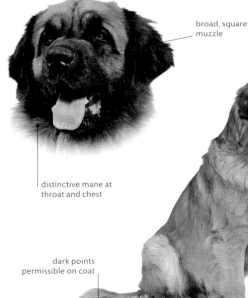

broad, square
muzzle

distinctive mane at
throat and chest

dark points
permissible on coat

rounded feet with
webbed toes

Color types

Height: 26–31½in (65–80cm)	Weight: 75–110lb (34–50kg)	Temperament: Intelligent, friendly

well-feathered ears

forehead must not be wrinkled

light yellow to red-brown coloration

underside of tail may be slightly lighter in color than coat

bushy tail, never held high

rough, not shaggy, coat

extensive feathering on back of forelegs

muscular hindquarters

hind legs are well angulated, appearing parallel when viewed from behind

black pads on feet

Place of origin: Germany	First use: Driving cattle, guard dog	Origins: 1800s

Rottweiler

Enormously powerful and muscular, this breed has a calm, self-assured expression that reflects a tranquil temperament. Its coloration is black, with distinctive symmetrical tan markings. It is responsive to training and an enthusiastic worker.

HISTORY The Rottweiler was developed in the German town of Rottweil, where it was used as a butcher's dog, for droving, and for guarding cattle. Now one of the most popular dogs in the US, this breed came close to extinction in the early 19th century.

REMARK The breed retains strong territorial instincts and can be fierce if aroused.

relatively small, pendent ears, set wide apart

tan markings on muzzle

arched forehead

well-developed occipital bone

skull broad between the ears

broad, deep chest with well-sprung ribs

broad, powerful hindquarters

forward-sloping pasterns

hind feet larger than front

Height: 23–27in (58–69cm)	Weight: 90–110lb (41–50kg)	Temperament: Protective, determined

Place of origin: Poland	First use: Guarding flocks	Origins: 1700s

Owczarek Podhalański

Although large and heavy, this sheepdog breed is surprisingly quick and agile. The usual coloration is solid white, although cream is also found, and both straight- and wavy-haired forms occur. This sturdy animal is well able to withstand the severe winter weather of its native Poland.

HISTORY Received wisdom claims the Italian Bergamasco (see p.131) as this breed's ancestor, but its more likely forebears would seem to be the very similar sheepdog breeds of neighboring Czech Republic and Hungary.

REMARK A placid nature is one of the key characteristics of this breed, and individuals prone to irritability are likely to be disqualified from the show ring. The Owczarek has now been adopted for military and police duties in North America.

OTHER NAMES Tatra Mountain Sheepdog.

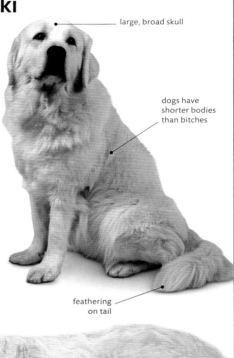

large, broad skull

dogs have shorter bodies than bitches

feathering on tail

hair on head and muzzle is shorter than body hair

strong neck

heavily boned forelegs

white- or cream-colored, thick, dense coat

large, thick-soled feet

Height: 24–34in (61–86cm)	Weight: 100–150lb (45–68kg)	Temperament: Independent, friendly

Place of origin: Belgium	First use: Guard dog on barges	Origins: 1500s

Schipperke

The Schipperke is relatively small for a member of the spitz family of dog breeds, but its attractive appearance has the distinctive features of this group. The outercoat is long, thick, and harsh, forming a ruff at the neck. In the US, solid black is the only acceptable color, although in other countries, additional colors are also permitted.

HISTORY The Schipperke has always been a small breed. It was used originally as a guard dog on barges and also perhaps to encourage barge ponies to renewed efforts. Its name is thought to derive from a corruption of the Flemish word for "little bargeman."

REMARK Most Schipperke are born tailless.

very mobile, erect, triangular ears

foxlike head with pointed muzzle

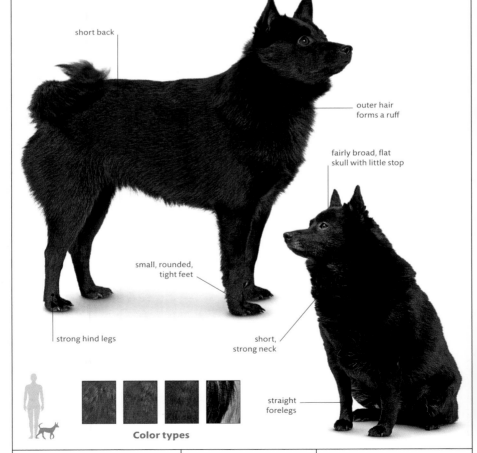

short back

outer hair forms a ruff

fairly broad, flat skull with little stop

small, rounded, tight feet

strong hind legs

short, strong neck

straight forelegs

Color types

Height: 10–13in (25–33cm)	Weight: 12–16lb (5.5–7.5kg)	Temperament: Alert, loyal

| Place of origin: France | First use: Baiting bulls | Origins: 1800s |

French Bulldog

This small, compact breed has a large head and distinctive batlike ears. It has suffered less from the breeding extremes that have afflicted its English relative (see p.39).

HISTORY These dogs are descended from the toy bulldogs of the 19th century, some of which were taken to France.
REMARK Overweight individuals may have trouble with their breathing.
OTHER NAMES Bouledogue Français.

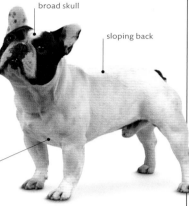

broad skull

sloping back

well-muscled body with barrel-shaped chest

Color types

| Height: 12in (31cm) | Weight: 22–28lb (10–13kg) | Temperament: Affectionate, playful |

| Place of origin: France | First use: Hunting game, guard dog | Origins: 300s |

Dogue de Bordeaux

Descended from ancient mastiff stock, the Dogue de Bordeaux is a very powerful breed with a well-furrowed face and a head so massive it ranks among the largest in the canine world.

HISTORY The sheer strength of this mastiff led to it being pitted against bulls in circus spectacles.
REMARK Careful breeding has pacified these dogs. A special breeding program was established in the 1960s.
OTHER NAMES French Mastiff.

massive, broad skull

powerful hindquarters

undershot jaw with black or red muzzle

ears set well back on head

Color types

| Height: 23–27in (58–69cm) | Weight: 80–100lb (36–45kg) | Temperament: Determined, fearless |

Place of origin: France	First use: Guarding sheep	Origins 2000 BCE

Pyrenean Mountain Dog

Sometimes confused with the Pyrenean Mastiff (see p.274), this enormous yet elegant breed can be distinguished by the color of its markings, which may be badger, wolf-gray, or pale yellow. Often, however, it is all white with distinctive black eye rims. The coarse coat enables it to withstand the severest climatic conditions.

HISTORY Of ancient, French origin, this breed is thought to have descended from the old heavy shepherd dogs found in the Pyrenees.
REMARK This giant takes three or four years to reach full maturity.
OTHER NAMES Great Pyrenees, Chien des Pyrénées.

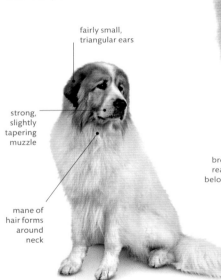

fairly small, triangular ears

strong, slightly tapering muzzle

mane of hair forms around neck

broad chest reaches just below elbows

straight, well-muscled forelegs

Height: 26–32in (65–81cm)	Weight: 90–125lb (41–57kg)	Temperament: Watchful, loyal

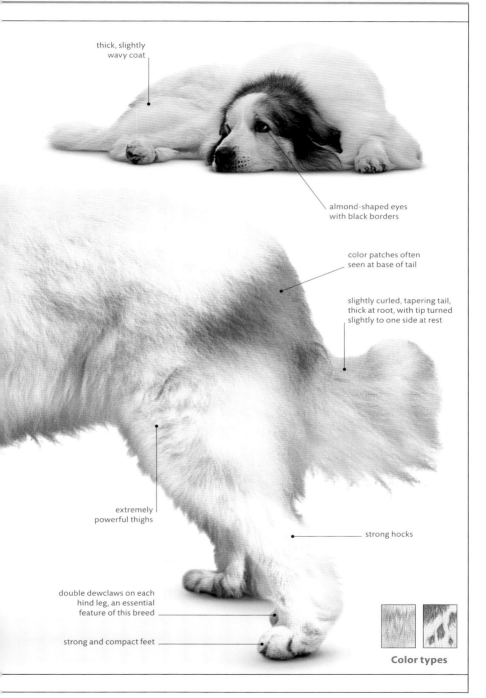

thick, slightly
wavy coat

almond-shaped eyes
with black borders

color patches often
seen at base of tail

slightly curled, tapering tail,
thick at root, with tip turned
slightly to one side at rest

extremely
powerful thighs

strong hocks

double dewclaws on each
hind leg, an essential
feature of this breed

strong and compact feet

Color types

Place of origin: Hungary	First use: Guarding sheep	Origins: 800s

Komondor

The distinctive corded coat of the Komondor reaches down to the ground. The breed is similar in appearance to its Hungarian relative, the Puli (see p.129), although much larger and with a thick-boned skeleton.

HISTORY The Komondor is well suited to its traditional role as a flock guardian. Its coat helps it to blend in with the sheep, until it leaps out at unsuspecting predators. Its name may derive from *komondor kedvu*, which means "sombre" or "angry."

REMARK The coat of the Komondor is particularly demanding. It must never be brushed or combed, for example; instead, the hair is divided into cords and trimmed to suit.

corded coat with the sensation of felt

black nose

medium-size ears

slightly arched profile to skull

adult coat starts at six to nine months; coat may take two years to become fully corded

large, powerful feet

tail extends down to hocks

Height: 26–32in (66–81cm)	Weight: 80–135lb (36–61kg)	Temperament: Protective, loyal

| Place of origin: Hungary | First use: Guarding flocks | Origins: 1200s |

Kuvasz

A working dog developed specifically as a flock guardian, as opposed to herder, the Kuvasz is a sturdily built dog with a medium-boned frame of beautiful proportions. Its coat is dense and must be pure white or ivory in coloration. Its ears are folded and lie close to the head, which is large without being bulky and has a rounded stop.

HISTORY The precise ancestry of the Kuvasz is not known. Its origins lie in Tibet, from where it traveled to Hungary via Turkey. In general appearance, it is similar to the Maremma Sheepdog (see p.271) and the Pyrenean Mountain Dog (see pp.260–261) and may share a common ancestry.

REMARK The Kuvasz has a natural affinity with children, is very protective, and forms a strong bond with its owner.

elongated, but not pointed, head

large black nose with open nostrils

straight muzzle

V-shaped ears with slightly rounded tips

medium-length, muscular neck without dewlap

wavy hair on body and legs

deep chest and long, well-sprung ribs

catlike feet with well-developed pads

| Height: 22–26in (56–66cm) | Weight: 80–110lb (36–50kg) | Temperament: Loyal, wary |

| Place of origin: Hungary | First use: Guarding flocks | Origins: 1800s |

Mudi

Less well known than its older and much better established countrymen, the Puli and Komondor (see pp.129 and 262), the Mudi is a versatile flock guardian and herder. It is both heavier and taller than the Puli, and the absence of the corded coat makes caring for the Mudi easier. The coat is usually black, but white is not uncommon, and a "pepita" form exists with an even distribution of both colors throughout its coat.

HISTORY The development of the Mudi seems to have been unplanned. It is a versatile and favorable blend of the ancient sheep-herding dogs of its Hungarian homeland. It became recognized as a separate breed in the 1930s.
REMARK Tail length in puppies is very variable, from a bobtail up to a full-length tail.
OTHER NAMES Hungarian Mudi.

erect, triangular ears

straight, short back

coat length about 2in (5cm) on body

small, rounded feet

hair on legs and muzzle shorter than on body

Color types

| Height: 14–20in (36–51cm) | Weight: 18–29lb (8–13kg) | Temperament: Adaptable, friendly |

| Place of origin: Italy | First use: Water retriever | Origins: 1300s |

Lagotto Romagnolo

This breed was developed as a gundog, but today, it is more highly valued for its truffle-hunting skills, being able to locate these valuable fungi growing underground.

HISTORY *Lagotto* translates as duck dog, revealing its original quarry.
REMARK Recognized officially in Italy only in 1993, the breed is now gaining an international following.
OTHER NAMES Romagna Water Dog.

Color types

prominent eyebrow arches

large, triangular ears

woolly, rough waterproof coat

rounded front feet and well-arched toes

| Height: 16–19in (41–48cm) | Weight: 24–35lb (11–16kg) | Temperament: Friendly, quiet |

| Place of origin: Switzerland | First use: Herding goats | Origins: 500s |

Appensell Mountain Dog

One of four breeds of Swiss mountain dogs or sennenhunds, the Appenzeller is a hardy, well-built dog that can be distinguished from the other similar breeds by its tail, which is typically curled back over its thigh.

HISTORY This dog is thought to be descended from the now extinct Molossus.
REMARK This dog has the unusual ability to both herd and guard livestock.
OTHER NAMES Appenzeller Sennenhund.

characteristic, curled tail

tan markings above each eye

white area on chest

blaze must be present on head

symmetrical facial markings

well-muscled hindquarters

| Height: 19–23in (48–58cm) | Weight: 50–55lb (23–25kg) | Temperament: Lively, loyal |

| Place of origin: Switzerland | First use: Driving cattle | Origins: 1800s |

Entlebucher Mountain Dog

The Entlebucher Mountain Dog is the smallest member of the sennenhund group. All four sennenhunds share the same symmetrical coloration of black, tan, and white.

HISTORY A native of the Swiss town of Entlebuch, this breed was traditionally used to drive cattle to market.
REMARK Renowned for its gentle attitude to children, it makes a fine pet but must be exercised regularly to prevent it from becoming obese.
OTHER NAMES Entlebucher.

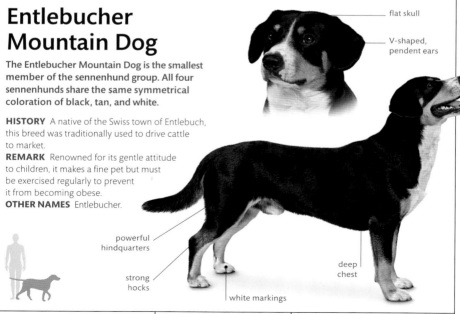

flat skull

V-shaped, pendent ears

powerful hindquarters

strong hocks

white markings

deep chest

| Height: 16½–20in (42–50cm) | Weight: 45–66lb (20–30kg) | Temperament: Obedient, friendly |

Place of origin: Switzerland	First use: Pulling weavers' carts	Origins: 100 BCE

Bernese Mountain Dog

This is the best known of the Swiss mountain dogs, or sennenhunds, and it can be readily distinguished from the other varieties by its coat. This is long and slightly wavy in appearance, without being curly. In terms of coloration and markings, it is identical to the other forms. A white blaze on the head extending between the eyes, and a white chest marking known as a cross, are essential characteristics. White paws, ideally extending no farther than the pastern, are also preferred, as is a white tip to the tail. These affectionate and responsive dogs make good family pets if they have adequate exercise.

HISTORY It is possible that crosses between native Swiss herding dogs and guard animals brought to Switzerland by the invading Roman legions laid the early foundations for this breed. In more recent times, Bernese Mountain Dogs have worked on farms, notably in the canton of Berne, frequently acting as draught dogs on market days by pulling carts laden with produce.

REMARK This breed has established a strong following in continental Europe but is not so widely kept elsewhere in the world.

OTHER NAMES Berner Sennenhund.

flat skull with slight furrow apparent

long, sloping shoulders

markings well defined, even in pups

Puppy

rounded, compact feet

Height: 23–27½in (58–70cm)	Weight: 87–90lb (40–44kg)	Temperament: Attentive, friendly

soft, silky-
textured coat,
with good sheen

compact
body shape

characteristic white
chest marking

bushy tail can
extend to just
below hocks

broad, strong,
muscular
hindquarters

medium-
length, strong,
muscular neck

Place of origin: Switzerland	First use: Pulling farmers' carts	Origins: 300s

Great Swiss Mountain Dog

This is the largest member of the four sennenhund breeds and has a smooth coat and distinctively long tail, which is held below the level of the back. Like the other group members, its coloration is basically black and tan, the tan areas bordered by both black and white markings. White areas form a blaze, extending down to the chest, and are also present on the toes and on the tip of the tail.

characteristic tan markings above the eyes

HISTORY This dog has a long history on Swiss farms. It declined during the mid-1800s, however, and by the turn of the 20th century had almost vanished. The few pure-bred individuals left were crossed with smooth-coated St. Bernards (opposite). They are now once again well established and were introduced into the US in 1968.

REMARK Despite their size, grooming their coats is easy and straightforward.

OTHER NAMES Grosser Schweizer Sennenhund.

triangular ears set high on head

long tail terminates in white tip

broad, powerful chest

dense, shiny topcoat with thick undercoat

rounded, compact feet with well-arched toes

Height: 23½–28½in (60–72cm)	Weight: 130–135lb (59–61kg)	Temperament: Active, calm

| Place of origin: Switzerland | First use: Searching and rescuing | Origins: 1000s |

St. Bernard

The St. Bernard is a dog of imposing proportions—tall, broad, massively boned, and heavy—but it is always dignified in expression and carriage. Both smooth- and rough-haired forms of this breed exist, white and red, or red and brownish yellow being the most favored color combinations.

very muscular neck

Smooth-haired form

very dense, smooth-lying hair

HISTORY The St. Bernard is descended from the Roman Molossus, which was the original mastiff stock introduced into the Alps by the Romans some 2,000 years ago. The first St. Bernard was bred at the Hospice of St. Bernard de Menthon about 1,000 years ago.
REMARK This powerful dog requires careful handling when out walking on a lead.
OTHER NAMES St. Bernhardshund.

slightly arched, massive skull

short, square muzzle

black shading on the ears and face common

deep chest

Rough-haired form

dense, flat hair

large, compact feet with strong toes

| Height: 24–28in (61–71cm) | Weight: 110–200lb (50–91kg) | Temperament: Tranquil, benevolent |

Place of origin: Croatia	First use: Carriage dog	Origins: 1400s

Dalmatian

color of eye rims matches that of spots

A bold, spotted patterning offset against a clear, white background makes this perhaps the most distinctive of all dog breeds. Black-spotted Dalmatians are far more common than their liver-colored counterparts. The spots should be round in shape, clearly defined, and not overlapping. Those on the extremities should be smaller in size than elsewhere on the body. Dalmatian pups are pure white at birth and develop their spots only later.

HISTORY This breed originated in Dalmatia, the region after which it is named, in what is now Croatia. It became very popular as a carriage dog in the 1800s, trotting alongside carriages and acting as a deterrent to highwaymen.

REMARK The Dalmatian has attracted considerable attention through Dodie Smith's book *A Hundred and One Dalmatians*, which was first made into an extremely popular children's cartoon film in 1961 by the Walt Disney Studios. Unfortunately, the breed has a higher than usual incidence of congenital deafness.

sleek, glossy coat

short, hard, dense hair

ears are set high on head and taper to a rounded point

rounded, well-arched, catlike feet

marking on ears should be well-broken spots

straight forelegs

elbows held close to body

rounded hindquarters

tail should reach level of hocks

Color types

Height: 22–24in (56–61cm)	Weight: 50–55lb (23–25kg)	Temperament: Quiet, alert

| Place of origin: Italy | First use: Guarding flocks | Origins: 100 BCE |

Maremma Sheepdog

White is the predominant color of this majestic sheepdog, sometimes with ivory or pale fawn shadings evident, notably on the ears. It is a muscular, powerful dog with a long, somewhat harsh coat. Its head is large and bearlike.

HISTORY This breed may be descended from the earliest flock guardians and may have been kept in the Maremma and Abruzzi regions of Italy since before Roman times.
REMARK This majestic breed is highly intelligent but is not easy to train, having a rather independent and aloof character.
OTHER NAMES Pastore Abruzzese.

large, conical head

thick ruff of hair

strong, medium-length back

tail has dense covering of hair

large shoulders and thick legs

close-fitting, slightly wavy coat

hind feet more oval than front feet

| Height: 23½–28½in (60–73cm) | Weight: 66–100lb (30–45kg) | Temperament: Responsive, protective |

| Place of origin: Italy | First use: Guard dog, dog-fighting | Origins: 100 BCE |

Neapolitan Mastiff

This ancient breed of dog has a slow, ponderous, bearlike gait, in common with other mastiff-type breeds, and a very large head. From the head, prominent dewlaps of skin extend in folds down to the neck, thus producing a multi-chinned appearance. In spite of its aggressive history as a fighting dog, the Neapolitan Mastiff is generally a calm, placid, and friendly animal, especially with people whom it knows well.

HISTORY The ancestry of the Neapolitan Mastiff may extend back to the Molossus breed of Roman times. Its enormous strength has seen it used for fighting, although it has also been a guard dog and a beast of burden, pulling carts. It was only in 1946 that steps were taken, by painter Piero Scanziani, to safeguard the breed's future. He established a kennel for the breed and did much to promote its survival.

REMARK Like most giant breeds, the Neapolitan Mastiff is sadly quite short-lived, with a life expectancy of just 7–10 years.

OTHER NAMES Mastino Napoletano.

broad, flat skull

deep, spherical shape to the head

dewlap hanging from lower jaw to midpoint of neck

small, well-spaced ears, positioned forward on head

very muscular, short, stocky neck

long, well-sprung ribs

broad, muscular croup with slight slope apparent

tail is thick at root

broad, well-muscled chest

oval feet with close-arched toes

short, dense, fine coat, with hard texture and good sheen

forefeet slightly larger than hindfeet

Color types

| Height: 26–29in (65–75cm) | Weight: 110–150lb (50–68kg) | Temperament: Protective, alert |

Place of origin: Italy	First use: Farm work	Origins: 1100s

Cane Corso

Descended from mastiff stock, this breed is related to the Neapolitan Mastiff (opposite). It has proved to be a versatile working dog, used as a cattle herder and livestock guardian. It has, however, now become more popular simply as a companion.

HISTORY The breed had nearly died out by the 1970s but was rescued just in time.

REMARK Its ancestry probably extends back to mastiffs kept in ancient Rome. As with other similar dogs, it does have a tendency to drool.

OTHER NAMES Dogo di Puglia, Cane Corso Italiano.

strong, square muzzle

long broad thighs

Puppy

straight, powerful forelegs

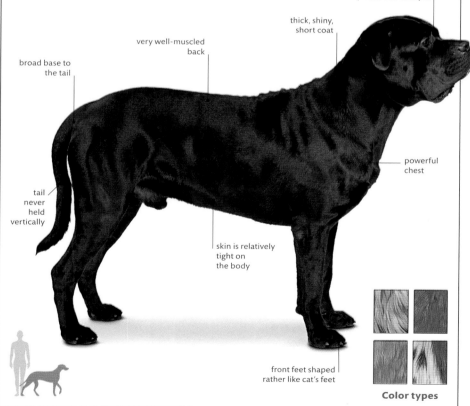

large head with a well-defined stop between the eyes

thick, shiny, short coat

very well-muscled back

broad base to the tail

powerful chest

tail never held vertically

skin is relatively tight on the body

front feet shaped rather like cat's feet

Color types

Height: 24–27in (60–68cm)	Weight: 88–110lb (40–50kg)	Temperament: Protective, loyal

Place of origin: Spain	First use: Guarding flocks	Origins: 3000 BCE

Pyrenean Mastiff

Although the Pyrenean Mastiff is slightly smaller than the Pyrenean Mountain Dog (see pp.260–261), they share a common ancestry. The Mastiff is a robustly built, symmetrical dog with a large head, powerful neck (often with excessive dewlap), and a deep body, all supported on very sturdy legs.

HISTORY Like the Pyrenean Mountain Dog, the Mastiff descended from dogs brought to Spain by early Mediterranean seafarers.

REMARK For its enormous size, this breed has a relatively small appetite and is light on its feet.

OTHER NAMES Perro Mastin del Pireneo.

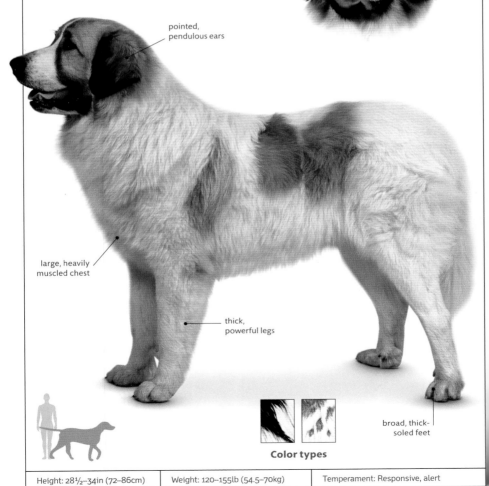

heavily boned, broad skull

pointed, pendulous ears

large, heavily muscled chest

thick, powerful legs

broad, thick-soled feet

Color types

Height: 28½–34in (72–86cm)	Weight: 120–155lb (54.5–70kg)	Temperament: Responsive, alert

Place of origin: Spain	First use: Guarding livestock	Origins: 800s

Spanish Mastiff

This breed has the typical mastiff appearance: a broad head with a relatively short muzzle, a massive chest, and a characteristic dewlap on the neck. The ears are pointed and pendulous but are not large.

HISTORY These dogs have been used to guard farm stock in the hills of Spain for centuries. The origins of the breed may lie with ancient mastiff stock brought to the region by the Romans. It has now attracted attention from dog owners in other parts of Europe and in the US.

REMARK The Spanish Mastiff is not usually aggressive toward people but may be combative with other dogs.

OTHER NAMES Mastín Español.

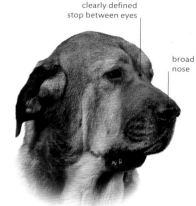

clearly defined stop between eyes

broad nose

ears set well back on head

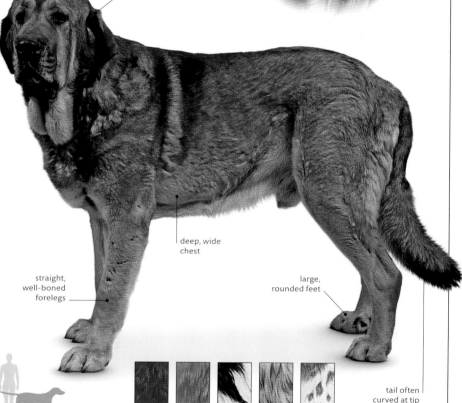

deep, wide chest

straight, well-boned forelegs

large, rounded feet

tail often curved at tip

Color types

Height: 26–29in (66–74cm)	Weight: 110–135lb (50–61kg)	Temperament: Obedient, protective

Place of origin: Balearic Islands	First use: Guarding farms	Origins: 1700s

Perro de Pastor Mallorquin

A well-defined head and a tapering muzzle give this breed a distinctive appearance. The tail is long and tapering toward the tip. Both long- and short-haired forms exist.

HISTORY The Perro de Pastor Mallorquin is native to the Balearic Islands, off the coast of Spain, and is a utility animal.

REMARK This dog was bred to withstand the heat of the Mediterranean sun and can be fierce and aggressive.

OTHER NAMES Ca de Bestiar, Majorca Shepherd Dog.

finely chiseled facial features

powerful back

muscular thighs

well-boned forelegs

prominent, hard nails

Color types

Height: 24–29in (62–73cm)	Weight: 77–88lb (35–40kg)	Temperament: Pugnacious, brave

Place of origin: Balearic Islands	First use: Baiting bulls, fighting	Origins: 1800s

Perro de Presa Mallorquin

This mastiff-type breed is fierce and formidable, heavily muscled, and with powerful, gripping jaws. The coat is very short and sleek, usually yellow in color, with patches of lighter or darker colors.

HISTORY The popularity of this dog has declined with the outlawing of bullbaiting and the decline of dogfighting.

REMARK This breed needs good training from a very early age.

OTHER NAMES Ca de Bou, Majorca Mastiff, Majorca Bulldog.

massively broad head

sleek, tight-fitting coat

wide, heavily muscled chest

sturdy, powerful legs

Color types

Height: 20–23in (51–58cm)	Weight: 66–84lb (30–38kg)	Temperament: Independent, fierce

| Place of origin: Israel | First use: Guarding livestock | Origins: 2000 BCE |

Canaan Dog

This medium-size, robustly made, spitz-type dog has been indigenous to the region encompassed by modern Israel for centuries. The ancestors of today's Canaan were pariah dogs, which have traditionally been domesticated to act as flock guardians, protecting the tribespeople's goats against jackals and other predators.

HISTORY A program to breed these dogs so that the puppies resembled their parents in appearance (breeding true) was begun from 1935 by a Dr. Menzel and her husband. Most of the stock seen around the world today originated from the Shaar Hagai Kennels in Jerusalem.
REMARK In spite of its feral origins, this dog is easily trained.
OTHER NAMES Kelef K'naani.

broad, erect ears with rounded tips

almond-shaped, dark brown rims

straight, strong forelegs

hard pads

muscular neck

thick, brushlike tail curves over back

straight forelegs

short to medium-length coat

rounded, strong feet

powerful nails

Color types

| Height: 19–24in (48–61cm) | Weight: 35–55lb (16–25kg) | Temperament: Intelligent, resourceful |

Place of origin: Portugal	First use: Guarding flocks	Origins: 1800s

Estrela Mountain Dog

powerful head
and rounded skull

Two distinct coat types are associated with this breed. The longer-coated form displays more abundant feathering than its smooth-coated counterpart, although a double-layered coat affords both of them excellent protection against the worst of the elements. The large size and a loud bark could make them intimidating, but they are usually friendly dogs.

HISTORY This breed is named after the Estrela region in central Portugal, where it was traditionally used as a flock guardian.
REMARK This is not a demonstrative breed. Like all powerful dogs, it requires thorough training.
OTHER NAMES Cão da Serra da Estrela.

Short-haired form

long, well-furnished tail

slightly sloping croup

very powerful shoulders

Long-haired form

solidly muscled, straight legs

hind dewclaws present

Color types

Height: 24½–28½in (62–72cm)	Weight: 66–110lb (30–50kg)	Temperament: Loyal, active

Place of origin: Portugal	First use: Guard dog	Origins: 1800s

Rafeiro do Alentejo

This powerful dog has a body not unlike that of a St. Bernard (see p.269) but has a head shaped like a bear's. This is the largest of the Portuguese breeds and is an imposing animal.

HISTORY This breed originated in the Alentejo region of southern Portugal. The Spanish Mastiff (see p.275) may have contributed to its ancestry, along with the Estrela Mountain Dog (opposite).
REMARK This breed is now quite scarce and regarded as vulnerable.
OTHER NAMES Portuguese Watchdog.

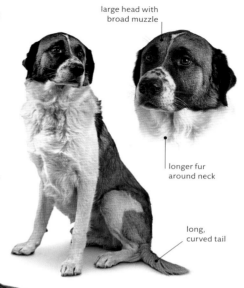

large head with broad muzzle

longer fur around neck

long, curved tail

solid, muscular back

short, stocky, powerful neck

well-boned, straight forelegs

distinctive markings, often spotted in appearance

smooth-coated legs

Color types

Height: 25–29in (64–74cm)	Weight: 77–132lb (35–60kg)	Temperament: Alert, independent

Place of origin: Portugal	First use: Guarding and herding flocks	Origins: 1500s

Portuguese Cattle Dog

This rugged, powerfully built dog has traditionally been used as a herding animal in the rocky, less accessible parts of Portugal. Its rather long body has a strong, weatherproof, coarse outercoat over a finer, thicker undercoat, making it ideal for the often harsh conditions of this region.

HISTORY The isolated nature of the area of Portugal where this dog originated—Castro Laboreiro—makes it likely that only local breeds were used in its development.
REMARK This breed is still widely employed in its homeland for herding and guarding stock.
OTHER NAMES Cão de Castro Laboreiro.

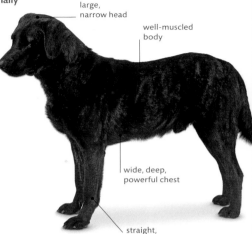

large, narrow head

well-muscled body

wide, deep, powerful chest

straight, well-boned legs

Color types

Height: 20–24in (51–61cm)	Weight: 50–75lb (23–34kg)	Temperament: Alert, brave

Place of origin: Russia and Finland	First use: Hunting big game	Origins: 1700s

Russian-European Laika

This is a powerfully built dog, characterized by its black-and-white coloration and pricked ears. If present, its tail is distinctively curled, but this breed is often born without a tail.

HISTORY The Russian-European Laika evolved near the border shared by Russia and Finland. Already an intrepid moose and wolf hunter, crossings with the fearless Utchak Sheepdog widened its role to encompass bear hunting.
REMARK This breed has a lot of energy and is not a dog for city life.
OTHER NAMES Karelian Bear Laika, Russko-Evropeĭskaya Láĭka.

large, prominent, upright ears

conical head

tail curled (if present)

wide, thick-soled feet

broad, powerful chest

Height: 19–23in (48–58cm)	Weight: 45–50lb (20.5–23kg)	Temperament: Independent, brave

| Place of origin: Russia | First use: Hunting bears | Origins: 1800s |

East Siberian Laika

This member of the laika family is large, squarely built, and has a slightly spiky coat that stands away from the body. Its head is broad, its expression is alert, and its ears are large and erect.

shorter hair on head

Color types

HISTORY This breed was used for pulling sledges, as well as for hunting such quarry as bear, elk, and reindeer.
REMARK Laikas were used as test animals in the early Soviet space experiments.
OTHER NAMES
Vostotchno-Sibirskaia Laika.

well-spaced, erect ears

well-arched toes

thickly muscled neck

| Height: 21–25in (53–64cm) | Weight: 40–50lb (18–23kg) | Temperament: Obedient, loyal |

| Place of origin: Russia | First use: Hunting bears | Origins: 1800s |

West Siberian Laika

The long legs and wolflike face of the West Siberian Laika give it an apparent lightness of bearing that belies its power and immense endurance.

erect ears

prominent nostrils

tightly curled tail

HISTORY This breed is more firmly established than its East Siberian relative (above) and is certainly more numerous.
REMARK West Siberian Laikas possess great hunting instincts and are not even intimidated by bears.

short, dense double coat

Color types

| Height: 21–24in (53–61cm) | Weight: 40–50lb (18–23kg) | Temperament: Active, lively |

Place of origin: Russia	First use: Pulling sleighs	Origins: 1800s

Siberian Husky

Although smaller and lighter than some other breeds of sled dog, the Siberian Husky is quick and athletic, agile and strong, as well as a tireless worker. This medium-size dog has a dense and woolly undercoat, well protected by a covering of tougher guard hairs, giving the dog a fullness of form and providing excellent insulation against the raw cold of its Siberian homeland.

HISTORY Siberian Huskies were developed by the Chukchi people of northeast Asia as their only means of transportation.
REMARK Communal howling is a feature of this breed. An amazing range of coat colors and markings is permitted.
OTHER NAMES Arctic Husky.

medium-sized, triangular ears

almond-shaped eyes, sometimes blue

medium-length muzzle

thick, bushy tail

strong, deep chest

shoulder fits tightly to rib cage

relatively long legs

well-furred, slightly webbed, oval feet

Color types

Height: 20–23½in (51–60cm)	Weight: 35–60lb (16–27kg)	Temperament: Dependable, energetic

| Place of origin: Russia | First use: Herding reindeer | Origins: 1600s |

Samoyed

This far-northern breed has a very full coat, consisting of a long, weather-resistant outercoat covering an extremely dense and woolly undercoat. Samoyeds make popular and attractive pets, as well as being highly valued as sled dogs.

HISTORY Today's breed is said to derive from just 12 dogs brought out of the Arctic by explorers and travelers. The basic Samoyed was developed by the once-nomadic Samoyede tribe, who now live in the area of Asia east of the Ural Mountains.
REMARK Antarctic explorers Scott and Amundsen both used Samoyeds.
OTHER NAMES Samoyedskaja.

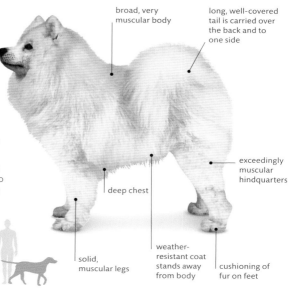

broad, very muscular body

long, well-covered tail is carried over the back and to one side

exceedingly muscular hindquarters

deep chest

solid, muscular legs

weather-resistant coat stands away from body

cushioning of fur on feet

| Height: 18–22in (46–56cm) | Weight: 50–65lb (23–29.5kg) | Temperament: Companionable |

| Place of origin: South Korea | First use: Hunting | Origins: 1000 |

Jindo

This breed is named after the island of Jindo, lying off the southwest coast of South Korea, which is where it was developed.

HISTORY Jindos share their ancestry with the New Guinea Singing Dog (see p.291).
REMARK These dogs are now recognized in Korean law as a National Treasure.
OTHER NAMES Korean Jindo, Jindo-kae, Jindo-kyon.

males have larger heads than females

Color types

medium-length, double coat

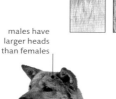

upright, triangular, forward-pointing ears, extending out to the sides

brown eyes

rounded feet with strong pads

| Height: 18–22in (46–56cm) | Weight: 30–50lb (13.5–22.5kg) | Temperament: Alert, loyal |

Place of origin: China	First use: Guard dog, pulling carts	Origins: 100s

Chow Chow

The rough-coated form (shown here) is most commonly seen; its coat is profuse, thick, and straight. The smooth-coated form reveals the squarely built, hugely muscled outline of this courageous and powerful dog. The Chow Chow is bred in solid colors from tan or red to silver-gray or black, while white is rare.

HISTORY Although popular in China for at least 2,000 years, the Chow first appeared in Britain only in the late 19th century. In its homeland, it was used to pull carts and as a guard dog. Its fur was also a valuable commodity, as was its flesh for human consumption.

REMARK The unusual tongue of the Chow Chow is, like that of the Shar Pei (opposite), blue-black in coloration.

broad, flat skull

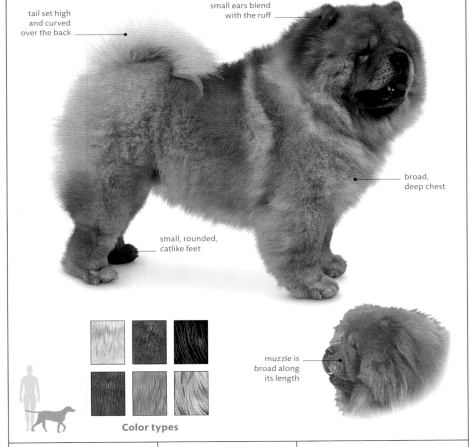

tail set high and curved over the back

small ears blend with the ruff

broad, deep chest

small, rounded, catlike feet

muzzle is broad along its length

Color types

Height: 18–22in (46–56cm)	Weight: 45–70lb (20–32kg)	Temperament: Alert, independent

| Place of origin: China | First use: Dogfighting | Origins: 1500s |

Shar Pei

The bristly coat of this dog is quite distinctive, but the folds of loose skin covering its body and especially its head, giving it a permanent frown, are by far its most striking feature.

HISTORY This ancient breed is thought to result from crosses between mastiffs and certain Nordic breeds. It was in danger of extinction until a Hong Kong fancier established stock in the US and elsewhere.

REMARK The loose skin was originally developed for the gruesome purpose of making the animal impossible to pin down in a dog fight.

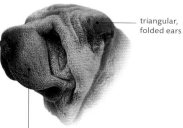

triangular, folded ears

relatively long, broad muzzle

dark, almond-shaped eyes

rounded tail set high on back

strong, short neck with loose skin

deep, broad chest

ear tips point toward eyes

abundant, loose folds of skin

Color types

Shar Pei pup

| Height: 18–20in (46–51cm) | Weight: 35–45lb (16–20kg) | Temperament: Independent, aloof |

| Place of origin: Japan | First use: Hunting big game | Origins: 1600s |

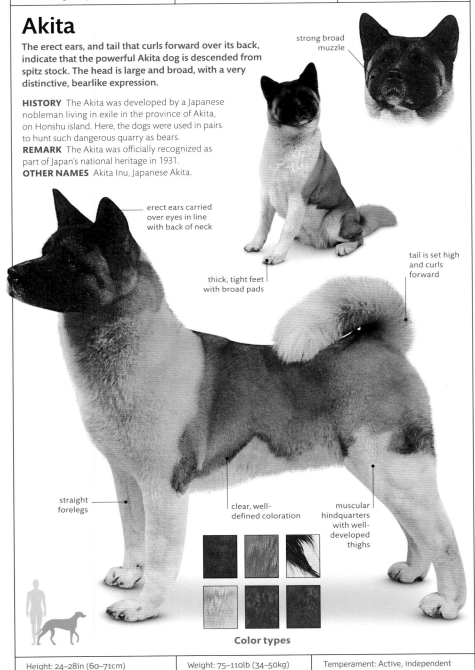

Akita

The erect ears, and tail that curls forward over its back, indicate that the powerful Akita dog is descended from spitz stock. The head is large and broad, with a very distinctive, bearlike expression.

HISTORY The Akita was developed by a Japanese nobleman living in exile in the province of Akita, on Honshu island. Here, the dogs were used in pairs to hunt such dangerous quarry as bears.

REMARK The Akita was officially recognized as part of Japan's national heritage in 1931.

OTHER NAMES Akita Inu, Japanese Akita.

strong broad muzzle

erect ears carried over eyes in line with back of neck

tail is set high and curls forward

thick, tight feet with broad pads

straight forelegs

clear, well-defined coloration

muscular hindquarters with well-developed thighs

Color types

| Height: 24–28in (60–71cm) | Weight: 75–110lb (34–50kg) | Temperament: Active, independent |

Place of origin: Japan	First use: Hunting small game	Origins: 1000 BCE

Shiba Inu

This dog is similar to the Akita (opposite), but it is smaller in size, its name translating from the Japanese as "small dog." The keen and alert appearance results from the broad forehead, pointed muzzle, and triangular ears that incline slightly, forward.

HISTORY The origins of the Shiba Inu breed go back more than 2,000 years in Japan, with the possibility of Chow Chow (see p.284) blood in its ancestry.
REMARK The Shiba Inu is the most commonly kept of the native breeds in Japan.
OTHER NAMES Brushwood Dog.

small, well-shaped oval eyes

tapering muzzle

short, level back

thick, sickle-shaped tail

harsh, double coat

Color types

Height: 14–15½in (36–40cm)	Weight: 20–30lb (9–14kg)	Temperament: Independent, industrious

Place of origin: Japan	First use: Dogfighting	Origins: 1800s

Tosa Inu

A sturdy, very powerful frame and a well-muscled physique, coupled with capable jaws and solid teeth, combine to make the Tosa Inu a formidable combat dog in its native Japan.

HISTORY Many of the Tosa's physical characteristics reflect its mastiff origins; it is, however, a modern fighting-dog breed dating only from about the 1860s.
REMARK This rare breed is named after Tosa province, on the Japanese island of Shikoku, where it was first bred.
OTHER NAMES Tosa Fighting Dog.

well-developed cheek muscles

tail positioned high on back

short, close-lying coat

broad muzzle with powerful jaws

Color types

Height: 24½–25½in (62–65cm)	Weight: 200lb (90kg)	Temperament: Stoic, relentless

Place of origin: Japan	First use: Retrieving game, ratting	Origins: 1700s

Japanese Terrier

This terrier has a relatively small head and distinctive tricolored coat. It is predominantly white with black and tan areas of the coat proportionately small in size, creating an attractive, speckled appearance.

HISTORY Descended from the Smooth Fox Terrier (see p.212), which was introduced to Japan in 1702, the subsequent development of this breed centered on the cities of Kobe and Yokohama.
REMARK In Japan this dog can be seen working as a waterfowl retriever.
OTHER NAMES Nippon Terrier.

smooth, short coat with random speckling

ears folded forward and set high on head

long, straight forelegs

Height: 13in (33cm)	Weight: 10–13lb (4.5–6kg)	Temperament: Affectionate, adaptable

Place of origin: Japan	First use: Hunting large game	Origins: 1000 BCE

Ainu

Resembling the Akita (see p.286), although smaller in size, the Ainu's foxlike head shape and curled tail carriage are typical spitz characteristics. Although not encouraged, a dark bluish tongue may occur, as with the Chow Chow and Shar Pei (see pp.284–285).

HISTORY Developed in Japan by the Ainu people, this handsome breed is thought to be the oldest of all the Japanese dog breeds.
REMARK Careful training and socializing can make this dog a good companion and home guardian.
OTHER NAMES Hokkaido Dog.

small, pricked ears

short, broad muzzle

broad, deep chest

short, thick coat standing off from the body

Color types

Height: 18–22in (46–56cm)	Weight: 45–65lb (20.5–29.5kg)	Temperament: Brave, loyal

Place of origin: Tibet	First use: Guarding flocks	Origins: 900s

Tibetan Mastiff

The formidable size of the Tibetan Mastiff makes it an excellent guard dog, yet it is responsive to training and usually proves gentle, even with children. Its distinctive, high-set tail curls to one side. In Tibet, it is customary for the dog to wear a red yak's hair collar as a sign of its status.

HISTORY It is possible that many of today's European mastiff breeds are descended from the Tibetan Mastiff, which spread eastward with the armies of Alexander the Great.
REMARK The female Tibetan Mastiff may come into season only once rather than twice a year, as is usual with other breeds.

broad, massive head

high-set tail

fairly long, thick, double coat

strong, muscular body

sturdy legs

very large, powerful feet

Color types

Height: 24–28in (61–71cm)	Weight: 140–180lb (64–82kg)	Temperament: Brave, loyal

Place of origin: Canary Islands	First use: Dogfighting	Origins: 1800s

Canary Dog

Bearing a strong likeness to the Perro de Presa Mallorquin (see p.276), the Canary Dog is a powerfully built, square-headed, mastiff-type dog. Fawn or brindle is the usual coloration, although white markings are also seen, and the coat itself is short and rough over slightly mobile skin.

HISTORY The ancestry of the Canary Dog involved crosses between the extinct Bardino Majero and the Mastiff (see pp.232–233), the latter being developed in Great Britain and introduced into the Canaries in the 1800s. The Canary Dog was used for dogfighting.

REMARK Having almost become extinct following Spain's ban on dogfighting and its declining use as a cattle herder, the Canary Dog is today being seen more often overseas.

OTHER NAMES Perro de Presa Canario.

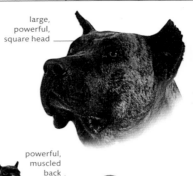

large, powerful, square head

powerful, muscled back

Adult and puppy

slightly raised rump

blunt, broad muzzle

very broad, heavily muscled chest

short, coarse-textured coat

strong, heavily boned legs

Color types

Height: 21½–25½in (55–65cm)	Weight: 84–106lb (38–48kg)	Temperament: Determined, forceful

Place of origin: Morocco	First use: Guard dog	Origins: 1000s

Aidi

White is the preferred color for this breed, although it does occur in a variety of colors. The coat is dense and fleecelike, offering protection from the searing desert heat and freezing cold nights in the Atlas Mountains of Morocco.

HISTORY The ancestors of this breed were probably introduced from Spain. It has served as guard dog and tracker, locating game that the faster Sloughi (see p.199) can then run to ground.

REMARK The Moroccan Kennel Association is helping to ensure the survival of the Aidi.

OTHER NAMES Chien de l'Atlas.

muscular neck

heavily plumed tail is desirable

straight, well-boned forelegs

tail extends to level of hocks

Color types

Height: 21–24in (53–61cm)	Weight: 50–55lb (23–25kg)	Temperament: Alert, highly strung

---

Place of origin: New Guinea	First use: None (pariah)	Origins: Unknown

New Guinea Singing Dog

This dog is a pariah, meaning it was semi-domesticated but could also live wild. It is of medium size with a coat of various shades of red, sometimes with white markings.

HISTORY It is native to New Guinea, being found with tribes in both the lowlands and highlands and is prized for its distinctive, musical voice.

REMARK This breed does not like prolonged handling.

broad head

plumed tail

white sometimes present on coat

muscular physique

Color types

Height: 14–15in (35–38cm)	Weight: 18–22lb (8–10kg)	Temperament: Aloof, unpredictable

DESIGNER DOGS

THERE IS OFTEN confusion around the description of "designer dog," and it might seem that such dogs are simply crossbreeds, resulting from the mating of two different recognized breeds. Yet these matings are not carried out randomly in the vast majority of cases but have deliberate aims behind them.

The idea is typically to combine the characters of the two breeds, to create a type of dog that will be a better pet, and maybe to make it cuter, too. This is especially significant now that most breeds are no longer being kept for the original purposes for which they were bred. Their sizes are not standardized.

Place of origin: Australia	First use: Guide dog	Origins: 1989

Labradoodle

The Labradoodle marked the starting point that triggered the increasing number of designer dog crosses that exist today. It came about as the result of a quest to create a hypoallergenic guide dog in Australia and entailed matings of Labrador Retrievers (see p.65) with Standard Poodles (see p.250), although smaller poodles have now also been used.

HISTORY Prior to this, Labradoodles had been bred in the US in the 1950s but generated little interest.
REMARK Labradoodles today may be paired with each other, resulting in a more standardized appearance.

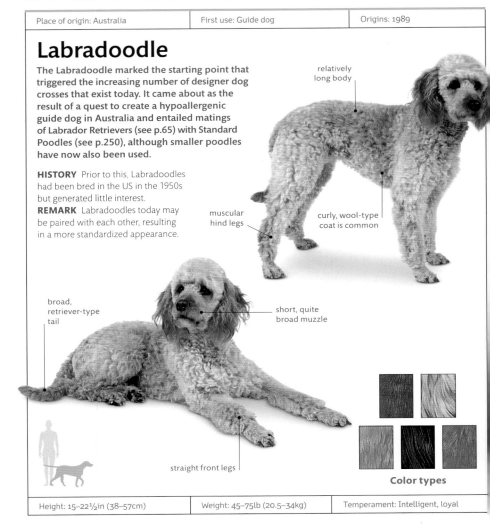

relatively long body

curly, wool-type coat is common

muscular hind legs

broad, retriever-type tail

short, quite broad muzzle

straight front legs

Color types

Height: 15–22½in (38–57cm)	Weight: 45–75lb (20.5–34kg)	Temperament: Intelligent, loyal

Place of origin: US	First use: Companion	Origins: 1960s

Cockapoo

The origins and appearance of the Cockapoo are varied, because of the range of ancestral breeds that could contribute to their breeding. It might be either the American (see p.56) or English (see p.59) form of the Cocker Spaniel, for example, combined with either Miniature (see p.44) or Toy (see p.43) Poodles. Again, the result can be dogs that tend not to shed and may be hypoallergenic.

HISTORY These were one of the first crosses to become popular, even before the Labradoodle (opposite) itself.
REMARK Standard Poodles (see p.250) tend not to be used in this case, because of their larger size.
OTHER NAMES Cockerpoo, Cockerdoodle, Spoodle.

expressive eyes

hair clipped back to minimize grooming

long, pendulous ears

straight, well-boned forelegs

low-set, long tail

relatively compact body shape

Color types

Height: 14–15in (35–38cm)	Weight: 20–25lb (9–11kg)	Temperament: Friendly, lively

Place of origin: US	First use: Companion	Origins: 1990s

Goldendoodle

These popular dogs are the result of matings between Golden Retrievers (see p.64) and poodles, often Standard Poodles (see p.250). Light colors tend to be favored, but the range can be wide.

HISTORY Both miniature and standard forms of the Goldendoodle have been created, with this size difference due to their poodle ancestors.
REMARK The style of coat can be wavy, curly, or shaggy, varying even in littermates.
OTHER NAMES Groodle.

broad skull with evident crest

powerful neck

feathering on the tail

straight, well-boned forelegs

attractively colored, wavy coat

well-spaced, dark eyes

Color types

Height: 21–24in (53–61cm)	Weight: 45–100lb (20–45kg)	Temperament: Friendly, loyal

Place of origin: US	First use: Companion	Origins: 1980s

Puggle

Although not likely to be hypoallergenic, as it does not have a poodle ancestry, the Puggle has become one of the most popular designer dogs today. It combines the Pug (see p.49) with the Beagle (see p.142) and so is always short-haired, like its ancestors.

HISTORY A breeder in Wisconsin is credited with creating the first crosses of this type. The Puggle's popularity soared during the first decade of the 21st century.

REMARK As has become accepted practice, so the name of the Puggle (Pug + Beagle) combines that of its parents, meaning that it is usually possible to figure out the ancestry of designer dogs on this basis.

OTHER NAMES Beagle-Pug.

rounded skull

large, floppy ears

wrinkling on the face

distinct stop in front of the eyes

sloping back

thick tail, not tightly curled

short muzzle

barrel-shaped body

legs longer than a Pug

Color types

Height: 13–15in (33–38cm)	Weight: 18–30lb (8–14kg)	Temperament: Lively, energetic

Place of origin: US	First use: Gundog	Origins: 1980s

Labradinger

Fashion has played a part in the world of designer dogs, with some crosses proving more popular than others. Literally hundreds have been made, and some are much rarer than others, which means it may be hard to track down the resulting puppies. The Labradinger can prove to be both a versatile gundog and active companion, in view of its ancestry.

HISTORY The Labradinger is the result of crossing a Labrador Retriever (see p.65) with an English Springer Spaniel (see p.62).
REMARK This is one of the less sought-after crosses, possibly because unlike the Puggle (opposite), it does not have a stand-out appearance.
OTHER NAMES Labradinger Retriever, Springador, Springerdor.

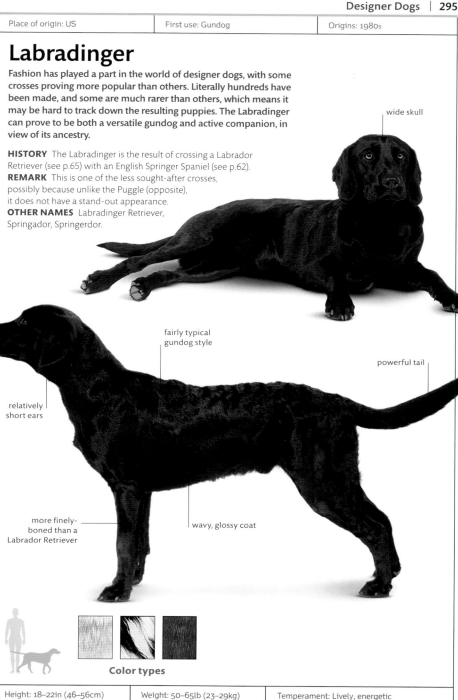

wide skull

fairly typical gundog style

powerful tail

relatively short ears

more finely-boned than a Labrador Retriever

wavy, glossy coat

Color types

Height: 18–22in (46–56cm)	Weight: 50–65lb (23–29kg)	Temperament: Lively, energetic

DOG CREDITS

Dorling Kindersley is greatly indebted to the many owners and breeders who allowed their dogs to be photographed for this book; without their help and enthusiastic cooperation, it could not have been produced. While every effort has been made to accredit all those involved, the publisher will gladly incorporate additional information in future editions. The dogs and the names of their owners are listed in page order.

COMPANION DOGS
- **34** *Kyi Leo* D. Weber
- **35** *Bulldog* C. Thomas & G. Godfrey
- **36** *Cavalier King Charles* T. Boardman; Hull; *King Charles Spaniel* (head) D. Fry
- **37** *Chihuahua* S. Lee
- **38** *Mexican Hairless* S. Corrone; H. Hernandez; Terry; L. Woods; *Inca Hairless* C. & B. Christofferson
- **39** *Havanese* K. Olausson; *American Eskimo Dog*
- **40** *Giant German Spitz* A. Fiebich; M. Horhold; *German Spitz: Mittel* Bodimeade
- **41** *German Spitz: Klein* K. Hill & Trendle; *Pomeranian* Powell & Medcraft
- **42** *Keeshond* M.R. West; *Continental Toy Spaniel: Phalene* J. Meijer
- **43** *Continental Toy Spaniel: Papillon* Urquhart & Urquhart; *Toy Poodle* S. Riddett & Moody
- **44** *Miniature Poodle* Treagus
- **45** *Löwchen* K. Donovan
- **46** *Italian Greyhound* S. Dunning
- **47** *Basenji* J. Gostynska; *Volpino Italiano* A . Hammond
- **48** *Pekingese* Stannard
- **49** *Pug* N. Tarbitt; *Shih Tzu* J. Franks
- **50** *Chinese Crested Dog* (Hairless) Moon; (Powder Puff) S. Wrenn
- **51** *Tibetan Spaniel* J. Lilley; *Tibetan Terrier* T. & A. Medlow
- **52** *Lhasa Apso* L. Chamberlain; *Japanese Chin* J. Jolley
- **53** *Japanese Spitz* S. Jones; *Maltese* U. Campanis-Brockmann
- **54** *Bichon Frise* S.M. Dunger; *Coton de Tulear* P. Zinkstok & H. & R. Bonneveld
- **55** *Bolognese* L. Stannard;

GUNDOGS
- **56** *American Cocker Spaniel* (sitting) L. Pichard; (standing) W. Weymans
- **57** *Chesapeake Bay Retriever* P. Taylor-Williams
- **58** *Clumber Spaniel* R. Furness;

(standing) S. Queen, Monaghan, S. Boden
- **59** *Cocker Spaniel* (puppy) T. Morgan & N. Memery; (black and white) M. Robinson; (standing) L. & P. Doppelreiter-Baines
- **60** *Curly-coated Retriever* A. Skingley
- **61** *English Setter* Grimsdell
- **62** *Gordon Setter* M. Justice; *English Springer Spaniel* D. & J. Miller; (standing) C. Woodbridge & T. Dunsdon
- **63** *Field Spaniel* G. Thwaites; (standing) C. H. and J. Holgate; *Flat-coated Retriever* A. Youens
- **64** *Golden Retriever* R.A. Strudwick; C. Carter
- **65** *Labrador Retriever* M. Prior; C. Coode
- **66** *Pointer* A. Morgan
- **67** *Slovakian Rough-haired Pointer* L. A. H. and A. J. H. van Heynsbergen; *Spanish Water Dog* D. Galbraith
- **68** *Welsh Springer Spaniel* J. Luckett-Roynon; *Sussex Spaniel* C. Mitchell; (standing) Mr & Mrs J. C. Shankland
- **69** *Nova Scotia Duck Tolling Retriever* G. Flack
- **70** *Old Danish Pointer* E. Karlsson
- **71** *German Spaniel* L. Ahlsson
- **72–73** *Weimaraner* F. Thibaut; (standing) C. Mutlow
- **74** *German Wire-haired Pointer* M. J. Gorrissen-Sipos
- **75** *Small Münsterländer* G. Petterson
- **76–77** *Large Münsterländer* K. Groom
- **78** *Dutch Partridge Dog* S. Boersma; J.P.A. vd. Zanden; *Kooiker Dog* L.A. & B. Williams
- **79** *Stabyhoun* E. Vellenga; *Wetterhoun* J.P. Visser
- **80** *Irish Water Spaniel* G. Stirk
- **81** *Irish Red and White Setter* S.J. Humphreys
- **82** *Irish Setter* Napthine
- **83** *Braque St. Germain* J.P. Perdry
- **84–85** *Braque Francais: Gascogne* Y. Bassot
- **86** *Braque d' Auvergne* L . Ercole; (standing, prone) P. Zvaigzne
- **87** *Braque du Bourbonnais* J. Regis; (sitting) I. Širmeniene
- **88** *Épagneul Francais* W. Klijn; G. de Moustier; *Épagneul Picard* M. & P. Lempereur
- **89** *Épagneul Breton* E. Reeves
- **90** *Épagneul Pont-Audemer* Y. Fouquer; J.P. Tougard; (standing) Mr & Mrs Stalter
- **91** *Barbet* J.C. Valée
- **92** *Épagneul Bleu de Picardie* M. Debacker
- **93** *Wire-haired Pointing Griffon*

R. Antila; *Czesky Fousek* M. Hahné
- **94** *Hungarian Vizsla* J. Perkins; (standing) J. C. Van Brederode
- **95** *Wire-haired Vizsla* J. & L.V. Essen; (standing, prone) J. Delf
- **96** *Spinone* M. D. Wellman & A. J. Cook
- **97** *Bracco Italiano* Mr & Mrs M. E. Wilson
- **99** *Portuguese Water Dog* J. & R. Bussell
- **100** *Perdiguero Portugueses* Canil do Casal das Grutas

HERDING DOGS
- **101** *Australian Shepherd* J. Goessens
- **102** *Bearded Collie* J. Wiggins
- **103** *Border Collie* P. Haydock; *Lancashire Heeler* S. Whybrow
- **104** *Rough Collie* V. Tame
- **105** *Smooth Collie* P. Sewell; *Shetland Sheepdog* J. Moody
- **106** *Old English Sheepdog* (adult) J.P. & C. Smith; (puppy) Anderson
- **107** *Welsh Corgi: Cardigan* T. Maddox; *Welsh Corgi: Pembroke* Davies
- **108** *Australian Cattle Dog* (adult) S. & W. Huntingdon; (puppies) S. Smyth
- **109** *Australian Kelpie* P. Rönnquist; M. Nilsson
- **110** *Finnish Lapphund* S. Bolin; (youngest) S. Dunger; *Lapinporokoira* B. Schmitt
- **111** *Caucasian Shepherd Dog* P. Juilla
- **112** *Beauceron* M.V. Rie
- **113** *Briard* (fawn) Snelling; (black) R. Bumstead; *Pyrenean Sheepdog* Per Toie Romstad
- **114** *Berger de Picard* C.V. Doorn; (brindle) J.C.P. Bormans
- **115** *German Shepherd Dog* (head, sitting) W. & J. Petrie
- **116–117** *Hovawart* (black) K. Srenhols; (golden) A. Göranson
- **118** *Giant Schnauzer* Wilberg; (standing) M. F. Seewald
- **119** *Polish Lowland Sheepdog* M. de Groot; *Schapendoes* J. Wierda-Gorter; (head) C. Roux
- **120** *Dutch Shepherd Dog* J. Pijffers; M. Vermeeren; *White Swiss Shepherd* A. Maryse
- **121** *Sarloos Wolfdog* C. Keizer
- **122** *Belgian Shepherd Dog: Groenendael* J. Luscott
- **123** *Belgian Shepherd Dog: Laekenois* Hogarty
- **124** *Belgian Shepherd Dog: Tervuren* K. Ellis & A. McLaren
- **125** *Belgian Shepherd Dog: Malinois* (head) S. Hughes
- **126–127** *Bouvier des Flandres* K.S. Wilberg; (standing, sitting) P. Aerts

- **128** *Swedish Vallhund* J. Hammar;
Iceland Dog A.S. Andersson
- **129** *Puli* M. Crowther; Butler;
Pumi (black) P. Johansson; (gray
and cream) I. Svard
- **130** *Karst Shepherd* M. Luttwitz;
Šarplaninac P. Gvozenovie
- **131** *Bergamasco* B. Saraber;
(puppy) M. Andreoli
- **132** *Catalan Sheepdog* M. Guasch Soler
- **133** *Portuguese Sheepdog* Borges,
M. Loureiro; Canil do Magoito;
Canil da Valeira; Cunha,
M.L.N. Lopes; Gomez-Toldra

HOUNDS
- **134** *Catahoula Leopard Dog*
M. Neal
- **135** *Plott Hound* J.M. Koons;
B. L. Taylor & M. Seets; *Bluetick
Coonhound* D. McCormick;
R. Welch & B. Slaymon
- **136** *English Coonhound* M. Seets;
J. Mantanona
- **137** *Redbone Coonhound*
J. & C. Heck; C. Elburn
- **138–39** *Black and Tan Coonhound*
K. & A. Shorter; D. Fentee &
R. Speer Jnr.
- **140** *Treeing Walker Coonhound*
L. Currens; J. Girnor & W. Haynes
- **141** *American Foxhound*
(sitting) A. Cannon
- **142** *Basset Hound* N. Frost;
Beagle M. Hunt
- **143** *Foxhound* The Berks and
Bucks Draghounds
- **144** *Deerhound* D. & J. Murray
- **145** *Otterhound* Smith; (head,
standing) R. Ganna
- **146** *Greyhound* U. & C. Schmidt
- **147** *Whippet* Oliver; S. Horsnell;
(standing) E. C. Walker
- **148** *Dunker* (sitting, standing) Almerud
- **149** *Haldestövare* G. Lerstad
- **150** *Hygenhund* R. Langland;
Finnish Hound T. Olkkonen; A Vilpula
- **151** *Drever* L. Jönsson;
Schillerstövare (refer to publisher)
- **152** *Hamiltonstövare* D. Cook
- **153** *Smålandsstövare* (sitting) K. Skolmi
- **154–55** *Miniature Dachshund*
(long coat) L. Mears; (smooth
coat) B. Clark; (wire coat) P. Seymour
- **156** *Hanoverian Mountain Hound*
I. Voegelen; *Bavarian Schweisshund*
I. Voegelen
- **157** *Polish Hound* A. Marculanis
- **158–59** *Irish Wolfhound* (gray)
Smith; A. Bennett
- **160** *Kerry Beagle* J. Sugrue; T. O'Shea;
M. O'Sullivan; P. Daly; J. Kelly
- **161** *Lurcher* C. Labers
- **162–63** *Bloodhound* Richards
- **164** *Billy* (head) A. Benoit

- **165** *Basset Fauve de Bretagne*
(head) N. Frost
- **166–67** *Grand Bleu de Gascogne*
Braddick
- **168** *Petit Bleu de Gascogne* (refer
to publisher)
- **169** *Petit Griffon Bleu de Gascogne*
(refer to publisher)
- **170** *Chien d'Artois* A. Lopez;
N.Bellet
- **171** *Basset Bleu de Gascogne*
J. Nenmann; *Basset Artésian
Normand* B. Hemmingsson
- **172** *Grand Gascon-Saintongeois*
(refer to publisher)
- **173** *Grand Basset Griffon Vendéen*
N. Frost & V. Philips
- **174** *Grand Griffon Vendéen*
G. Lamoureux; D. Boursier
- **175** *Briquet Griffon Vendéen*
D. Fabre; *Griffon Nivernais*
D. Duede
- **176** *Anglo-Francais de Petite
Vénerie* A. Dubois
- **177** *Griffon Fauve de Bretagne*
M. Imbert & D. Carrat
- **178** *Porcelaine* R. Lavergme
- **179** *Jura Laufhund: Bruno*
P. Guenole
- **180–81** *Jura Laufhund (St. Hubert)*
M. Aigret
- **182** *Hungarian Greyhound*
T. Christiansen; *Berner Laufhund*
R.J. Luchcmeijer
- **183** *Schweizer Laufhund* O. Bonslet
- **184** *Luzerner Laufhund*
M.B. Mervaille
- **185** *Serbian Hound*
I. Vicentijevic; *Posavac Hound*
Z. Marinkovic
- **186** *Montenegrin Mountain
Hound* D. Milosevic
- **187** *Serbian Tricolored Hound*
R. Andelkovic
- **188** *Italian Hound; Cirneco dell'Etna*
D.H. Blom
- **189** *Pharaoh Hound* J. Gostynska
- **190** *Ibizan Hound* Carter & Donnaby;
F. Benecke
- **191** *Sabuesco Español* (head, sitting)
J.C. Palomo Romero
- **192** *Spanish Greyhound* J.F. Olij
& J.W. Luijken; L. Rapeport
- **193** *Podengo Portugueses Pequeño*
Macedo, L. Vaz; Reis, A.S. Oliveira
- **194** *Podengo Portugueses Medio*
Canil G. Oleganense; Canil de
Veiros; Canil do Vale do Criz
- **195** *Saluki* (black) Ziman;
(grizzle) Spooner
- **196** *Borzoi* A.G.C. Simmonds
- **199** *Sloughi* (sitting) L. Vassalo
- **200** *Kai Dog* M. Malone
- **201** *Rhodesian Ridgeback*
M. & J. Morris

TERRIERS
- **202** *American Toy Fox Terrier*
(standing) A. Mauermann
- **204** *American Staffordshire
Terrier* K. Hahn; *Boston Terrier* R. Lutz
- **205** *Airedale Terrier* G. Francois;
Bedlington Terrier A. Yearley
- **206** *English Toy Terrier*
(standing) T. Wright; *Manchester
Terrier* (head, sitting) E. Eva
- **207** *Border Terrier* (head) Dean;
Norwich Terrier Mr & Mrs S. Philippe
- **208** *Staffordshire Bull Terrier*
(standing) G. & B. McAuliffe
- **209** *Dandie Dinmont Terrier*
P. Keevil & S. Bullock; *Cairn
Terrier* K. Holmes
- **210** *Lakeland Terrier* J.C. Ruiz
Mogrera; Hedges; *Norfolk Terrier*
(standing) N. Kruger
- **211** *Parson Jack Russell Terrier*
(standing) J.P. Wood; *Wire Fox
Terrier* J. Palosaari; G. Düring
- **212** *Smooth Fox Terrier*
L. Bochese; *Welsh Terrier*
P. M. J. Krautscheid
- **213** *Skye Terrier* P. Bennett;
(puppies) D. & J. Miller
- **214** *West Highland White Terrier*
(standing) S. Thompson; J. Pastor &
M. Gonzalbo
- **215** *Yorkshire Terrier* H. Ridgwell
- **216** *Sealyham Terrier* A. Klimeshova;
Australian Terrier I. Coppée
- **217** *Australian Silky Terrier* I. Leino;
Mr & Mrs De Bondt; *German Hunting
Terrier* B. Andersson
- **218** *German Pinscher*
R. & M. Collicott; Boyer
- **219** *Affenpinscher* A.J. Teasdale;
Miniature Pinscher Y. Hulpiau
- **220** *Miniature Schnauzer* P. Gowlett;
(standing) D. L. and M. May
- **221** *Kromfohrländer* (short coat)
M. Schaub; (long coat) H. Hoppert
- **222** *Irish Terrier* A. Noonan &
Williamson; (standing) N. Pesola
- **223** *Soft-coated Wheaten Terrier*
A. Buscher & A. Lammering
- **224** *Glen of Imaal Terrier*
(standing) M. V. Wiele; *Kerry Blue
Terrier* Campbell
- **226** *Cesky Terrier* (sitting)
D. Delplanque

WORKING DOGS
- **227** *American Bulldog* S. Leclerc
- **228** *Olde English Bulldogge*
(refer to publisher)
- **229** *Chinook* T.J. and G. Anderson;
D. & C. Hendricks;
- **230–31** *Alaskan Malamute* Lena-
Britt Egnell
- **232–33** *Mastiff* D. Blaxter; (dark

brindle) B. Stoffelen-Luyten
- **234** *Bull Mastiff* J. & A. Gunn
- **235** *Bull Terrier* Youatt; *Eskimo Dog* E. & S. Hammond
- **236–37** *Newfoundland* Cutts & Galvin; (black and white) Cutts
- **238** *Dogo Argentino* Roelofs; (standing) P. H. C. Bakkereren
- **239** *Fila Brasileiro* E.H. Vlietman
- **240** *Greenland Dog* M. Dragone; M. Demoor
- **241** *Norwegian Elkhound* (standing) A. Meijer; *Black Norwegian Elkhound* N. Bonaunet
- **242** *Lundehund* M. Jansson; *Norwegian Buhund* R. W. J. Thomas
- **243** *Finnish Spitz* Gatti; *Karelion Bear Dog* P. Gritsh
- **244** *Swedish Elkhound* A. Johansson
- **245** *Swedish Lapphund* R.A. Wind-Heuser; *Norbottenspets* (standing) A. Piltto
- **246–47** *Dobermann* (head, sitting) B. Schellekens & S. Franquemont
- **248–49** *Great Dane* (fawn with black mask) D.J. Parish; (harlequin) N. Marriner
- **250** *Standard Poodle* E.A. Beswick; (prone) L. Woods & J. Lynn
- **251** *Boxer* Mr & Mrs Cobb; *Eurasier* (standing) J. Bos Waaldijk
- **252–53** *Landseer* G. Cutts
- **254–55** *Leonberger* (head, standing, prone) F. Inwood
- **256** *Rottweiler* Hine; T. Barnett; Y. Bekkers

- **257** *Owczarek Podhalański* G.V. Rijsewijk
- **258** *Schipperke* L. Wilson; (head, standing) Lefort
- **259** *French Bulldog* J. Keates; *Dogue de Bordeaux* (standing) A.E. Neuteboom
- **260–61** *Pyrenean Mountain Dog* (standing) I.& W. Spencer-Brown
- **262** *Komondor* P. & M. Froome
- **263** *Kuvasz* J. De Jong
- **264** *Mudi* (refer to publisher)
- **265** *Appensell Mountain Dog* W. Glocker; (head) C. Wentzler *Entelbuch Mountain Dog* C. Fransson
- **266–67** *Bernese Mountain Dog* A. Hayden; (puppy, prone) A. Hearne
- **268** *Great Swiss Mountain Dog* H. Hannberger; (standing) A. & O. Thomas
- **269** *St. Bernard* (short-haired) H. Golverdingen; (long-haired) T. Hansen
- **270** *Dalmatian* K. Goff; R. & H. Tingey
- **271** *Maremma Sheepdog* T. Barnes
- **273** *Cane Corso* W. van den Berg
- **274** *Pyrenean Mastiff* G. Marin
- **275** *Spanish Mastiff* Camps & Ritter
- **276** *Perro de Pastor Mallorquin* J. M. Martinez Alonso; *Perro de Presa Mallorquin* J.J. Calderón Ruiz; E. Lurbe; M. Calvino Breijo
- **277** *Canaan Dog* (sitting, prone) M. Macphail
- **278** *Estrela Mountain Dog* P. Olsson; E. Bentzer

- **279** *Rafeiro do Alentejo* Gomes, J. Oliveira
- **280** *Portuguese Cattle Dog* Canil do Casal da Granja; Amorim, J.M.P. de Lima; Macedo, L. Vaz; *Russian-European Laika* S. Enochsson; B. Vujasinovic
- **281** *East Siberian Laika* (head) L. Milic; *West Siberian Laika* S.Enochsson
- **282** *Siberian Husky* S. Hull
- **283** *Samoyed* C. Fox
- **284** *Chow Chow* P. Goedgezelschap; U. Berglöf
- **285** *Shar Pei* B. & C. Lilley
- **286** *Akita Inu* A. Rickard
- **287** *Shiba Inu* M. Atkinson; *Tosa Inu* F. Kappe
- **288** *Japanese Terrier* (head) M. Delaye
- **290** *Perro de Presa Canario* D. Kelly; Grupo los Enanos
- **291** *Aidi* M. Bouayad (Cluc Chien Atlas); *New Guinea Singing Dog* A. Riddle; P. & F. Persky

DESIGNER DOGS
- **293** *Goldendoodle* James Harrison
- **294** *Puggle* Sharyn Prince
- **295** *Labradinger* Jemima Dunne

USEFUL ADDRESSES

American Kennel Club (AKC)
101 Park Avenue, New York, NY 10178
www.akc.org

United Kennel Club, Inc. (UKC)
100 E. Kilgore Rd., Kalamazoo, MI 49002
www.ukcdogs.com

Assistance Dogs International
www.assistancedogsinternational.org

The Humane Society of the United States
1255 23rd St. NW, Suite 450,
Washington, DC 20037
www.humanesociety.org

Canadian Kennel Club
200 Ronson Drive, Suite 400, Etobicoke, ON M9W 5Z9
www.ckc.ca

The Kennel Club
10 Clarges Street, London, W1J 8AB
www.thekennelclub.org.uk

Australian National Kennel Council
DOGS ACT, PO Box 815, Dickson ACT 2602
ankc.org.au

Dogs New Zealand (Dogs NZ)
Level One, Tottenham House,
7 Kilkerran Place, Porirua 5022
www.dogsnz.org.nz

GLOSSARY

Angulation
Angle formed by the meeting of bones at a joint.

Barrel
Rounded chest shape.

Bat ears
Erect ears, wide at the base and rounded at the tips, pointing out.

Bay
Call of hounds in pursuit of quarry.

Beard
Long, thick hair around the jaws.

Belton
Blue-lemon flecked coloration associated with English Setters.

Bite
The positioning of the upper and lower teeth relative to each other.

Blaze
White marking running down forehead to muzzle.

Bobtail
Naturally short tail associated with individual dogs of certain breeds.

Brindle
Combination of light and dark hairs, resulting in darker streaking.

Brisket
Area of the chest between the forelegs, including the breastbone.

Broken-coated
Rough, wire coat.

Brush
Bushy tail.

Butterfly nose
Nose of two colors.

Button ears
Semi-erect ears, folding over at their tips.

Clip
Type of trim, associated particularly with poodles.

Cobby
Short-bodied and compact.

Conformation
Overall shape, resulting from combined relationship of all of a dog's physical parts.

Coupling
Region extending from the last rib to the pelvis.

Cow-hocked
Hocks point in towards each other.

Croup
Area of back closest to tail.

Culotte
Long hair at the back of the thighs.

Dewclaw
Claw on the inside of the legs, often removed in young puppies.

Dewlap
Pendulous, loose skin under the throat, as seen in the Bloodhound.

Double coat
Guard hairs protruding through softer, insulating layer beneath.

Drop ear
Ears that hang down, close to the sides of the head.

Elbow
Joint below shoulder.

Entropion
Eye abnormality causing almost continual irritation.

Fall
Hair hanging down over the face.

Feathering
Long fringes of hair on the ears, body, legs, and tail.

Flews
Pendulous upper lips.

Frill
Longer hair present on the lower neck and front of the chest.

Grizzle
Bluish gray color.

Guard hairs
Coarser outer hairs.

Hackles
Hair on the neck and back, raised to show aggression or fright.

Hare feet
Relatively long and narrow feet.

Harlequin
Black or blue patches set against white, as seen in the Great Dane.

Haunches
Back of thighs, in contact with the ground when the dog is sitting.

Hock
Hindleg joint—the dog's heels.

Jowls
The fleshy part of the lips and jaws.

Leather
Ear flap.

Lobular
Lobe shaped.

Loins
Region from last rib to back legs.

Mane
Long hair on and around the neck.

Mask
Dark, mask-like shading on head.

Merle
Marbled coat pattern, caused by darker patches on lighter background of same basic color.

Muzzle
Portion of head in front of eyes.

Occiput
Highest part on back of skull.

Pastern
Lower part of leg, between wrist and foot.

Plume
Soft hair on the tail.

Point
Immovable stance of a hunting dog, indicating location of game.

Points
Body extremities, usually referring to the coloration of ears, face, legs, and tail.

Roached
Convex arching of the back.

Roan
Mixture of white and another color, in even proportions.

Rose-eared
Typically small ears, which fold down and show the inside.

Ruff
Long, thick hair encircling neck.

Sable
White coat, shaded with black.

Sabre tail
Tail in the shape of a semi-circle.

Saddle
Black markings in the shape and position of a saddle.

Soft mouth
A characteristic of hunting dogs, indicating ability to retrieve game without damaging it.

Stand-off coat
Long, heavy coat standing out from body, as in the Keeshond.

Stifle
Hindleg joint, the angle of which is important in breed standards.

Stop
Depression between the eyes, where skull and nasal bone meet.

Ticking
Coat pattern in which spots of color stand out against the basic background color.

Trim
Grooming that entails clipping or plucking.

Whelping
Giving birth to puppies.

Withers
Highest point of the shoulders, behind the neck.

INDEX

ACKNOWLEDGMENTS

THE AUTHOR AND PUBLISHER are indebted to a number of institutions and people, without whom this book could not have been produced: Mia Sandgren, Magnus Berglin, Thomas Miller, Maria Bruga, Steve Fielder, Jovan Serafin, Luis Isaac Barata, Luis Manuel Calado Catalan, Dr. J.L. Slack, Anita Bryant, Sergio Montesinos Vernetta, Ann Houdijk, Antonio Consta, Jose Carrera, Steven Boer, Egon Erdenbrecher, Mr. & Mrs. Lawlor, Mr. K. Bent, E. Vanherle, Dr. Herbert R. Axelrod, John Miller, M. Peonchon, Patrick Schwab, Mme. Dhetz, Stella Smyth, Mandy Hearne, Heather Head. Special thanks are also due to Sabine Weiss of SDK Verlags GmbH; Susanne Marlier of the Fédération Cynologigue Internationale; Susanne Lindberg of the Norsk Kennel Klub; M. Noblet of the Société Centrale Canine; Mme. Mila; Mme. Durando of the Société Canine of Monaco, and Her Serene Highness, Princess Antoinette of Monaco.

Commissioned photography by Tracy Morgan, except for: **6 Alamy Stock Photo:** The Print Collector / Ann Ronan Picture Library / Heritage-Images (bl); **7 Alamy Stock Photo:** Chronicle (cra); PA Images (b); **8 Alamy Stock Photo:** ukartpics (cb). **Shutterstock.com:** Ksenia Raykova (br); **10 Dreamstime.com:** Tetiana Nazarenko (cl); Andrea Vance (cr). **Shutterstock.com:** Henry During (b); **11 Dreamstime.com:** Erix2005 (bl); Zita Stankova (cra); Lopolo (br); **14 Dreamstime.com:** Retsel2526 (cra); **28 Kisaki Nakatsukasa:** (tc); **93 Dreamstime.com:** Waldemar Dabrowski (br); **141 TFH Publications, Inc.:** (t); **148** (t&b); **149** (t&c); **150** (t); **151** (crb); **153** (c); **169 Marc Henrie:** (b); **183** (t&b); **203 Dreamstime.com:** Sergey Lavrentev (crb). **Shutterstock.com:** Ysbrand Cosijn (br); **221 Dreamstime.com:** Judith Dzierzawa (br); **241** (br); **245 Neil Fletcher:** (br); **250 Dreamstime.com:** Ttretjak (tc); **264 Sandra Russell:** (t); **292 Kisaki Nakatsukasa:** (tr) **Endpaper images:** Front & Back: **Dreamstime.com:** Andrey Pavlov; **Getty Images / iStock:** GlobalP

All other images © Dorling Kindersley
For further information see: www.dkimages.com

The author would like to thank the many kind dog fanciers around the world who have allowed their dogs to be photographed. A particular debt is due to Tracy Morgan who, with the help of her husband, Neil, undertook the bulk of the photography, and to Andrea Fair who arranged the overseas trips. He would also like to thank Neil Fletcher, Marc and Fiona Henrie, James Harrison, Bob Gordon, and Jonathon Hilton for their input at various stages of the book. Thanks go to everyone at Dorling Kindersley, Richmond, who have contributed: in particular Jonathan Metcalf, Carole McGlynn, Constance Novis, Mary-Clare Jerram, Gill della Casa, Spencer Holbrook, Vicki James, Anne Thompson, and Sam Grimmer. Also, all the members of the team at DK India who have been involved with this title, including Saloni Talwar, Saumya Agarwal, Arunesh Talapatra and Shipra Jain. Last, but not least, thanks to Rita Hemsley for her typing skills, and Les Crawley, John Mandeville, and Darrin Lunde for their invaluable contributions.

Dorling Kindersley would like to thank: Lemon Graphics, Alastair Wardle, Pauline Bayne, Elaine Hewson, and Sharon Moore for design assistance; Mike Darton and Amanda Ronan for proofreading; Michael Allaby for indexing; Julia Pashley for picture research; Helen Townsend, Angeles Gavira, and Lucinda Hawksley for editorial assistance in the first edition, and for this edition: Priyanka Sharma, Senior Jackets Editorial Coordinator; Vagisha Pushp and Adhithi Priya for picture research; Nandini Desiraju for editorial assistance.

SMITHSONIAN ENTERPRISES
Kealy Gordon, Product Development Manager
Jill Corcoran, Director, Licensed Publishing
Brigid Ferraro, Vice President, Business Development and Licensing
Carol LeBlanc, President

SMITHSONIAN REVIEWER
Darrin Lunde, Collections Manager, Division of Mammals, National Museum of Natural History

David Alderton grew up in a home surrounded by pets and originally trained to become a veterinary surgeon. An allergic dermatitis acquired in his final year of study at Cambridge University forced a change of career however, leading him into the field of writing and broadcasting about animals instead. David's books have currently sold some seven million copies in 31 languages, and he has been awarded the Maxwell Medallion by the Dog Writers' Association of America. His international television credits include the special program that celebrated the centenary of the famous Crufts Dog Show, titled *Thank You, Mr Cruft.*